D1539726

MEDICAL TREASON

MEDICAL TREASON

NURSES ON DRUGS

Joyce E. Strom-Paikin, R.N.

NEW HORIZON PRESS
Far Hills, New Jersey

HICKSVILLE PUBLIC LIBRARY
169 JERUSALEM AVE.
HICKSVILLE, N.Y.

Copyright © 1988 by Joyce E. Strom-Paikin

All rights reserved. No part of this book may be reproduced or transmitted in any form whatsoever, including electronic, mechanical, or any information storage or retrieval system, except as may be expressly permitted by the 1976 Copyright Act or in writing from the publisher. Requests for permission should be addressed to New Horizon Press, P.O. Box 669, Far Hills, New Jersey 07931.

Library of Congress Catalog Card Number 89-60104

Strom-Paikin, Joyce E.
  Medical Treason

ISBN 088282-043-5
New Horizon Press

362.293
S

This book is dedicated to my mother, Elizabeth Walker Bartlett, RN, Class of 1944, Buffalo, New York and to all Nurses for their dedication to our profession along with a special thank you to my husband Lester Paikin for lovingly supporting this story and believing in my abilities.

AUTHOR'S NOTE

The story you are about to read is true. All these cases are based on my experiences. I have taken the liberty of changing names and the identifying characteristics of people, hospitals, and schools in order to protect the rights of the people I have had as patients, their families, and those professionals with whom I have worked and from whom I have learned. In some cases, the people in this book are composites, and in a few instances the chronology has been altered.

I have written this account in the first person using my name. Years ago I made the decision to put my licenses and credentials on the line in order to help others, especially those in the nursing profession.

Nursing is currently going through tremendous changes and crises. We have numerous internal problems. Many of them will be addressed in this book. It is not meant to betray medical, personal or professional confidences, but to clearly reveal critical areas of drug addiction within medicine, a subject that needs to be carefully and truthfully examined.

ACKNOWLEDGEMENTS

Paul Flurschutz, Cayuga Community College for believing in me.

Stella White, RN, BSN, my college nursing director and a mentor.

Judge Peter E. Corning, Auburn, New York, who supported my growth.

St. Joseph's Hospital, Syracuse, New York, for giving me the opportunity to develop both critical care and psychiatric nursing skills.

Charlotte Preston, RN, MSW, for working with me over the past four years.

Julia Trenker, RN, MSN, former Assistant Administrator of Nursing, Broward General Hospital, Ft. Lauderdale, Florida for her friendship and professional association.

South Florida Nurse Educators, Inc., Margate, Florida for years of growth, exposure, and the offices I have held.

Lester Paikin, my husband of six years, who never stopped believing in me.

The Hollywood Pavilion, Hollywood, Florida and the Care Unit of Coral Springs, for staff and admitting privileges and the opportunity to learn and grow.

Raymond Moody, MD, Ph.D., friend and colleague with IANDS—The International Association for Near Death Studies.

The American Nurses Association, the Florida Nurses Association, and the National League for Nursing for all of their assistance.

The Florida State Board of Nursing and the Intervention Project for Nurses, especially Judy Ritter, RN, MSN, Ann Cantazarite, RN, and Jean Kelly, RN, for all of their assistance.

Roger Goetz, MD and the Impaired Physicians Program, state of Florida, a special thank you.

To all of the nurses who have shared their experiences, dealt with the pain of recovery, and allowed me to work with them individually or within a group process, a very special thank you.

To the nurses and doctors who have given their life for others, a very special thank you.

To all of the doctors, nurses, and professional nursing and psychological organizations who have supported my research and allowed me to present it at national and international conferences, a very special thank you.

To all of the medical professionals still in denial or passing judgments—a special prayer and hope that you will receive help before it is too late.

"Scalpel! Retractors! Sutures!" Dr. Vorhees's voice called out the perfunctory orders loudly. I felt frightened remembering his earlier threat of performing surgery on me. Was he pretending or really going to do it. Panic stricken I waited "Number 8 oral endotracheal tube," the nurse anesthetist bellowed, adding, almost as a last minute thought, "and for God's sake, turn on the respirator!"

The breathing machine filled the room with loud, life-giving swishing sounds. The doctor's panicking voice could barely be heard above it. "Thrust the jaw forward. Now, insert the tube." Commands kept coming.

Finally, a gag reflex occurred. "Good," the doctor said. A sigh of relief passed through his lips. It was still too soon to totally relax. Too much could still go wrong. "Slide it in very carefully," he instructed. "I think we have it. Attach the life support to the machine and set the dials for control. Pentathol stat."

The needle penetrated the IV tubing already in my vein. I thought it was my right arm and wondered if I was correct. *What did it feel like?* I questioned myself in a sleepy daze. *Perhaps like a slippery, smooth snake winding its way through a dark tunnel.* My hand wanted to move, but I was paralyzed. Something heavy lay on my wrist, like a brick.

"That's fine," the familiar voice praised quietly. "Go slow and make this as real as you can," he cautioned.

The voices were clear but distant. Far, far away. I could hear my lungs filling and emptying with the life-sustaining air. Air sounds like wind in a tunnel. *No control,* I thought. *I have no control. Perhaps I am dying. Maybe this is the near death experience I have heard about. It is so peaceful here.* I wanted to stay.

"Nasogastric to low suction." A nurse's voice penetrated my thoughts. I recognized the voice. Soft. Commanding, yet deferential, knowing her place on the team. The voice was reassuring. I felt the slippery snake passing through my right nostril into my stomach lining. A frightening noise permeated my quiet space. Suctioning turned on and off at regular intervals. My stomach rumbled; I began to retch violently, trying to cough up the tubes that filled my breathing and eating passages. I felt another tube emptying urine from my bladder; others filled my veins with painkilling medications.

"Where the hell is more pentathol?" the doctor's voice bellowed angrily again.

Yes, bring me drugs, I thought as I began gasping for air. It wasn't peaceful anymore. I was frightened.

"I'm coming," the nurse answered. She didn't sound so reassuring. "I'm injecting it now, doctor, into the main fluid IV."

"Thank God. We nearly lost this mean-aarterial line, and we still have to put the swanz gans pulmonary wedge line in." The doctor seemed to be talking to himself. "The next time I call you, young lady, you had better come running." *You always have to tell the nurses what to do, doctor,* I thought. *Put them in their place.*

Peace suddenly fell over me. My mind went blank. *Where am I?* I asked in the last momentary split second of consciousness. In that split second in time I remembered who I was.

I know. I know. My mind raced back to the injection

Dr. Vorhees gave me. Then my body went flacid, succumb-ing to a deep, drug-induced state; my mind was no longer on earth or in heaven. My spirit lingered someplace in between.

ONE

The alarm rang. I was wide awake, anxious. As a new graduate I was preparing for my first real day on duty in the Intensive Care Unit of Trinity Hospital. Nurse's training was behind me, although I did not yet have my license. With State Boards two months away, I was filled with great expectations of saving lives and helping critically ill patients recover.

My uniform, cap, white stockings, and shiny school pin had been laid out the night before. During my restless sleep I had admired the purity of the color. After four years of wearing a pink pinafore over a pink uniform I finally felt like a real nurse.

Birds chirp merrily at 5:30 in the morning. Dragging through school I had never before noticed them. Suddenly, I felt really alive and eager to begin my new day. There was a nervous knot in my stomach. I couldn't eat breakfast.

I forgot my cap as I ran out to my red Chevette. Racing back to the apartment, I tried not to awaken my roommate, Karen, and grabbed the clear plastic carrier with my nurse's cap. The drive went smoothly: there weren't, and would not be, any cars on the highway for another hour.

I had to report to Nursing Service first. As I approached the hospital I noticed the staff parking lot had already filled. Living at the hospital, parking in the student parking lot had never been a problem for me. I didn't even own a car the first three years of college. Today I noticed just how many cars belonged to employees. The knot in my stomach grew tighter; I couldn't be late for work on my first real day on duty.

I stole a glance at my watch, the new one with the black band and large sweep second hand. It had been a graduation gift from my mother, who was also a Registered Nurse. I had completed my RN at my mother's school of nursing. Unlike her, I had also earned a Bachelor's degree and was eagerly looking forward to a Master's degree.

Seven minutes. My heart began to pound as I drove up and down the aisles of the lot. Finally I found a space between a white Porsche and a tiny, red MG and whipped my small car in. Out of breath, I pulled open the heavy hospital doors and sped along the medicinal, shiny halls.

I nearly wiped out a lab technician on his early morning rounds as I ran in the direction of Nursing Service. As I reached for the door handle, recollections of stress reduction courses flashed back through my mind.

"Good morning," I smiled at the secretary in the office. "I'm Joyce Strom, GN for the Intensive Care Unit." The statement sounded so good that I flashed a grin of pride. Apparently the secretary was not quite as taken with me as I was. She proceeded to open her typewriter and shuffle papers.

"Have a seat over there," she indicated with her eyes. "I will tell Miss Holcomb you are here."

I was sure that the secretary could hear my heart pounding as I sat on the cold, green plastic chair in the corner. I remembered my initial meeting with Miss Holcomb during my first week of training. Just the thought of it produced a wave of nausea in me. Miss Holcomb was the Director of Nurses and a graduate of this same school nearly forty years ago. "Intimidating" was hardly the word for her. We students had been convinced she was still a virgin.

I could see her in my mind. Large, wide hips. Broad hands. A deep, almost masculine voice. Hair the color of snow, cropped close to her ears. I couldn't remember what color her eyes were—only the small pinpoint size of the dark pupils.

"Miss Strom," the secretary's voice startled me. "Miss Holcomb will see you now."

I must have looked dazed and confused.

"Go right into her office," she prompted. Even the sign, "Nursing Director," on the front of the office was intimidating.

"Good morning, Miss Holcomb," I said timidly.

"Yes, good morning," she answered. "The unit surely can use an extra pair of hands today. They have a full house up there. A bad accident last night. Two were DOA (dead on arrival), but we managed to save three. Well, come along. I'll take you up."

She strode out the door with me in her wake. I noticed the clock said 7:10; I was afraid that I had missed Report. We rode the elevator in silence to the third floor. Miss Holcomb seemed larger and taller than I had remembered. As the doors of the elevator opened, she took giant strides down the hall.

"Come along," she called over her shoulder. I ran to keep up with her. Suddenly, the double doors to my new world appeared before us:

INTENSIVE CARE UNIT. Authorized Personnel Only
Visiting Hours: 1:00–1:20 p.m., 4:00–4:20 p.m.,
and 8:00–8:20 p.m., only.

Miss Holcomb pushed through, leaving the doors to swing back at me. We stood in the reception alcove of the unit. Distant respirators and cardiac monitors hummed and beeped, as Miss Holcomb entered the small staff room off to the left. While I remembered the room as a student, it looked different to me today. A thick, blue cloud of smoke stung my eyes. The room was crammed full of folding chairs and unfamiliar faces.

"Girls," Miss Holcomb interrupted, "this is Joyce Strom, one of our new graduates. She is a new pair of hands to the unit. Take her under your wing." Looking at me, she added, "This is Marilyn, your head nurse. She'll help you. Well, good luck." Before I could nod or say thank you, the director disappeared through the doors.

Marilyn was abrupt. "Have a seat." She held her report chart in her hands and tapped it until I found a chair. Then she added, "Tina, you be her buddy for the day and keep her out of my hair."

"Swell," Tina mumbled as she motioned me to come closer. I suddenly felt very comfortable and unwelcome. I wondered where my feelings of euphoria had gone. "I'll take your assignment," Tina whispered.

A tired looking night nurse spoke monotonously of a patient in bed four: ". . . BP (blood pressure) every 15 (minutes); TPR (temperature, pulse, respirations) every hour; CVP (central venous pressure) every 15 (minutes); MAP (mean arterial pressure) every 15 (minutes); changed dressing prn (as needed); suction every 2 (hours) and prn (as needed); turn every 2 (hours) and prn (as needed) . . ."

This must be one of the accident victims, I concluded. A nurse in the corner wrote furiously. I decided this was her patient. I looked at the night nurse; she was weary and her uniform was bloodstained. The contrast of my own starched, clean whites was obvious, even to me.

". . . MFV (main fluid vein) running at 150 (drops) per minute and piggyback at 25 per minute . . ." the night nurse continued without taking a breath. I wondered what her name was and from where she had graduated. I couldn't see her school pin. ". . . patient admitted at 3:30 a.m. and stat (immediate) chest X ray done showing a collapsed right lung. Vitals every 15 'til stable. Output down to 30 per hour . . ."

As I listened, I racked my memory banks to sort out the terms. I also noticed that no one was paying any attention to me. For the time being, I felt comfortable and not as awkward as I had when I'd first entered the unit.

"Bed five," the night nurse continued. Tina began to write rapidly. I wondered if this would be my patient or hers. I listened closely.

". . . BP dropped at 4:30 and Dr. Kim, from on-call, ordered a stat type and cross match. Two units (blood) ordered. Type A positive. First unit hung at 6:00. We took credit for it. No adverse effects noted. The second was hung at 7:00 for you to take credit for. Vitals every 15 and not stable yet. Output down. Gave lasix 20 mg. IV push. Output 250 (cc's) last hour. KVO (keep vein open) at 15 drops a minute right arm. 490 (cc's) Ringers lactate off left arm 'til blood in . . ."

I was suddenly glad to have a buddy taking this report; even a hostile buddy was better than being left on my own. The acrid smell of coffee filled the air. I wanted a cup desperately. My stomach began to growl. Skipping breakfast had not been a good idea after all. Other nurses got up and helped themselves, but I felt conspicuous and sat still.

Report raced on. I wanted to ask questions, but knew they would have to wait until I was alone with Tina, who was engrossed in her 3 × 5 cards. Finally, report was over. The night nurse closed the kardex and handed it to Marilyn, whose huge, diamond-stud earrings sparkled in the dim light. I looked at my watch again: 8:00 already.

"All right, Joyce," Tina sighed wearily, "let's find you a locker." She led the way out. "You won't need that cap here," she added as an afterthought. "They only get in the way, so we don't wear them."

I felt disappointed, but placed the carrier in the top of a locker. Tina turned and left. I raced after her. Once inside the main unit I stopped. The big open room had twelve filled beds circling the large nurses' station. People milled about. Comatose bodies were attached to machines, respirators, and monitors. Tubing hung everywhere. My heart and breath quickened. I was finally working in the intensive care unit as a nurse. The beginning of my dream, I thought.

TWO

"There's no time to daydream, Strom," Tina growled. "Let's get to work and meet your patients so these girls can get out of here. Now," she began, not looking directly at me, "you've got beds number five and six. I'll take seven and eight. You couldn't possibly handle number eight yet, although five will keep you busy."

Her attitude was making me nervous. I wondered what I had done to set her off, or if she was always this unfriendly. She seemed agitated and nervous. I noticed that her hands were shaking, but then she had consumed three cups of coffee during report. One cup of coffee always makes me nervous, so I rationalized that she, like me, had probably not eaten and was suffering the effects of the caffeine. My stomach growled to remind me.

Tina was talking to a night nurse, Mary. "So, you had a hell of a night? Oh," as an afterthought she suddenly turned to me, "this is Joyce . . . a new one." I stood quietly, nodding my head and smiling.

"Welcome to the pit. I'm Mary." The tall brunette shook my hand. "So, what have you got?"

Before I could answer, Tina spoke. "We're buddying; beds five and six are hers. Five will probably take her all morning." Mary nodded affirmatively. I wondered what the rest of the day would be like.

"Okay," Mary began giving her bedside report to both of us. "Bed five is stable now. He was on every 15, but I've increased him to every 30. Watch the urine. It's still down. Call Dr. Monroe, as Kim is off now. I did his a.m. (morning) care and changed the abdominal dressing, so he's all set for a little while. There is 250 MF (main fluid IV) to go. I'm a little behind. Catch it up. Okay?" She went on about my next patient. "Bed six is alright except that I'm sick of looking at her. She needs to be suctioned frequently. Control her when she fights the respirator."

I wanted to interrupt and ask how to control her, but I knew that I would have to read the medication orders. She probably had Pavulon to anesthetize her muscles while the respirator breathed for her.

"Her IV is on time," Mary continued. "Are there any questions?"

Tina asked nothing, so I remained silent.

When Mary turned to leave, Tina reminded me of unit protocol. "The IV's must be on time. If they aren't, that's sufficient reason for writing you up. This one at bed five is behind, so catch it up."

I took my card to compute the math for the drops per minute on the IV and taped it to the IV pole. The clock now said 8:40. I had still done no hands-on nursing. I was eager to begin my patient care, to read the charts, and to have a hot cup of coffee.

Tina and I agreed to assist each other with the beds and baths. By 9:30 we had completed the routine work, stopping only for the periodic thirty—or sixty-minute vital signs. I was greatly relieved when she suggested that we stop for a coffee break. I felt dizzy from tension and hunger, and I had a burning sensation in the soles of my feet. Tina showed me the unit refrigerator and cookie drawer. I was famished. I made some toast and poured the coffee. We sat in the lounge in silence until a nurse entered whom I had not seen before.

"Hi," Tina called out. "Lois, this is Joyce Strom. A new graduate in the unit."

A strong-faced woman, whose short auburn hair was slightly streaked with gray, introduced herself. "I'm Lois Stevenson, the unit supervisor. Welcome. We sure can use another pair of hands."

The comment made me cringe. I was beginning to wonder if I was a unit nurse or part of a robot. Lois lit a cigarette and blew puffs of smoke in the air. I was not a smoker. My eyes began to water.

Lois took a sip of her coffee before speaking. "I'll put you on the time sheet and give you this weekend off." Weekends off to a nurse are considered so valuable that I could hardly contain my joy. "After that," she shook her head, "the rules apply to you the same as anyone else. You get every other weekend off and you will share the holidays."

I knew that I had been spoiled in training, with most weekends and holidays free. But I also knew that nursing is a twenty-four-hour job, seven days a week.

"Let me know when your Boards are scheduled," Lois continued. "Any special requests you have must be in writing to me in advance of the monthly schedule. I prefer them at least two to three weeks before. It is your responsibility, once the schedule is posted, to swap with someone else if an emergency arises. But I am here to help you." She puffed on her cigarette again and ground the butt into the filled, dirty metal ashtray.

"Thank you, Mrs. Stevenson," I replied quietly.

"You may call me Lois."

I tried to feel comfortable with her. Supervisors like Miss Holcomb always intimidated me. Doctors intimidated me. Everyone with a license, power or authority made me feel insecure. I was still suffering from *studentitis*. Lois seemed warm, compassionate, caring, and trustworthy. Looking more closely at her, I saw that she was almost as tall as I, but thinner. Her pant uniform hung on her. Her makeup was scant. I couldn't make up my mind how old she was, although I was sure she was younger than she looked. I didn't recognize her school pin. Afraid to ask any personal questions, I sat silently.

Tina swung her feet off the chair, signalling that our break was over. Back in the ward, we worked fast and furiously. Before I knew it, it was 1:00 and time for lunch. It wasn't until the afternoon care was finished that I had some quiet time to read my patients' charts.

I enjoyed the chance to read the case histories and lab studies in the charts. I stopped only to take the vital signs of my patients every half hour. They were resting comfortably and probably gratefully, having the solitude of some uninterrupted rest. ICU psychosis is a very real problem. Patients need a minimum of ninety minutes to sleep before the REM (rapid eye movement) state. Without REM, patients become psychotic and often act in a bizarre and disoriented fashion.

My patient in bed six was a frail, tiny woman of seventy-eight who had been admitted for the removal of a malignant tumor in her descending colon. The colostomy she'd had was only one of her numerous problems. Since surgery she had developed septicemia (a blood dyscrasia—infection) and was consistently intubated on a MA-1 respirator. The unit policy was that any patient who needed a respirator for more than ten days had to have a tracheosotomy. She had been trached two weeks before. She was filled with rales in her lower left lobe (lung) and cultures were positive for pseuydomonas—a bacterial infection. Massive doses of antibiotics were being infused piggyback into her main fluid IV.

The evening shift began to drift in through the doors at 2:30. The noise level in the unit rose once again. I noticed a male nurse, which I thought was refreshing. While men still made up only two to three percent of the nursing profession, it was strongly felt that our internal problems would improve as more men entered our ranks.

I was distracted by an unfamiliar voice. "Hi, there," was all I heard as I spun around to find a warm, smiling, familiar face. "I'm Lisa, remember?" she asked. I nodded.

I would never forget Lisa; she was in charge many times when I worked in the unit as a student.

"I certainly do," I said, "and I'm so happy to see a smiling face."

Lisa seemed to be aware of my message. "It's pretty tough being the new kid on the block in here, huh?" I nodded as she added, "Now you know why I prefer evenings or nights. Just too much chaos for me on the day shift." I said nothing, but the smile on my face and the glint in my eye told her I agreed. "Well, you'll be with us soon enough, and after two weeks of days, you'll be grateful to be with us." Without another word, she headed off for the nurses' lounge and report.

I liked Lisa and, for the first time that day, I felt accepted. Only two years older than me, she had also graduated from Trinity. She had been the president of her class and well liked. I was an entering freshman when she was a senior. While I never knew her intimately, she took all the students under her wing.

Giving report on my patients to the afternoon nurse, I realized that my shift was over. I had survived my first day "on duty" in the intensive care unit. I also had a throbbing tension headache, and was grateful to finally go home.

Tina was in the locker room. I thanked her for her help, but she was lost in thought. I needed to use the restroom before I left the hospital. As I was washing my hands I suddenly noticed a small vial on the floor, next to the wastepaper basket, and I leaned over to pick it up. Vials were a common sight in the hospital, especially in the unit. Anything from normal saline to sterile water to demerol, vistaril, or morphine could be found in a vial. I didn't think anything of the small bottle as I picked it up to throw it in the wastebasket. After all, someone else had probably done the same thing and missed.

The bottle felt unusual. My fingernail caught on a rough spot on the bottom. I picked it up to eye level and pointed it in the direction of the bathroom light. The vial was marked "Demerol—100 mg." Upon closer inspection, I noticed the bottom of the vial had been cut all the way around and then glued back together. I wondered why someone would take the time to do such a thing.

A knock on the restroom door interrupted my thoughts. I tucked the bottle into my pocket, knowing full well that if I were caught and inspected I would be in trouble. Vials were not supposed to be disposed of in the restroom wastebasket. Vials, ampoules, syringes, and needles were to be thrown into a special container at the medication counter and then destroyed by the hospital separately. It prevented contamination.

At the time I had no idea why I confiscated the bottle. I unlocked the door, smiled to an unknown nurse, and headed for the time clock. It was 4:00 p.m. The end of a very long and arduous day. I was off duty and going home. I forgot about the bottle in the bottom of my uniform pocket.

THREE

Two weeks passed quickly. They were emotionally draining. I felt the tension of the unit and my co-workers up the back of my neck. I had worked eight straight days and was physically exhausted. The unit was always busy. Always hectic.

My roommate, Karen, and I kept missing each other, which also frustrated me. Karen worked nights on OB (maternity) while I was still on the day shift. With no love interest in my life and no family close by, I was at loose ends.

Late at night lying in bed, I thought about my life. Books and notes lay all over our apartment. In my spare time I tried to study for State Boards. Our class graduated in May and would take those dreaded exams only two months later in the beginning of July. With such close proximity to the tests, we should have been knowledgeable and confident. But the dread and fear of those two-day-long exams had hung over my head since the beginning of nursing school. Instead of concentrating on the textbook, though, I found my mind drifting.

I remembered with pride the pink uniform with the pink and white pinafore I had worn for three years. Each year another pink ribbon was added to the cap. Finally, that cap was turned in for the white cap with the black band now sitting in my plastic hand carrier.

The instructors of my nursing school were all graduates of the original hospital school of nursing. Nationwide, these three-year diploma programs, as they were called, were closing. Nursing was becoming centered in the community colleges and local universities. The courses, as well as the students and teachers, were more exciting. Our class had begun as a three-year, hospital-based, diploma program, but, halfway through our second year, we transferred to the community college. By our senior year we were attending the university. Although we graduated from Trinity with a diploma and a RN, we also received a Bachelor's degree in nursing from the university. We had the option to complete a Master's degree at the university for a MSN in nursing. Someday, I hoped to do just that.

It was at the community college where I began my nursing career that I met Eric. He was an engineering student who played football on the college team. Eric had the superb body of an athlete. What he lacked in educational skills he made up for in a whirlwind of parties, dates, and dances.

As the psychiatric textbook lay open on my lap I wondered what Eric was doing now. He had transferred to Ohio State. Then we lost touch. Eric was my first love and the man who introduced me to my own sexuality.

When the alarm rang early the next morning, I wondered how I could drag my aching body out of bed to face another day of crisis in the unit. Then I remembered that I was scheduled to have off the next three days. Finally—a weekend, plus a Friday. It didn't even bother me that I was not dating anyone. Had I been, I would have been too tired to go out. *At least tomorrow morning I can sleep*, I thought, pushing my body out of bed into the cool, early morning twilight.

Standing and stretching I heard the usual sounds of birds singing. I wondered what they saw that was so joyful. The way my body felt, it was hard to imagine ever feeling rested and refreshed again. Nursing school had never been as physically intense as this. Somehow I found the stamina to dress and go to work.

As I swung the heavy doors open I was suddenly aware of unusual activity in the unit. Looking around, I noticed the curtains were pulled around bed four. Dr. Kim, a surgical resident, was at the bedside. Beside him stood Phil Baker, a new intern. Marilyn stood at the foot of the bed with Tina and Melanie next to her. Lois was close by. Then, I saw the crash cart.

In bed four was a nineteen-year-old auto accident victim. She had been in the unit for two weeks. She had never regained consciousness from the time of the accident. Only the respirator kept her heart beating and her lungs breathing. Her EEG's had been flat, which probably meant that her brain stem was torn. She was very young and her parents kept praying for her recovery. No one wanted to turn the respirator off. Taking care of her had been emotionally draining for all of us. We were not much older than she. It was hard to envision the ending of a young life; it hit too close to home.

Melanie turned and looked at me.

"It's almost over," she murmured.

"Thank God," I replied.

"Yes." She nodded sadly. Attractive, with a long blonde braid down her back, Melanie was one of the few nurses in ICU with whom I sensed a rapport.

For days I had been wishing the nineteen-year-old would die, but then I would feel guilty for thinking such an unethical thought. Medicine functions to save lives at all costs. *I must function the same,* I would remind myself. Suddenly the code ended. I breathed a heavy sigh of relief.

The patient had done for herself what no one else would do. She had arrested and died.

Lois caught my eye. As she walked by me she snapped, "Strom, I want to see you at the end of the shift in the nurses' lounge." She kept on walking away as she spoke. I couldn't even respond before she was around the corner and out of sight.

The staff placed the crash cart back against the wall in clear view of all the patients' beds. Tina and Shelly, who had worked nights, did the post mortem care on the lifeless young body. I felt a surge of panic in my chest and my face reddened. I wondered what Lois wanted.

The tension headache took over again as I asked myself, *Why do I let people get to me?* Even in nursing school I had accepted every criticism and negative statement about me as absolutely correct. My mind raced over the past two weeks. Had I done something wrong? Was my nursing care poor? By 8:00 a.m. I was becoming paranoid with my own delusions and negative thoughts. The day became long, tedious, and unsettling.

Finally it was 2:30. Lois came out of the lounge and asked me to come in. She and Marilyn were sitting smoking in the coffee room. Together, they had filled the room with a deep, blue haze that burned my eyes. Tears began to well around my contact lenses. I blinked hard, trying not to appear upset. *They have good news for me or are going to switch me to evenings,* I said over and over to myself.

The silence was as thick as the smoke. I watched each of them light another cigarette. The suspense escalated. My head throbbed. My eyes hurt. My chest was ready to explode. I hated feeling out of control. Absent-mindedly, I noticed that Marilyn wore a gold chain studded with tiny sapphires, and Lois sported a Cartier watch.

Finally, Lois spoke. "Strom," she began, using my last name as we had done in school. It seemed so cold and impersonal. "We asked you to come in here today, because we find it necessary to talk with you."

My heart raced even faster. My gut instinct had been correct. This encounter was going to be very negative.

Lois inhaled deeply on her cigarette. The chunky gold rolex watch on her arm sparkling. Shaking my head, I wondered how anyone could tolerate the lung pressure of foreign inhalant. "In the two weeks that you have been here, you have completely alienated everyone. No one likes you. No one wants to buddy with you," she sneered.

What had I done? I wondered. The tears began to well up in my eyes. I felt my defenses rising, but was too numb to respond.

Marilyn took over. "Your patient care," she said sharply, "leaves much to be desired. You are a disgrace to this nursing school and we just wanted you to know that if you don't improve you will not stay in the unit."

My face flushed with emotion. I was stunned. Again, I asked myself *Why? Why was this happening to me . . . and why now?*

Lois blew more smoke into my face. Her accusations began anew. "You have not kept your IV's running on time and we know that Tina told you that was a requirement your first day here."

I wanted to answer that no one kept their IV's on time, but that we all tried and covered for each other. Surely Lois knew that. But the words just would not come out.

Lois continued. "We have already written you up on that violation."

Marily began again. I wondered if they had prepared this routine. They seemed to have it down as to who would start and who would finish. "We have also noticed that you are flirting with the doctors and respiratory therapists. We want to remind you that you are here to give constant bedside nursing care to as many patients as we choose to assign to you, not to carry on with the males in this unit." Her dark eyes flashed with anger.

The charge was absolutely false, but I still could not speak. It was Carol who was always sitting on the laps of residents and making sexual overtures to them. Had they confused me with Carol? My tears began. A gentle stream, but rapidly building to a rushing flow.

"You are the low man on this totem pole, Strom," Lois added vehemently. "Therefore, you are going to work the July Fourth holiday plus every weekend for the next month. We are also putting you on the night shift with the next time sheet for one month. Longer if you don't shape up," she concluded.

I was stunned. The month of nights along with working every weekend seemed excessive. I didn't mind working the holiday, but what had I done to provoke such an attack, with so much punishment, in two brief weeks?

Marilyn spoke again: "And, Strom, we expect you to stay at the bedside of your assigned patients. No matter what. If you must leave, you wait until someone relieves you. This rule applies to coffee breaks, meals, and bathroom privileges. Quality care is the primary goal of this unit. If you cannot accept that, then I suggest you leave."

It struck me suddenly. They wanted me to leave! I felt numb. My hands were so cold they tingled. My head began to swim.

"Get out of here, Strom," Marilyn snapped. "You're on probation right now. I have had enough of looking at you for now, so just leave."

I didn't have to be asked twice. Reeling, I headed for the nurses' lounge and bathroom. Once inside I began to cry; then I began to vomit. My head throbbed.

I washed my face and swollen red eyes with cold water. The evening shift bustled around in the locker room. I knew Report would begin soon. Somehow, I had to pull myself together and go back into the unit to report to the evening nurse taking my patients.

I hid out in the bathroom until everyone left. Slipping out of the locker room, I saw Sally's plump figure at the bedside of one of my patients, a man named Hermes in his early eighties, who had a ruptured aortic aneurysm. The nursing care was routine: read all of the monitors and document the results and times correctly. But the nursing responsibility called for more decision-making: assess any change in his condition and notify the charge nurse and physicians accordingly. Sally was measuring his CVP when I approached her.

"Where the hell have you been?" she hissed, her reddish hair almost bristling. I started. It wasn't like Sally to be so irritable. I wondered if she was one of the nurses who complained about me.

"Sorry," I sniffed. "I was in the bathroom."

"Have you got a cold?" she asked, not looking up.

"Yes," I replied, hoping she wouldn't look at my puffy eyes. "How's Mr. Hermes?" I changed the subject.

"His CVP is up. Circulatory overload. I'm going to give him twenty milligrams of lasix and see if we can nip this in the bud." She drew up a syringe with the lasix and injected it into the main fluid IV. "That should help him within the next hour." Sally turned away from the bed and headed for my other patient.

Mrs. Wolf was a sweet old lady. She was sixty-four years old, and her history was extensive because of numerous cardiac problems. This time she had been admitted to the unit for a pacemaker. The machine worked on demand: if her heart skipped a beat, the pacemaker kicked in and produced one. Everything seemed to be going smoothly; Mrs. Wolf was ready to be transferred to the floor. Her doctor had already written the discharge notes. I had hoped to transfer her before the end of my shift, but the medical floor still didn't have a bed. I told Sally all of this and apologized for leaving her with the job.

"Code Blue!" The call made us all jump. Suddenly the unit came alive. Everyone ran to push the heavy crash cart over to a bed. I turned. The bed they were running to was Mr. Hermes's.

Quickly, Sally moved to his bed. The cardiac monitor

was no longer showing the cavernous sinus rhythm of
PVC's (premature ventricular contractions); it now
showed V-tack. "He's in ventricular tachycardia," Sally
yelled. "He is going into cardiac arrest."

"What happened?" I asked Sally as she raced to the
head of his bed.

Sally didn't answer. The look of fright on her face was
enough. Sally had been a critical care nurse for over a
year. She worked in our unit and in CCU (Coronary Care
Unit). Obviously, something more than a Code was happening.

"Sodium bicarb," Marilyn yelled.

"Paddles," screamed another nurse.

I backed up. People pushed me out of the way. I found
myself next to Mrs. Wolf and turned to reassure her. The
cubicle drapes around Mr. Hermes were drawn in order to
provide privacy.

Mrs. Wolf stared at me. Tears tricked down her face.
"Everything will be all right," I whispered, patting her
hand and trying to sound confident.

"Child," she whispered back, "at my age death sneaks
up on you."

I shook my head. "You are not going to die, Mrs. Wolf.
You have a nice heartbeat now. You are going to go home
soon." I fumbled for words of comfort and support. Behind
me the commotion grew. The other patients were awake
and listening.

By now the small area was filled with twenty doctors,
nurses, and respiratory therapists. I heard the "stand
clear" and then the electrical zap of the paddles. My skin
crawled. Again, the "stand clear." And, again, the sound
of the paddles.

"Come on. Get that heart going," a male voice bellowed.

"Stand clear." Zap, again.

The monitor whirred. I was already attuned to the
sounds of heart rates, so when it hissed out a loud, flat
tone, I knew it was asystole. Mr. Hermes was dead.

"Damn it," screamed the attending physician, "who the hell gave potassium chloride?"

I froze. My mind raced. *Postassium chloride? Did I give it to Mr. Hermes?* I thought. *No,* I answered myself. *Sally gave him lasix, but he had been stable on my shift.*

I held onto Mrs. Wolf's bedrail. Had I overlooked something in the wake of my confrontation with Lois and Marilyn? Had I given medication without documenting it?

The male voice behind the cubicle curtain continued. "I asked," he snarled, "who the hell gave potassium chloride?"

I could only hear mumbling: *Would I be blamed for this one too?* I wondered. I stood still, not daring to move.

The next voice I heard was Lois's. "Dr. Jones, perhaps we can discuss this over here. I'll take the nurses' notes with me."

"I want some answers," he demanded angrily, "and I want someone's hide for this."

Potassium chloride causes instant cardiac arrythmia. The heart muscle needs potassium, but in the proper dosages. I was confused. And scared. Before I could decide what to do, Sally called me.

"Get over here, Strom," Sally said in a nervous, low voice. Her voice sounded like it would crack.

Everyone else had left the bedside. Lois and Dr. Jones headed for the desk; others went back to their patients. The cart was pushed back against the wall, and a nurse I didn't recognize was restocking it.

Sally closed the cubicle firmly. I looked at Mr. Hermes laying silently on the bed. Blood still oozed from his IV's. The burns from the paddles stained his chest bright red. I could almost visualize his chest moving in and out, but his lifeless body had no life signs.

Sally began the post mortem care. "What happened?" I asked.

Suddenly Sally looked up at me with tears in her eyes. "I think I killed him."

"What?"

"Ssssssh . . ." She glanced around, afraid of being overheard.

Somehow, I regained my composure. Almost whispering, I asked her, "What do you mean, you think you killed him?"

She began to sob. "Oh, God. I thought I gave him lasix, but look over there." She pointed.

I looked at the bedside table, where standard supplies were kept. The lasix was still sitting on his bedside stand unopened. Next to the lasix was a vial of potassium chloride. It was empty.

"You gave potassium chloride?" I asked.

She nodded. "I think so. God, what am I going to do?"

"Look, it was a mistake. It could have happened to any of us." I tried to sound reassuring.

"Don't you understand," she began to cry, "I killed a patient." She began to sob heavily. I held her up as she covered her face with her hands.

"Sally, look, get yourself together. You have to tell them." I felt enormous pity for her. I tightened my arm around her shoulder.

"Tell them," she exclaimed, straightening up. "How the hell do I tell them? Didn't you hear Dr. Jones?"

"You have to," I replied. "What can they do to you?"

"Start by taking my license away," she said shakily. "Then, I can be sued by the family, the doctor, the hospital, and God knows who else." She began to cry again. "I'll never work as a nurse again. What am I going to do?"

I was frightened. What would I do in this situation? I began doing the post mortem care on Mr. Hermes. I had to busy myself. I filled his bedside wash basin with warm water to give him his last bath before wrapping the body for the morgue.

"I could just not say anything," Sally said, reaching over for another washcloth. She began to wash Mr. Hermes' right side as I did his left. "They will never know," she went on. "They'll never be able to prove anything."

I washed his legs, then his genitals. I removed the foley catheter. "Did you document the lasix?" I asked.

She thought for a moment. "I don't remember."

I snipped the small tubing attached to the foley, allowing the internal balloon filled with normal saline to deflate. As I gently slid the foley out of his flacid penis I reminded her, "They'll probably do a post, you know."

"A post?" she asked, watching me work as she held the washcloth in a tight grip.

"An autopsy," I said.

"Oh, God, you're right. They *will*. But they already know it was potassium chloride."

"No," I continued while removing the IV's and re-placing his dentures in his lifeless mouth. "They *suspect* potassium chloride."

Her tears began again. "I don't have a choice, do I, Joyce?"

I shook my head. "No. You had better tell them." Suddenly I knew that I would.

I tied Mr. Hermes's hands and feet together with the gauze from the post-mortem kit. *How frightening it can be to have a nurse's responsibility,* I thought. *In a split second we must make life and death decisions. In a split second we can also make mistakes.*

I looked up at Sally, who stood wringing the wash-cloth. Reaching toward her I gently took the cloth from her hands. She continued to wring her hands. "Sally, I can finish up here."

She stared back at me. "Thank you. I better go tell them now."

She hesitated a minute. "Could you come with me?" My stomach tightened. I certainly didn't want to, espe-cially after the horrendous scene I'd had earlier with Lois and Marilyn. Sally shook with fright. "Please," she pleaded. I nodded slowly, "Give me a few minutes."

I thought of how brave she really was. As I wrapped

the plastic liner around Mr. Hermes's body and carefully covered him, my mind went back to the session with Lois and Marilyn. What they had said to me didn't feel real. Now, as I stood at this man's bedside, I wondered if they were trying to tell me that critical care nursing is a very serious and demanding responsibility. Was that the purpose of that scene with me? Was there some redeeming value in it?

I caught up with Sally, who had almost reached the nurses' station where Lois and Dr. Jones sat reviewing the charts. "I have to talk to you, Lois," she stated, her voice cracking.

Lois and Dr. Jones looked up. They looked at me quizzically.

"I think I killed Mr. Hermes," Sally said quietly. With that, she began to slip to the floor. Lois and Dr. Jones raced around to cushion her fall.

"Bring an ammonia ampoule," Lois ordered, staring at me.

I ran to the nurses' desk and came back with a small glass ampoule. Lois broke it and passed it under Sally's nose. Sally coughed and choked. Her eyes watered. Lois held the ampoule away from her. The strong odor irritated her eyes also.

"Are you all right?" she asked with genuine concern.

Sally nodded. Dr. Jones helped her to her feet. Lois, Dr. Jones, Marilyn and I walked Sally into the nurses' lounge and placed her on the sofa in a reclining position.

Dr. Jones finally spoke first after Lois gave her a glass of water. They all liked Sally. She was a good nurse and they knew it. "What happened?" he asked.

Sally couldn't look at them. She stared at her water glass held in both of her trembling hands. "Mr. Hermes's CVP was up so I gave him twenty milligrams of lasix. At least, I thought I did. But," she paused, taking a sip of water to regain her composure, "I must have given him the potassium chloride."

All three professionals listened silently. Everyone

knew the ampoules looked the same. But it was a nursing responsibility to read and reread all medications before administering them.

Dr. Jones finally broke the silence. "Mr. Hermes was an elderly man who was already clinically dead due to his aortic aneurysm. I am not sure what would be accomplished by doing an autopsy."

Lois and Marilyn nodded in agreement. Neither Sally nor I could believe our ears. In nursing school we had been taught that doctors would never protect a nurse. When it came to licenses, the nurse would always lose hers first. But, from the way Dr. Jones was talking, it sounded like he was going to protect her.

"I think we will just list the cause of death as cardiac arrest," he said soberly.

Sally looked at him. The tears in her eyes said what she couldn't put in words.

"I am so sorry," she cried.

Dr. Jones patted her hand. "I know you are. You are a good nurse. This was a terrible mistake, but it need not leave this room. Without an autopsy we will never be sure anyhow."

Sally was shocked. "Thank you," was all she could say.

I remained silent.

Lois spoke up. "This will stay in this room. Sally, you are too valuable to us. A tragedy like this is something you will have to live with. You will have also learned an important lesson."

Sally nodded again saying "thank you" to Lois and Marilyn. She turned back to Dr. Jones. "I am so sorry."

"I know you are, young lady." Dr. Jones took the chart from Lois and wrote the time and cause of death. "Notify the family," he said. He looked at Sally once again and in silence, left the room.

"Why don't you take a few days off?" Lois asked when Sally realized the full impact of what had happened.

"Yes. I will," she replied. "I need the time." She

looked searchingly at me. "Would you walk me to my car?"

I looked at Lois, who nodded her permission. "Take fifteen minutes, Strom," she said curtly.

Quickly, we left the building and found Sally's beat-up car nestled uncomfortably among the rows of exotic imports with MD and RN license plates which dominated the parking lot. I wondered silently how struggling young nurses and interns could afford such beauties.

"It will never be the same for me," Sally wept, opening the rusty car door and sliding in.

I reassured her as best I could. "Look, what you really need now is some rest."

She nodded. "I don't know how to thank you." Exhausted myself, I watched her drive away.

Finally, I punched my time clock at 4:30 p.m. I didn't see Lois, Marilyn or Dr. Jones again that day, and I thought myself fortunate. Leaving the unit, I thought about the day, especially my meeting with the two nurses and what had happened to Sally. Driving home, I tried to concentrate on the road, but questions spun endlessly through my mind. Why had they let Sally off? Why had they attacked me? What power did these doctors and nurses have to chastise me or to forgive Sally? Why had Mr. Hermes died? Was his death due to the error of a nurse?

My mind raced over the previous weeks. Yes, I was new to the unit and critical care nursing, but I had not made any mistakes that I could think of. Sally had made a gross nursing error, yet she had only received a scolding. Still, my conscience was clear. Sally would have to live with her mistake for the rest of her life.

For the next three days I considered requesting a transfer out of the unit. However, I knew that I didn't want to be a nurse in any other area of the hospital. In fact, all of the speciality units were full. Only the medical/surgical floors were open, and I didn't want to work with ten or more elderly, incontinent, bedridden patients every single day. The critical care unit was where I wanted to be. There, I felt I was doing something skilled and life saving.

Besides, since I would be working nights for a while, I could probably avoid both Marilyn and Lois when they came on duty.

FOUR

Saturday was a gorgeous, hot, balmy, summer day. Karen and I lay on the beach feeling the sand under our toes and the water clinging to our oil-ladened bodies. We briefly attempted to study for State Boards, but the sand and blue-green water won out.

"Karen, can I talk to you about a problem I'm having in the unit?" I asked when I felt we were both sufficiently relaxed.

"Sure," she replied, slowly repositioning her lithe body face up towards the afternoon sun. "What's up?"

I began tracing circles in the sand. "I'm not sure what the problem is, so I guess I'll just start at the beginning," I said hesitantly.

"It started the first day in the unit when I was assigned to work with Tina on the buddy system. The funny part of it is, I really like the nursing that goes on up there, but I'm beginning to feel that something else is going on and I am intentionally not part of it."

I recounted my experiences, including the confrontation with Lois and Marilyn. With the exception of her breathing and an occasional stir of her body towards the sun, Karen was silent. As I expressed my views and feelings I began to feel that perhaps I was blowing things out of proportion.

Karen didn't answer; so I finally asked, "How is everything going for you on maternity?"

Karen hesitated, "Better than ICU is treating you. I really enjoy Labor and Delivery the most. It is so exciting to be a part of the birth of a new life. Of course, there are some unhappy moments. We've had one stillborn and two Downs Syndromes since I've been there. We also had a close call with a Frank breech delivery."

I sighed heavily. Was Karen avoiding my question? "How does the staff treat you?" I asked.

"Like a new graduate, I guess. They're not overly friendly. They seem cautious about me. After all, it's their license I work under until I receive mine. They offer me the chance to learn and do procedures, though. I give meds, assist in the deliveries, and I have finally learned both vaginal and rectal dilation." Karen finally laughed. "Remember when we thought as students we would never get the hang of centimeters?"

I chuckled too. "I never did," I said. "Maybe I should have been more interested in maternity." As an afterthought in my defense I added, "Perhaps I should have begun my nursing on the floors or in another area. What do you think, Karen? Should I hang in there or should I just transfer out before it's too late?"

Karen could have been a psychologist. She didn't answer directly. "Well, what do *you* think? I think you have to decide that for yourself. Weigh out the situation carefully."

I lay on the blanket in silence, thinking of my choices and options. Leaving would be humiliating and an admission of failure. My pride and ego were beginning to tell me that I really shouldn't give in to the pressure. Perhaps the pressure was nothing more than a way of weeding out nurses who couldn't stand up under the constant crisis of the environment.

"I really don't want to leave," I said out loud. "I know that I can be a good critical care nurse. Maybe I should try to forget Lois and Marilyn and warm up to the others."

Then a peculiar idea entered my head. Before I realized it, I was voicing it. "You know, I almost wonder if Marilyn and Dr. Vorhees are having a relationship." It seemed to be more of a question than a comment. "Maybe she thinks I'm after him," I added. "He has been giving me strange looks, and he's always touching my arm when he comes to the bedside."

"You've gotten that too," Karen laughed, bringing me back to my full senses. "So do we. Christ, the attendings are worse than the residents, and they are all married. Why do doctors and nurses always play little sexual games?"

"Ummmmm. Could be that's what's behind the intimidation message."

"Well," Karen went on, "it *is* common. I wish we had a course in nursing school on how to cope with doctors," she added.

I picked up on it. "How to communicate with doctors without having intercourse?" We both laughed hysterically, thinking of whom the instructor would be and of the classroom demonstrations.

Karen expressed my thoughts. "You know, Joyce, maybe our problems have a lot to do with the sexes."

"What do you mean?"

"Doctors are usually men and nurses are usually women, in spite of the two to four percent of opposite sexes in each profession. Put men and women together working side by side, day after day, and what do you have?"

I knew where she was going. I thought of other businesses. "Many corporate structures find the co-workers having affairs, don't they?"

"Of course they do. But the stress is higher here. We are really two individual professions working together in some of life's most exciting experiences. Sexual contact is probably just a way of maintaining our sanity in the life and death tragedies of our daily routine. And the fallout— the hazing and backstabbing—is going to be greater. Prob-

ably more so for you, Joyce, because critical care sees the
worst of it."

"Next to the emergency room," I added.

Karen was right. The tension was so great that sex
was often the only way to release the stress.

"Do you think nurses will ever understand that our
profession is a business?" I asked. "You know something,
Karen, we may be the new grads on the block, but I
recently learned in a lecture that the consumers of our
services are not the patients, but the doctors."

"Wait a minute," she corrected me. "We don't call
them 'patients' anymore. Not since the Nurse Practice Act
of 1974, and you know that will be a question on the
boards."

"Right. Clients. Patients are now clients. And clients
are consumers of our services." It was difficult for me to
change my language.

"So," Karen wanted to know, "how can a doctor be
the consumer of our services?"

"The instructor said that doctors look to us to fill
their orders and need us to be there when they cannot." I
didn't give Karen time to respond. "I know we are care-
givers, but we are still our own corporation, just like
football players. Why don't we use our strength and
power? Why do we always submit?"

Karen sighed. "Women have always submitted to
men. I wonder if it will ever change."

I wondered too. At least I was feeling better and in
more control of my life and destiny. "Thanks, Karen." I
leaned over and patted her shoulder. "You've been a big
help to me and a good friend."

She sat up and looked at me. "I love you, Strom.
You're my best friend. You'll be okay in the unit. Just don't
compromise yourself."

She was right. "I love you too, Karen. So, have you
had enough sun?"

For some reason, the timing didn't seem right to tell

Karen about Mr. Hermes's death and Sally's mistake. Something in my gut told me to keep it quiet.

She nodded, looking at her watch. "Four p.m. Just enough time to go home, wash our hair, grab a bite and hit the campus lounge."

"Sounds great." I even knew what I would wear. A pink silk skirt with matching blouse and wide white belt. After weeks of white, the belt was enough white for this evening.

With her chestnut, shoulder-length hair, blue eyes and a petite figure, Karen always looked great. Our friendship had grown long after I admired her stunning beauty.

I was still terribly insecure. Always towering above everyone in school, I think I was born 5'9". My hair was long and dirty blond. My hazel eyes, light skin, and freckles were evidence of my English-Swedish heritage.

The campus lounge parking lot was crowded and I could smell marijuana when we arrived at 9:30 p.m. Our college was still a place to go to meet old classmates and swap stories about work. We also met the underclassmen who had to finish nursing school. Interns and residents hung out there, too.

The dimly lit lounge always seemed tinged with romance. Beer kegs lined the corner. We always wondered if we would meet someone new. Karen and I speculated regularly about a Prince Charming, who would sweep us off our feet. Romance had not been a part of either of our lives in more than a year. Lately I longed to be held by a tall handsome man. Preferably with blond hair and blue eyes.

Karen found an old friend. I mingled. The talk was of the upcoming boards. Apprehension and fear of failure loomed in the air along with the increasing odors of pot, beer, perspiration, and cigarette smoke. I was beginning to get bored.

"Hi, don't I know you?"

I turned around, coolly. "That cliche is pretty old, don't you think?"

The man was taller than me. I didn't raise my head to look at him directly.

"I know you're familiar to me," he went on. "Aren't you a nurse?"

I nodded. "Yes, and I work at Trinity in ICU."

"Then that must be where I have seen you. I'm a first year resident in surgery. I just began working at Trinity for my surgical rotation. My name is Paul Thompsom."

Then I looked up into the most sensuous, beautiful, deep-blue eyes I'd ever seen. His hair was dark, almost black. His smile was soft. Glowing. Charming. And even in my high heels I had to crane my neck to meet his eyes.

"My name is Joyce Strom," I smiled, reaching out to shake his hand. Shaking hands is a comfortable way to assess a person's self confidence. A weak, light handshake means insecurity to me, while an overly strong, pumping shake is aggressive. A firm, gentle shake is comfortable.

Paul's hand clasp was strong, firm, but also gentle. Only, he didn't let go as our eyes met again and locked. "Would you like to dance?" he asked.

Breathlessly, I nodded "yes." He walked me to the dance floor, and my heart began to race as he whisked me into his arms, his strong, masculine body next to mine. He smelled of Calvin Klein's "Obsession," which I bought for my father every year. I loved it.

"Where are you from?" I asked, trying to make small talk, hoping he couldn't hear the pounding of my heart.

"A small town you probably never heard of," he smiled. His voice was quiet. Soft. "Endicott. It's just a little south of Binghamton."

I nodded. I was familiar with both. "I'm from Auburn," I breathed. "It's a small city on Owasco Lake."

He smiled as we moved easily across the dance floor. The lights bounced off his skin and hair. His eyes twinkled. I thought he was the handsomest man I had ever seen.

"So, do you like Trinity?" he asked, breaking into my thoughts.

"Yes. I trained there. I stayed on because I just can't imagine leaving the city."

He nodded. "I've requested a surgical residency under Dr. Vorhees at Trinity. He is the best open heart surgeon around. Open heart is my specialty."

"That's exciting." I wondered if he knew my heart was pounding. The music suddenly ended. I thanked him.

He didn't leave. He walked me back to a small table in the corner. We talked more: of his home, his dreams, and how he missed snow-mobiling and skiing in the winter. I talked about my dreams and ambitions to climb the critical care ladder. We danced most of the slow numbers. "I hate fast dances," he said. As he held me in his arms, my fantasies raced along with my adrenaline.

Karen came over to get me. It was time to go home. I introduced her to Paul. "Thank you for a wonderful evening," I murmured.

"Could I have your phone number?" he asked.

I was thrilled. He really did like me! I grabbed a cocktail napkin and wrote my number on it.

"I'll call you," were his last words. As Karen and I walked away, I turned and looked back at him. My heart melted.

I slept restlessly. But unlike the previous nights' dreams filled with Lois, Marilyn and the unit, these dreams were of Paul.

We decided not to go to church Sunday morning. Church was mandatory while we were in training since, although we trained at the university, we lived in the hospital student nurses' quarters and were required to attend the scheduled church services. Now, Karen and I did not feel the slightest bit of guilt for sleeping late.

She got up before I did. The smell of fresh coffee and

hot bagels brought me awake. I stumbled out to the kitchen.

"What shall we do today?" Karen asked as she spread cream cheese and lox over her bagel.

I slathered a bagel with cream cheese. "We could go back to the beach," I said between bites. "I felt so relaxed out there yesterday." I looked out the window. My mind wandered to Paul.

"You like him, don't you?" she asked, grinning.

I nodded. "He sure was good looking. I could feel my hormone system coming alive." It had been a long time since Eric. Too long. "I wonder if he'll call."

"Sure," Karen replied. "He liked what he saw."

"So did I," I blushed, adding, "And I liked what I felt."

By noon we were both sprawled on the beach. I still wondered whether to tell Karen about Sally's medication error. As my mind drifted off to the unit I brought up the meeting with Lois and Marilyn again.

"You know, Karen," I began, "I just remembered something else. Lois accused me of being a trouble-maker as a student. I think she even said something about the nursing school telling her that I was." Until now I had blocked that part of their accusations. Suddenly the full impact of everything they had said was coming back to my mind.

"That's not true!" Karen exclaimed. "You were a good student. The only trouble you got into was the time we all hung Sister Daniel's habit out the dormitory window in effigy. She was such a pain. She deserved it for locking all of us in for a weekend, because we failed her dumb psychiatry exam. Remember all of those stupid questions she asked us?"

I nodded but turned the subject back to my question. "Why would Lois say such a thing if it wasn't true?"

"Because they like to intimidate you. It was just as bad when we were students, remember? The trouble is, it still goes on. Call it hospital politics, female vindictiveness, jealousy, or whatever. It goes on everywhere in every hospital today. It stinks! But it's a well known fact."

I knew she was correct. In training we were always told that "constructive criticism" was for our own good. "Intimidation was the method they used to make a student a better nurse. If it's a planned approach for graduates, then I suppose it makes us better nurses too?" I didn't really believe those words.

"Sometimes," Karen answered, "but, most of the time, it is just politics or jealousy. You know, men tell it like it is to each other. But women play back-stabbing games and talk about each other."

In my opinion, Karen was right. All the men I knew openly expressed their anger and frustration at each other. Women with whom I was acquainted, on the other hand, never confronted anyone. I was guilty of the same dark behavior. I hated confrontations.

"Many nurses leave the profession every year," Karen said. "We are on the verge of a major nursing shortage worldwide."

I laughed. "How did we get on the subject of the nursing shortage" I inquired half-joking, realizing that my problem with Lois and Marilyn was mine to deal with.

"Women don't want to be nurses today," Karen stated, eager to begin a new subject. "When your mom graduated the only choice for women was teaching or nursing."

I nodded. She was right about that one.

"Being underpaid, overworked, understaffed, and underappreciated doesn't make our profession glamorous," she continued.

"There is nothing glamorous about bedpans, emesis basins, or surgical incisions," I concurred.

"True. But, we save lives."

"Right, Karen, but few people know that. Most don't understand the decisions nurses make or the responsibility we carry."

"You're right there, Joyce." Karen flipped over on her

blanket to sun her back. Hers was a delicate little body, unlike my gawky, tall one. She wore a size one dress. She resembled a doll I once owned, now long gone.

"Even on maternity the public thinks we just sit by watching women go through labor and then hand a baby to them. The responsibility and the pressures are strenous. It is a wonder we don't make more mistakes."

There was my opening. "Karen, there is something else I didn't tell you that happened in the unit last week."

She didn't answer, but turned her face toward me.

"The three-to-eleven nurse who took my patient assignments killed a patient."

Karen rolled over and sat bolt upright. "What?" She stared at me, open-mouthed. "What happened?"

"Sally was checking my patients when I came out of the nurses' lounge. She said that Mr. Hermes's CVP was elevated so she was giving him twenty milligrams of lasix. Apparently, she gave him twenty milligrams of potassium chloride instead."

Karen moaned. "Oh, my God. Twenty milligrams of potassium chloride is instant death."

"That is exactly what happened. He was coded and paddled three times, but he was dead."

"What did she do?"

"She told them what she had done."

Karen sat silently. Long moments passed. "I wonder if I would have done the same thing," she said softly.

I shook my head. "I hope we both would. It took guts."

"What happened to her?"

I repeated my last conversation with Sally. Karen's eyes widened. "I hope she'll be okay."

"I know," I said sympathetically. "I'm really concerned about her."

"Well," Karen paused, "I heard something equally upsetting happened a few weeks ago on maternity. Apparently, the anesthesiologist gave a spinal to a woman fully dilated and ready to push for delivery. Only he gave it too high. The woman delivered, but a few hours later she still had no feeling from the waist down. She's permanently paralyzed.

I cringed. "We do make serious mistakes, don't we?"

"We make serious decisions. Mistakes happen," she answered slowly.

"But people in the medical profession protect themselves and each other," I added, "maybe more than we should."

Karen disagreed. "I don't think so. Lawyers sue us at the drop of a hat. They are only interested in feeding off our errors. I'm not saying they should stop law suits, but most medical errors are *not* the result of incompetence."

"Karen, could you intimidate someone?" I asked.

"Not intentionally, but I wouldn't hesitate to challenge a nurse or a doctor if I thought he or she was making a grave error."

"If you made a gross medical error, would you report it?"

"I like to think so," she mused. "How about you, Joyce?"

I gazed into the white-capped ocean waves. "I can't intimidate anyone. I think it is cruel. But if I made a mistake," I turned back to meet her eyes, "I sure hope I could admit to it. You know, it frightens me to think how vulnerable we are."

She shook her head. "You're right. Nursing is no longer wiping brows and looking virginal in long-sleeved white uniforms." She paused. "So, did you join the ANA yet?"

She had been after me since our student days to join the American Nurses Association. "No," I replied slowly, "I just can't justify the fee and I don't see why we need to belong."

"Come on, Strom. The doctors all belong to *their* AMA! Whether you agree with them or not, they've joined ranks and they accomplish their goals."

"Like what?"

"Like lobbying for legislature in their favor. Or having good group malpractice insurance."

"We have malpractice insurance through the hospital." I stroked the sand with my fingers.

"I hope you're not relying only on that." Her voice rose slightly. "You had better get your own. Take your friend Sally. When it comes down to a law suit the hospital won't protect her. They'll protect themselves. And, in the end, the doctor won't protect her either."

"So you think she should carry her own insurance?"

"Absolutely. And it is not that expensive. Yet."

"You're full of good news today, Karen. Obviously you carry your own insurance?"

"Damn right, and disability insurance too."

"Why disability?"

"Because I have to take care of myself and provide for myself. If I can't work, who will take care of me?"

She had a point there. I could see the dollar signs growing in my head. Mentally adding up all of these costs, I realized that in order to get insurance I would have to use all of my next paycheck.

"And another thing," Karen continued, "your friend Sally would also have legal counsel from the State Nursing Association. Because when you join one, you join both."

"I always thought the ANA was out for itself and did nothing for us." I'd believed the gossip and rumors that flew through school. It would be years before I would realize that I was functioning on the novice level. It takes years to become an expert.

"The ANA is out for *us*," Karen pounded her hand on the sand for emphasis. "You have to C-Y-A yourself."

"Yup. Cover Your Ass." I nodded my head. "You're right, Karen. I will join the ANA and get insurance when I get my next paycheck."

"I'm going to hold you to it, Joyce." Karen lay back on the blanket, a cheshire grin on her face. "I hope your friend Sally is protected. She'll need it."

"Can we keep the news about Sally between us?" I asked.

"Sure," Karen nodded and positioned herself on her back again. She was already toasty brown while I was fast becoming beet red. The only brown on me was my freckles—thousands of which were growing by the second under the hot afternoon sun.

"So," I asked, "did you meet anyone special last night?"

Karen smiled, eyes still closed. "Yes. A law clerk. John Bivens."

"Karen," I practically shrieked, "why didn't you tell me?"

"Well," she laughed. "I haven't really had the chance."

"Tell me about him." I leaned toward her.

Karen described John, including his family, his home town, and his desire to run for politics someday. In one evening she had learned a great deal about him. I was amazed. Paul hadn't been as open with me.

I enjoyed the heat on my body, which I knew would burn later. I tried to forget the medical lectures I'd heard on skin cancer and premature aging. At twenty-two, my whole life lay ahead of me. Like death, illness was beyond my personal experiences. I was a nurse. Nurses never got sick. They took care of the sick.

Karen rambled on about John. I listened quietly, letting my mind wander to Paul. Would he call? Would I see him again? Would we make love someday? Would it be like Eric? I forgot about the hospital and all of its problems.

A cool wind forced me to open my eyes.

"Did you have a nice nap?" Karen asked. Already dressed in shorts and a tank top, she was shaking out her blanket.

I blinked hard. "Did I fall asleep?"

"You sure did," she replied. "While I was telling you

about John. Guess I bored you!" She laughed. I knew she was kidding.

But I was embarrassed. "What time is it?"

"Six forty-five," she said.

"How long did I sleep?"

She laughed again. "Long enough. And are you *red!*" She pointed at my torso exposed from bra to bikini pants. I was thoroughly burned.

"Second degree?" I asked, trying to remember the definitions for burn degrees. Burn questions were always on State Boards.

"No, first degree." She grinned. "Well, have you had enough sun?"

"As I stood up I knew I had more than enough. Fortunately, the drive home was not long.

The phone was ringing as I unlocked the apartment door.

"Oh, please let it be Paul," I prayed. I tripped as I reached the phone and knocked it off the receiver. "Hello, hello."

A male's voice answered, "Hello."

Was the voice familiar? Short of breath, I paused to listen to the voice. My heart began to pound. Karen came in just as I said "hello" again.

The man asked, "Is Karen there?"

My heart sank. "Yes. Just a moment please." I turned to her and handed her the receiver. Overhearing the first part of her conversation I knew it was John.

The rest of the night was bleak. John and Karen went to a movie. I ate alone in front of the television set. My body hurt from the sun.

I realized that I was sitting by the phone waiting for Paul to call. Reluctantly, I went to bed at 10:30 p.m. I had to work the next day. At 12:30, Karen came in. I tossed restlessly until morning.

FIVE

Whenever I came on duty I saw respirators blowing life into inert bodies, IV tubing hanging from all extremities, CVP (central venous pressure) lines from the subclavian vein on the right side of the neck, and MAP (mean arterial pressure) lines from the left artery in the wrist. The smell of aseptic betadine, old blood, purulent infections, septicemia, urine and feces blended in the air. Life and death intermingled. Blood surged through my veins in rapid excitement, as I wondered what the day would bring and whose life I might save.

State Boards were only two weeks away.

The night shift was quiet in comparison to other shifts. Lights were dimmed. Patients were sleeping, or trying to sleep, in between checks of their vital signs or changes of dressings.

Shelly was there. She worked nights one week a month. She was an LPN, and older than most of us in the unit. Whatever anyone asked of Shelly, she was there: quiet, efficient, and friendly. I liked her. As with Melanie, I sensed an immediate rapport between us.

During the slow times, we'd discussed her returning to school for an RN. She felt she was too old to try. "Besides," she added, her brown eyes twinkling, "I already make more per hour than anyone else in the unit!"

She was right.

"How's it going, Joyce?" she said as I approached the nurses' station.

"Okay. How're things here?"

"Fairly quiet."

"Good. Maybe I can get in some studying."

"Probably," she grinned.

My first patient, Mr. Williams, was a sixty-eight-year-old man who had undergone an exploratory and radical surgery for the removal of a tumor lodged originally in the head of his pancreas.

Mr. Williams's post-operative notes and prognosis were poor. The surgeons had discovered the malignant tumor extending from the pracreas into a portion of the stomach and much of the intestines. A radical surgical procedure, known as a "Whipple," was performed. In removing the malignancy the surgeons had also removed most of his stomach, his spleen, the duodenum (the first part of the small intestines), and his pancreas. The stomach, cut end of the pancreas, and common bile duct (from the liver) were connected to the jejunum (the second part of the small intestines). Mr. Williams' abdomen was essentially an empty shell covered with mounds of saturated dressings closed with heavy Montgomery straps. His skin was so badly jaundiced that it was bright orange. The sclera of his eyes were yellow. His bilirubin count was high. Too high. A foley catheter drained small amounts of old, blood-tinged urine. The main fluid IV, with a piggyback of whole blood, flowed into his right arm. A CVP protruded from his right subclavian vein. The MAP was taped into place on the left wrist. A number eight oral endotracheal tube connected him to an MAI respirator. I felt tremendous pity for him as I studied his body and chart.

Paul was the surgical assistant on the case. We had spoken on the phone three times by now, but had not been able to make a date. I was swinging the night shift while he pulled days in the OR. But he'd told me he would be

assigned to a twenty-four-hour rotation soon. Knowing we
would at least meet in the hospital picked up my spirits.

Kevin, the night shift respiratory therapist, set the
dials on the MAI. Mr. Williams's last blood gases showed
him to be acidonic with too much carbon dioxide and not
enough oxygen flowing through his body.

"What a shame," Kevin mumbled under his breath.
He looked at me as I nodded in agreement. We both knew
that Mr. Williams would probably not survive. But the
feeling of hope was still there.

Marilyn was making a point of ignoring me when she
came on duty at 7:00 a.m. My stomach clenched every
time she looked at me and then turned away in disdain. I
was losing weight from the nervousness. My body was
beginning to look gaunt. Lois spoke to me with some
civility, if not friendliness.

Sally was back from her leave. I noticed that she
avoided me. I caught her once in passing and asked her
how she was doing.

"I'm fine," she replied, avoiding eye contact.

I was curious. "Sally, has there been some trouble?"

"Look, Joyce," she said, "they let me off, so do me a
favor and just drop it. No one knows and we're keeping it
that way."

"Dr. Jones is going to protect you?" I said question-
ingly. "He as much as promised it."

She nodded. "This has been a nightmare for me. I
don't sleep. I dream constantly about it. I *am* getting some
help."

"Therapy?" I asked.

"Yes. She tells me I will be fine as time goes on. Just
promise me you won't tell anyone."

"I promise, Sally. I haven't repeated it or discussed it
with anyone other than my roommate."

Her face flushed in anger. "You told your roommate?
Doesn't she work in this hospital?"

I tried to sound reassuring. "It's okay, Sally. She

HICKSVILLE PUBLIC LIBRARY
169 JERUSALEM AVE.
HICKSVILLE, N.Y.

hasn't talked about it, either. She doesn't care about the unit. She has her hands full with maternity."

It didn't mollify her. "If word of this ever leaks out, I'll come after you," she growled. "I'll know you did it." She stormed off for the locker room.

Later, I saw her talking in low tones to Tina and Marilyn. I was sure they were talking about me.

I didn't know whom I could trust in the unit. I had caught the rumor that I was a cold and unfriendly person; it had extended to the physicians, X-ray and laboratory people.

Technically, I was still on the "buddy" system. But my co-workers left me increasingly to myself and assigned me long-term patients such as Mr. Williams, for whom no one else wanted to care. I was determined that I would beat the system. It would not defeat me.

The hardest part of working nights was trying to sleep days. By 3:00 a.m. I would find myself wanting to doze off. It was hard to keep alert and oriented. Sometimes I would pace the floor and consume many cups of coffee. Other nights, patients like Mr. Williams kept us all on our toes.

A new nurse appeared on night shift. Bob Morgan, RN, was one of the two males working in the unit. Nursing certainly could use an influx of men, not only to even out the current female statistics of ninety-seven percent but to equalize the pay scale and decrease the stresses of shortages and closed programs.

As I began to check Mr. Williams's chart, I mused that women today seemed to have no desire to enter nursing. They could be doctors, astronauts, or Supreme Court Justices. The choices for women were greater than ever before. For men they were even more plentiful. As Bob approached me, I wondered why this good-looking man chose nursing.

"Can I give you a hand?" he asked politely. He looked over at Mr. Williams. "It looks like you have your hands full."

"I certainly appreciate the help. Thank you for offering. My name is Joyce Strom." I put out my hand.

He shook it solidly. "Nice to meet you. I'm Bob Morgan."

"What brings you to the unit?" I asked, looking over at my patient. Mr. Williams was becoming restless and fighting the respirator. "Carol," I called out. "Better bring control meds." Our unit was still using team nursing rather than primary care, so the nurse assigned to the patient provided care while medications were given to all patients by one med nurse. Some, such as lasix, lidocaine, dopamine, and potassium chloride, were given by the bedside nurse. Knowing when to make the decision to administer life-saving medications is a crucial part of critical care nursing. I was eager to take a medication course so I could give meds, but my probationary status was going to delay that.

My stomach turned as I began to change the dressings on Mr. Williams's abdomen. The stench was awful. The sight of the incision made me wince. Purulent drainage mixed with bile flowed from his empty cavity. I could see clear through to his spinal cord. Using sterile technique to avoid introducing an outside contaminant, I asked Bob to find out where the control meds were. Mr. Williams was waking up and was both frightened and in pain.

"She's coming," Bob coolly announced, drawing the curtains of the bedside cubicle around him. "Here, let me give you a hand." He piled sterile dressings on, then closed the Montgomery straps. Carol finally came in and injected the medication into the main fluid IV line. Within moments Mr. Williams fell unconscious.

Bob and I became acquainted as we attended to our patients. He was tall and solidly built, with large, firm, muscular arms. He had a moustache and long sideburns. A cross between an army vet, a weight lifter, and a cowboy, I thought. I found myself drawn to him emotionally. He gave the impression that no one could intimidate him or dictate to him.

He was an ex-Marine, he told me, and was thirty-seven—older than the rest of us. Apparently the nursing staff and some of the physicians were having problems with him.

I'd learned that the unit had had another male nurse working there the previous year, Larry, an LPN who resigned suddenly. Larry had been the source of "gay" jokes. Unfortunately, since my mother's era in nursing, any men entering the profession were the targets of ridicule. They were automatically assumed to be "gay" simply because they entered a female-dominated profession. The myth still existed. The stressors for nurses are difficult enough. The stressors for male nurses are even more arduous. But I had the feeling that no one would ridicule Bob.

Before I knew it, I had related to Bob my confrontation with Marilyn and Lois. He listened quietly and attentively. "Be careful," he whispered. "Around here it is better if you keep your mouth closed and your eyes open."

Another warning. I wondered why. Bob took a break, leaving me to watch his patients and mine. Melanie was across the unit. Carol was both in charge and giving meds. The night shift was the only time when one nurse did both jobs.

I walked over to check Mr. Williams's vitals again. He was resting comfortably. Studying the nurses' notes, I noticed that Carol had given Demerol 100 mg. IV push at 1:15 a.m. The control meds of valium and morphine had been given at 12:05 a.m. I thought it was unusual for someone to receive those addicting painkillers so close together, especially when his doctor had left orders for prn's (whenever necessary). It frustrated me that I didn't know enough about ICU meds, but I brushed aside the thought. Carol certainly knew what she was doing.

When Bob returned, Melanie and I took a coffee break together. The small talk soon turned to hospital politics. "So, do you like the unit?" she asked, lighting a cigarette and blowing the smoke away from me.

"I think so," I replied meekly. "I have had my problems, but I suppose I will get used to it."

Melanie chuckled. "Oh, you mean the hazing?"

"Hazing?" I asked. "Hazing is what we did in sorority."

"Sure, and it's done here too."

For the first time in days I felt a ray of sunshine. "Do you mean that every nurse in the unit goes through some kind of hazing?"

"Of course," Melanie responded matter-of-factly. "Critical care nursing is very difficult and very stressful. Nurses have to be weeded out before too much time, energy, and money is invested in them."

"But, why?" I was confused.

"Well, the recruitment costs of a critical care nurse are approximately eight thousand to twelve thousand dollars each. Patients are sicker today. Their stays are shorter due to the DRGs (diagnostic related grouping) and we nurses have to be on our toes at all times. We make more money than the floor nurses, but we earn it."

I nodded. My bones were beginning to ache with tension. "Burnout is common, isn't it?"

Melanie shook her waist-length blond braid affirmatively. "We also have all kinds of games we nurses play like 'mine is better than yours.' "

"What do you mean?" My curiosity was aroused now.

"You know—nurses are always fighting over their degrees. My AAS in nursing or my BSN is better than your diploma—that sort of thing."

I sat silently. I agreed with her. The old concept of diploma schools for the training of nurses in hospitals was gone. Of course, three-year, hospital-based nurses had more hands-on experience; they were also free help for the facilities. The nursing shortage was not quite as evident when students could be used to fill the gaps. Now, the trend towards professionalism demanded a Bachelor's degree in nursing. I could foresee the day when it would be a Master's degree.

Melanie continued. "The hazing has to be done because we only want good, highly-skilled nurses working
with us bedside. We make crucial judgment calls. We
decide when to give medications. We even tell the interns
and residents how to write their orders. No one really
seems to know what we do, how much we know, and how
well we do it." I nodded my head affirmatively. She was
right.

Still, I thought, Lois and Marilyn had been harsh.
"Do you mean," I timidly asked, "that every nurse who
comes into the unit is called on the carpet somehow?"

She nodded. "You just had yours, huh?" Before I
could reply, she stated, "Mine was pretty intense, too. I
was told that everyone hated me and that I flirted with
doctors."

Relief flooded through me. Melanie's light blue eyes
twinkled as she relived her experience.

"How long ago was that?" I asked.

"Two years ago," she said. "And, I'm still here. Listen," she whispered, "just keep your eyes open and your
mouth closed and you'll make it here."

The second warning of the night. Suddenly Melanie
stood up and left the lounge. Our break was over. For the
first time, I felt a renewed spirit. I wasn't alone.

Mr. Williams was still sleeping. He had received one
hundred milligrams of Demerol for pain every two to three
hours, along with the morphine and valium for respiratory control. Carol raced from one bedside to the other
injecting fluids into IV tubings.

As the sun began to rise, I eagerly looked forward to
clocking out and going home. No matter how hard I tried,
I would never get used to those long nights. Before our
shift ended we had all given our patients their morning
care, including bedbaths and clean sheets. Team nursing
made it easier on the following shift.

Bob helped me silently. He seemed lost in thought as
he surveyed the unit. He went to the bathroom quite often,

but then so did Carol. I absentmindedly noticed and brushed my questions aside.

The day shift rambled slowly through the doors. Finally, report had been given and the night shift could leave. My locker was all the way in the back corner of the locker room. As I changed my shoes, I heard a low, whispered conversation. Not daring to breathe, I listened intently.

"Do you have it?" a female voice asked.

"Of course. It was a successful night," the other replied.

It seemed to me I recognized the voices. I concentrated harder.

"Dr. Vorhees will be pleased. We should get a nifty bonus," the first voice stated.

"Yeah, well great. Listen, do you have some coke for me?"

These nurses always amazed me as they inhaled their nicotine and consumed their caffeine in coffee and cokes.

"Not now," the first voice said, "but I will have it by Friday. Can you wait?"

"Sure," the other answered. "I only wanted some for my boyfriend."

How stupid can I be, I thought, realizing suddenly that "coke" was cocaine. Who were these two? The voices resumed.

"Did everything go okay on the night shift with the two new ones?"

"You mean Strom and Morgan?"

I froze.

"Sure. Which one do you think is the narc?"

Now I knew those voices: it was Carol and Marilyn.

"I don't know, but just be careful," Marilyn said. "It could be either one. Dr. Vorhees knows that Nursing Service planted someone here. We'll find out and deal with them accordingly."

"I hope it's not like Marie was dealt with," Carol whispered.

"Who cares," Marilyn angrily snapped. "We have to protect ourselves." Suddenly the conversation closed. "I'll see you tomorrow." The door opened and I heard footsteps leave.

I still didn't move from my spot. I was nauseated and confused by what I had just heard. I was also frightened. My mind raced. *Who was Marie? What was a narc? What was going on?* Footsteps started to come in my direction. My heart pounded. I was about to be discovered. The bathroom was in front of me. It had to be Carol.

Suddenly, the footsteps stopped. The door to the lounge opened. I heard someone leave. Petrified, I stayed there for fifteen minutes. When I finally peeked through the door, Marilyn's back was to me and Carol was nowhere in sight. Everyone else was busy at their bedsides with cubicles drawn.

I tiptoed out the door and around the corner. Fortunately, I had punched out on the time clock earlier. I raced down the hall and into the elevator. I didn't feel relieved until my car swung onto the highway.

The relief gave way to fear. Something serious was going on in the unit, and I was a target. I sighed heavily. From now on I would be cautious and watch everyone carefully.

Karen wasn't home. I checked the calendar we kept on the refrigerator to keep track of our own and each other's schedules, and saw she was on days.

Our message machine was blinking. I pressed the replay button. "Hi, honey, this is your mother. Just wanted to see how you are doing. I wondered if you would be coming home for a visit soon. Well, call me when you can. I love you." Click.

I felt awful for not phoning her more often. Although it was a five-hour drive home I knew I should schedule a trip on my next weekend. I promised myself to call her right after the messages were done.

The next voice came on loud and clear. "Hi, sweetheart. Just called to wish you a happy day. Can't wait to see you tonight. Love you." Click.

The voice was familiar and obviously not for me. I knew Karen was still dating John; I wondered if the relationship was becoming more serious than I was aware of.

Another voice interrupted my thoughts: "This message is for Joyce. This is Paul Thompson calling." My heart surged. I grabbed the arm of the chair and leaned closer to the machine.

"I wondered if we could make a date for Friday night," he continued. "If so, please call me at 447-9242 or page me at the hospital." Click.

I was so excited I began to jump around the apartment. *How could I possibly sleep now?* I asked out loud as I dialed his number. I reached his machine. "This is Joyce for Paul. Thank you very much. I would love to go out with you on Friday. The only problem I have is that I am working nights, so could we make it an early evening? If not, please call me and we'll make arrangements for another time." Click.

I raced around the apartment taking an inventory of myself and my wardrobe. My hair hung limp and lifeless. It was in great need of a trim. Since it was only 9:00 a.m., I telephoned my local hairdresser and got a 10:00 appointment. I forgot all about calling my mother.

Jan cut my hair a good inch. "Boy, you have been away too long," she commented, clipping chunks of hair with her scissors.

"I know. Lazy, I guess."

"What are you doing to your hair?" Jan asked. Jan always loved working on my hair. It is naturally curly and very thick, but it showed my lack of interest recently. "Your hair is limp and ragged. So many split ends. And no shine."

"I wear it up all the time," I commented.

"It shows," she retorted. "Aren't you eating or sleeping well?" she asked.

I shook my head. "My job is very stressful, and I've been on nights."

"Your hair looks it. And, while we're at it, so does your body." She stood back and looked at me. "Circles under your eyes. No make-up. You need the works."

I shook my head. "I guess I do. Can you help? I have an exciting date Friday night. The first in months."

Jan finished the trim and showed me how to use my curl to my advantage. The days of nurses' having to cut their hair to collar length or wear it off their shoulders were over. Today, almost anything—pants suits, jewelry, nail polish, even earrings—was allowed as long as it was in good taste and could not contaminate the patient or the nurse. Long hair had to be pulled back or up, but not cut. I loved my long hair hanging just below my shoulders. With Jan's cut I could pull it back and still have full curls around my face.

Jan pulled out a make-up tray. Her profession required more than just cutting, clipping, and curling. She had to know nutrition, skin types, hair texture, and the foundations of good skin care. She applied make-up taste-fully, lecturing me the whole time. I looked like a new person.

"Jan, you work miracles," I laughed, tipping her and purchasing the eye shadow and liner.

"Just get some rest, Joyce," she warned. "All of the make-up in the world can't hide the way you feel."

She was right. I knew it, but still felt too excited to sleep. I decided to take a walk. Exercise, I told myself, would be good for me. Nearby I found a lovely little boutique and, feeling lighthearted, I decided to splurge.

The small shop was filled with tasteful clothing. The smell of strawberries gently filled my nostrils.

"What a lovely shop," I commented to the thin, gray-ing lady in her sixties who'd greeted me as I entered.

"Thank you," she replied.

I told her I needed something for a special date. She

looked me up and down, then headed for a rack along the left side of the wall.

"What are your tastes?" she inquired.

I realized she couldn't tell that from my blue jeans and tee shirt which said "Love a nurse PRN" on it. "I like the Victorian look," I stated.

"I see you are a nurse. Well, the Victorian on you would be lovely; you're so tall. And, with that lovely hair . . ."

It had been a long time since anyone had paid attention to me or given me a compliment. I felt good—alive—happy. She handed me three outfits.

Walking into the dressing room, I held each one up and chose my favorite, quickly putting it on. "I like this one," I announced, not even looking at the price tag. It was an off-white cotton with hand-sewn lace around the skirt, the high neck of the blouse, and the wrists of the long sleeves. It was sensual, feminine, and sexy.

"How would you like to pay for this?" she asked, as I headed back into the dressing room to put on my jeans and tee shirt.

I momentarily cringed and then called out, "Master-card."

The dress was $195.00, before tax. I was too happy to care. I signed my name and took my package and new face home.

Finally I lay down, but my sleep was restless. I wasn't refreshed when I entered the unit that night at 10:45 p.m. I was on an adrenaline high of excitement. I met Paul just as I got off the elevator.

"I got your message," he smiled, those beautiful blue eyes dancing irresistibly.

"Is it a problem?" I asked, adding, "my working nights, I mean?"

"No. If we go out around 5:00 we can have you here by 11:00. Okay?"

I nodded, momentarily breathless. Then I gave him

directions to my apartment. "See you Friday," I called over my shoulder as I raced into the unit.

My spirits were high, and the night was very busy. I was assigned to an elderly man who had been admitted following a routine hernia repair. He had arrested on the floor and was intubated and on an MAI. He'd had a tracheostomy since he'd been on the respirator for more than a week. Mr. Smorel had been on Roberta's floor initially. Roberta and I graduated together. She worked both surgical pre-op and post-op. Since Mr. Smorel's tracheostomy he had been a unit patient for over two months. He had developed septicemia, pneumonia, and pseudomonas.

Mr. Smorel was passed from one nurse to another. One of the main problems working in a unit with a long-term patient is the feelings of hopelessness. Everyone dreaded being assigned to him. The staff fought long and hard to save him, especially the doctors. The nurses, however, were greatly frustrated and complained about him daily.

I was assigned two other patients—not uncommon for this unit, but not the ideal patient-nurse ratio. Technically, a critical care nurse should be assigned one-to-one or one-to-two. One-to-three stretched the quality of care; one-to-four, also not uncommon, jeopardized it. With three patients, I would be busy all night. But I was grateful that I didn't have Mr. Williams again.

At 2:07 a.m., Mr. Smorel arrested. The staff knew it was coming because he had been throwing PVC's (premature ventricular contractions) on and off during the day and evening shifts. The surgical intern on call, Dr. Bartlett, raced to the unit. Interns on call had very little,if any, sleep during their twenty-four-hour rotation. The surgical resident on call was Dr. Fowler, a third-year vascular surgeon who had nodded off in the nurses' lounge around midnight.

I was doing the vital signs on my patient in bed two when I noticed the monitor over Mr. Smorel's bed was in

V-tach (ventricular tachycardia). His ventricles were pumping the much-needed blood throughout his system, but the bottom part of his heart couldn't do that for long without a return to a sinus rhythm where the top part of his heart functioned again.

I called out "Code Blue" and raced for the crash cart. Shelly and the night charge nurse, Brenda, raced to my side. Adrenaline flowed through everyone. It was moments like this that made good critical care nursing so crucial. Life and death. Dr. Fowler raced in, still dressed in his greens. Three evening supervisors ran through the door. A Code always brought everyone out. The supervisors, dressed in meticulously clean white uniforms with caps placed on their picture-perfect hair, somehow looked out of place.

I placed the electrodes from the cart on Mr. Smorel's chest and began running the EKG strips. Brenda administered Sodium Bicarb IV push as ordered. There was no change in the heart rhythm. Dr. Fowler called for the paddles. Brenda lubricated them and handed them to him within a split second of his request.

"Stand clear," Dr. Fowler yelled. He placed the paddles on Mr. Smorel's exposed chest and then zapped the levers. Mr. Smorel's body jumped automatically. We all looked at the monitor. I quivered. His heart rate was still in V-tach.

Once again Dr. Fowler placed the paddles on his chest. Again the voltage was turned on. We all stared at the monitor, watching for a new pattern. The monitor was in a straight line. Asystole. Mr. Smorel was dead.

Sometimes it is hard for medical professionals to let death happen with dignity.

"Give him adrenaline," called Dr. Fowler. He nodded to Dr. Bartlett, who injected the large needle into the thoracic (chest) cavity. I winced as I watched the needle enter Mr. Smorel's heart. The syringe filled with blood; he was in the heart. Bartlett shook his head negatively. The monitor was still asystole. Everyone complimented each other on the fine job they had done. Brenda went off to fill out the paper work and notify the family. The supervisors left.

I peered down at the lifeless body. No one likes to lose a human life. Dr. Fowler called Brenda over. "Better ask for an autopsy," he said. Mr. Smorel's only relative, a nephew, sleepily approved of the request over the telephone. He agreed to come into the hospital in the morning and sign the release. Dr. Fowler and Dr. Bartlett walked away together. I could hear them talking. "Autopsies are valuable," Fowler said confidently. "Another learning experience." Bartlett agreed, nodding. Each hospital requires a minimum number of autopsies a year. Mr. Smorel would help that statistic at Trinity.

I did my post mortem care, checking vital signs of my other patients. Shelly was busy, but she gave me a hand wrapping Mr. Smorel in the plastic liner for his last trip in the hospital. On the night shift we took the patients to the morgue.

We pushed the cart through the hall. As on the day shift, the corpse was covered with a white sheet to give the illusion that a sleeping patient was being transported. Everyone always knew the difference.

The morgue in the basement of the building was eerie, and reeked of formaldehyde. A large porcelain table with a sink at the base of it filled the center of the room. Lockers lined the wall vertically and horizontally. We found an empty locker and placed Mr. Smorel inside, head first. The feet, with the name tag on the toe, were left out for the pathologist in the morning.

"I just want you to know," Shelly suddenly whispered, "that we all are aware of what you have been through."

I stared at her wordlessly.

"You looked good tonight, Strom. Hang in there. I think you just might make it."

"Like sorority?" I inquired.

She nodded. We turned to leave. "Thank you," I replied.

Getting past the 3:00 a.m. mark made the rest of the night easier. I found myself concentrating on Friday night, my dress, and Paul. Marilyn and Lois said nothing to me after report about how well I had responded to my first Code. I wasn't surprised.

SIX

Paul arrived right on time. I liked the way his eyes roamed over my body. I tingled as his eyes started with the top of my hair and moved slowly, deftly, down towards my feet. His eyes lingered momentarily at my breasts. Again, at my hips. The white dress hung delicately. Sensually. My curly hair hung softly around my face. Its new luster made me feel alive.

"You look gorgeous, lady," he exclaimed with unmistakable seductiveness in his tone.

I felt a surge of blood rush to my face. Lowering my eyes I murmured, "Thank you." I needed to talk if only to breathe. "I'm really glad to see you again," I added.

Paul laughed. "That makes two of us, lady. *I'm* glad to see *you.*"

I gazed at him. His eyes: the same luscious blue I remembered, with streaks of dark blue intermingled. The color and depth reminded me of the ocean. His hair was darker than I remembered. A slight wave fell over his right eyebrow.

His lips were moist, soft, placed squarely in the middle of his face above a slight dimple in his chin. He was dressed in a navy suit, a white shirt, and navy blue tie.

"Well," he said, interrupting my thoughts, "how about Carusso's? Is that okay with you?"

"I love Italian food," I offered. "In fact, I've never been there, but I hear it is great."

"It is, and you will love it," he replied, holding the door open for me. The evening sun was slowly sinking. I noticed the outline of a full moon against the still-light sky. Summer was in the air in the smell of roses and lilacs. And I liked the smell of Paul as I strode next to his tall frame in my three-inch heels. I felt attractive walking beside him.

He had a gorgeous car. "A Porsche?" I asked in shock. I thought all residents, like all student nurses, had cash flow problems.

Paul answered as if he were accustomed to the question. "I have a wonderful family who help take care of me. I don't like to flaunt it, but I am luckier than most."

I seated myself in the soft leather seats. Black inside; a bright red exterior. The classy car matched Paul.

We talked about the hospital on the way to Carusso's. Paul had rotated from General where he worked on the surgical resident's staff. "I like Trinity better," he said. "The caliber of patient and their ability to pay for services is far better than General. General is demoralizing."

"General is a county hospital. Someone has to take care of the poor and indigent patient." I had done a rotation at General during training. It was mandatory that we each experience the county hospital, a nursing home, an elementary school, and the public health nursing department. General was poor. The county and state governments supported it. People without insurance were transferred to General. Ambulance drivers had the dreary job of checking insurance coverage first and then transferring patients accordingly.

"I know." Paul continued weaving the Porsche in and out of the heavy Friday night traffic. "It's just not for me. I want to be an open heart surgeon, which is why I transferred to Trinity and Dr. Vorhees. I hope to go into private practice with him someday."

"Is that a possibility?" I asked, looking at Paul intently. He sounded determined. Sure of himself.

"Of course. Dr. Vorhees knows my family well. He and I get along just fine. Ah, here we are." He turned the car into a circular driveway.

A valet opened my door and helped me out. "Keep the car on the hill, Bobby," Paul called out, tossing the young man the keys.

"Yes, sir, Dr. Thompson," the boy said. "In your usual spot."

"I guess you come here often."

He held the door for me. "This restaurant is in the family."

"Are you Italian?" I asked.

"Partly," he replied.

"Good evening, doctor," the maitre d' said. "Your table is ready."

Paul gently took my elbow and led me across the room to a private table for two in a back corner. The room was filled with statues of Roman figures; pictures of Rome covered the walls. A small candle stood next to a fresh red rose in a bud vase centered on each white-linen-covered tablecloth. I had heard about Carusso's: the reputation was that it had delicious food and exorbitant prices.

Paul ordered a dry red wine—Sauvignon, vintage 1968. The old bottle was covered with dust when the waiter brought it out. He sniffed the cork, swiveled the wine in the glass, smelled the aroma, took a sip, savored it, then gave the waiter permission to fill our glasses.

"A toast," he offered, holding his crystal wine glass up next to mine. His words and the sound of the glasses clinking were filling my heart with joy. "To us—and my plan to get to know you better." His eyes twinkled as he smiled.

I could only nod as I raised my glass to my parted lips and took a sip of the excellent wine. "I would love that," I finally said.

Paul ordered for us: hot Italian bread; squid; Caesar

salad; veal marsala with broccoli and garlic on the side; fresh cannolis for dessert.

"Oh, Paul, I am stuffed." I sat back in my chair sipping my wine and felt the room begin to spin. I wondered how I could go to work in only a few hours. I contemplated calling in sick.

Paul read my mind. "Why don't you?"

"Why don't I what?"

"Why don't you call in sick?"

"I am tempted," I mused. I have never done it before."

"So do it," he smiled. "I'll make the night worth it."

My body flashed heat waves. Excitement raced through my groin. I suddenly wanted to hold this man, to feel his naked body near mine, to feel his firmness penetrate me.

I looked at my watch: 8:05 p.m. "If I am going to do it, I had better do it now."

He smiled. "Use the phone over there. It's quiet and no one will hear the background noise." He pointed in the direction of the ladies' room. I needed that too; I was nervous.

When the hospital answered, I asked for Nursing Service. After a long wait the evening supervisor came on the phone.

"Mrs. Kallin speaking. How can I help you?"

I lowered my voice, making it sound gruff and hoarse. "Mrs. Kallin, this is Joyce Strom. I am a nurse in ICU." I coughed for effect. "I am sorry I am calling so late." I coughed again. "I had hoped I would feel better by now." Again, a cough. I hoped I wasn't overdoing it. "I'm afraid I am too sick to work tonight."

"Well, that cough does sound bad. Actually, the unit is quiet now. I hope you feel better."

"Thank you," I coughed again. She hung up first. I felt relief and guilt.

Back at the table I found Paul leaning back in his chair watching me stroll through the main dining room. "Is everything all right?"

"Yes. I just feel guilty."

"Why?"

"Well, I've never called in before. In training we are indoctrinated that calling in sick when we are not is wrong and unfair to our co-workers."

"Everyone does it, Joyce."

"I know. At least the evening supervisor said the unit was slow."

"That's a consolation for you." He laughed. "Let's go dancing." He stood and walked me over to an adjoining lounge where a small dance floor lay in front of a three-piece band.

The band members all nodded to him. Paul was well known in here. In fact, I noticed that he had not paid the bill; we just moved into the other room where he ordered another bottle of the same wine.

He guided me to the floor. As he pulled me close I felt the strength of his arm around my waist. He pulled my chest closer to him. My face was right next to his. He squeezed my right hand with his left. His right hand began to roam gently over my back.

I tingled, passion rising in me. I felt the bulge between his legs press into my body. We circled the floor slowly. Suddenly he pulled his cheek away from mine and looked down into my eyes. His eyes were glassy. His head moved closer until his lips reached mine.

All too soon the kiss ended. Neither of us spoke a word. We continued to dance, his cheek on mine, the passion throbbing through both of us.

"Let's get out of here," he murmured as we walked back to the table.

I nodded.

We drove in silence to a large apartment building on a quiet, tree-lined street. "This is my place," he said, wheeling the Porsche into an underground garage and numbered parking space.

"Hmmm," I murmured.

On the fifth floor he led me into one of the most beautiful apartments I had ever seen.

Black leather furniture filled the white-carpeted living room. A marble fireplace loomed against the far wall. Large bay windows overlooked a private courtyard filled with trees, a fountain, and exotic shrubbery.

"I'll give you the tour," he said, leading me through the living room into a small formal dining room. A maple table for eight filled the area with heavy, maple chairs to match. The room was immaculate. A centerpiece of Venetian glass sat on the table. In the corner was a curio cabinet filled with crystal goblets of all sizes and shapes.

"This is exquisite," I breathed. The large kitchen sported a sterile-looking oven and open pit on top of the range. A microwave was built in overhead. In the center was a large wooden chopping counter surrounded by copper pots and pans hanging from overhead. A metal mesh basket filled with fresh fruit, hung near the refrigerator. "I have never seen anything so beautiful."

"Thank you. My cleaning lady was here today. She does most of my cooking, although I enjoy cooking when I can."

"You cook too?" I laughed.

We moved down a small hallway past a guest bath containing a sink and toilet. The wallpaper was silver with a green floral pattern, echoed in matching green and silver towels and accessories. "Did you do the decorating also?"

"Of course." He smiled. "One of my other loves." Then we were in the bedroom. It was filled with heavy dark maple furniture. A dresser and tallboy sat in one corner. Opposite was a small sofa for two and a large-screen television set. Another bowl of fresh fruit rested on the coffee table. Again Paul read my mind. "I love fruit. And I love this room."

Paul opened the door to his bathroom. A Roman tub filled half of the room. The tub was surrounded with small candles. He began to light them. Sweet fragrances filled the bathroom. A telephone was on the wall. The room, tastefully decorated in light blues, matched his eyes and his personality.

"This is absolutely breathtaking. I have never seen anything so beautiful."

He smiled, opened a cabinet and produced an unopened toothbrush. "I hope I am not being too presumptuous?" he asked.

I shook my head.

"Then let's take a bath together." He reached over and unzipped the back of my blouse; it fell to the floor. He removed my bra and began to fondle my breasts, squeezing the erect nipples.

His tongue floated over my neck and down the center of my breasts. Then he stood up and kissed me. Long. Hard. Passionately.

I unbuttoned his shirt, exposing the smooth silkiness of his skin with the dark hairs encircling his chest. He removed my skirt, then pulled me closer. Embracing in another kiss, I felt his fingers tenderly pull on my tiny bikini underwear. Within moments we were both naked and grasping at each other's bodies.

Paul lifted me and carried me to the bed. We sank into a blue comforter and matching throw pillows. We began to moan, and thrash. Our flesh blended into one. He entered me, gently but determinedly. My shyness was gone. It had been so long, and he felt wonderful.

We didn't talk. The thrusting movements increased. Our breathing became loud, rapid. Suddenly the climax occurred. I screamed in joy. The release of built-up tension, frustration, and excitement was overwhelming.

As he lay on top of me, I felt at peace with myself and with the world.

"You were wonderful," I whispered, kissing his neck. Our lips met.

"So were you," he murmured.

We lay on the bed in each other's arms. I had forgotten about my guilt over calling in sick. For the first time in a long time I was happy and at peace with myself.

Then we took a long bath in the Roman tub. By morning we had made love two more times. I was spent. Exhausted.

The morning sunlight streamed in his apartment window. "Did I oversleep again?" I asked, yawning and stretching.

He was smiling and nodding. "If you hurry we can make it to my parents' summer home by noon."

"Where?" I asked, heading for the bathroom. Then I added, "I don't have any clothes."

Paul laughed. " 'Where' is the Catskills. As for clothes—we'll stop by your apartment."

"Paul, I have to work tonight." The thought of leaving him and the offer to go away was depressing. Thinking about the unit and the night shift made my heart sink.

"Call in sick." His reply was matter-of-fact.

"Again! How can I?"

Paul laughed again. "Simple. Just pick up the phone and call in. You have the flu. Besides, if you need a doctor's note I'll give you one."

Now I laughed. "Sure. That will look real innocent." But I gave in to temptation. I didn't feel relieved until I'd completed the call to the day supervisor.

I loved the Catskills, the fresh air of the country, the lush, green hills. Paul wheeled the Porsche through winding roads at rapid speed.

By noon we pulled into a long dirt road that eventually circled in front of a large white house. "I thought you said this was your parents' summer *cabin?*" Behind the house I could see the outline of a lake.

"It is." He pulled alongside a Rolls Royce.

"What is your home like?" I was instantly embarrassed for asking.

Paul chuckled. "You are so innocent. Our home is

rather modest." He opened my door and led me up the path.

I half expected a servant to open the front door, but it was Paul's mother who came rushing out before he could turn the door handle. Mother and son embraced. It was obvious that they were very close. Paul introduced me to her. "This is Lorraine," he said affectionately. She was a lovely woman with the same dark hair and blue eyes.

Paul's father was working and unable to come up for the weekend. Lorraine made me feel comfortable. The large house had five bedrooms and four bathrooms. She led me to a yellow and white bedroom with a yellow canopied bed.

"This was my daughter's room when she was younger."

So Paul had a sister. "Where is she now?" I asked.

"Oh, Samantha is married and living in California. She has two children, but she comes home during the year to visit. I keep this room the way she left it. Paul's room is also the same as it was when he was in high school."

Lorraine proudly showed me pictures of her grandchildren, and of her children when they were small. We visited for over an hour before Paul reappeared in swimming trunks.

"Let's walk down to the lake and see if it is warm enough to water ski," he said, giving his mother a kiss.

"Go have fun, children," she called after us as she headed off for the kitchen.

I hurriedly changed into the bathing suit I'd brought from my apartment. A narrow cobblestone path gently turned down towards the lake. The last few steps went directly down to the water and a dock. Next to the dock was a motorboat equipped with water skis and an outboard engine.

"Do you ski?" he asked.

"Yes. I've been skiing on Owasco Lake since I was a child."

"Great." He walked into the water knee deep. "It's not too bad. Let's try."

"We need another person in the boat to spot us," I reminded him.

"Not really," he answered. "I'll drive and spot you."

I knew he was being reckless, but my heart overruled my common sense. Paul pulled me up on the skis from the dock on the first try. I felt the rush of cold water spraying up my legs and across my body. As Paul steered the boat out into the center of the lake I became brave and kicked off the left ski. I wanted to make rooster tails on one ski. Jumping the waves, I moved back and forth excitedly until my arms began to hurt.

Paul was staring straight ahead. I yelled at him, trying to get his attention, "Cut the engines and let me get off." He seemed lost in thought. Suddenly, I couldn't hang on any longer. The rope handle burned my skin as it slid away. I hit the water with a face-down crash that nearly made me lose consciousness.

My head bobbed around. I swallowed water and began to cough and choke. Paul was off in the distance, still travelling at the same speed. Only my life jacket kept me afloat. I tried to swim towards my skis, but I hurt. My back hurt. My face hurt. My hands hurt. Tears filled my eyes. I wondered how long it would be before Paul noticed I was gone. I found myself getting angry with him for being so reckless.

The boat came speeding back towards me. Paul pulled alongside, cut the engine and grabbed me. "Are you all right?" He looked upset.

"I think so." I didn't want him to know how sore I was. "I couldn't get your attention to tell you I was tired."

He lifted me into the boat. Wrapping a towel around me he offered, "I am so sorry."

I sat quivering until we reached the dock. When Paul locked the boat into its hoist he examined me. "You're hurt."

"I'll be okay."

He lifted me and carried me to the steps.

"I can walk," I offered.

Placing me on my feet he steadied me. Looking down into my eyes he suddenly kissed me. Tenderly, Passionately. I instantly forgave him.

Lorraine made potato salad and tossed greens. Paul cooked the chicken on the barbeque. My bruises were beginning to show. Both Paul and Lorraine asked me often how I felt.

We roasted marshmallows over a campfire on the sand by the water. The full moon cast a bright yellow trail across the lake.

"I thought *our* lake was beautiful," I commented, pasting a burned marshmallow between graham crackers with chocolate pieces. "This one is heavenly."

Paul sat quietly. We didn't need to talk. Silence added to the romance and beauty of the night. Around midnight he led me back to the house. At my bedroom he gently kissed me good night. Reluctantly, I watched him head off for his old room and shut the door.

On Sunday at ten o'clock, Lorraine prepared a huge breakfast. Relaxed and content, I could have slept away the day. She had already been to church. She was a vibrant woman, active and happy. I envied her lifestyle as I tried to see myself living it, married to Paul.

"No water skiing for you today," Paul announced over breakfast. "But," he added, "you can get even with me."

"How?"

"I'll ski and you can spot me."

"Who will pilot the boat?"

"My neighbor Tim. We went to high school and college together. He's home today. Just called."

"I'll spot you." I was falling in love with him.

Where did the last two days go? I wondered, walking into
the unit at 10:45 p.m. Sunday night. I wore a sweater to
cover the bruises on my arms. Fortunately, my face was
okay. *It was so wonderful,* I mumbled to myself as I surveyed the unit. I had spent two days out on a sick leave
living life to the fullest while bodies lay connected to
machines fighting for life.

Paul had brought me back into the city at 8:00 p.m. I
invited him to dinner after boards, but he told me he
would call. He wasn't sure of his schedule.

I floated into the unit too happy to care about anything.

"Are you feeling better, Strom?" Brenda asked. She
was the night charge nurse.

I nodded, then offered, "But my chest still hurts." It
wasn't a lie. My chest did hurt from the fall off the skis.
"Were you busy?" I asked, trying to concentrate on the
unit once again.

"Two codes. Three admissions. As you can see, we
have a full house."

I felt guilt—that emotion which became ingrained in
nursing students. Never leave your co-workers in the
lurch. Even if you were dying, your responsibility was to
be there. I thought about Florence Nightingale walking
through the battlefields of the Crimean War attending to
the physical and emotional needs of hundreds of soldiers.
Florence without sleep. Florence without play time. Florence sacrificing herself endlessly to help others. Florence
dying in the end, in her nineties, of a highly communica-
ble disease.

Brenda brought me back to reality. "Here's your
assignment. Let's get to report."

I had Mr. Williams again, along with two other patients. Beds two and three were stable enough. Mr. Williams was still very ill. His family sat in the waiting room
around the clock. They knew, as we did, it was a matter of
time.

At 3:20 a.m. the night supervisor came into the unit on her usual rounds. She and Brenda sat at the desk together talking and laughing. When the supervisor left Brenda met me in the nurses' lounge for a break.

"Want to hear a nice piece of gossip, Strom?" she asked.

I nodded. At 3:20 a.m. I wanted to hear anything to keep me awake and keep my thoughts on my job, not on Paul.

"The night supervisor just told me that the ER has quite a case downstairs. It would seem that a local well-known judge is having an important part of his anatomy repaired with sutures right now."

"What do you mean?" I asked.

"Well, apparently this judge has been having an affair with his secretary and his wife found out. She followed them in her car. When he was parked with his secretary on a quiet road she apparently rear-ended his car with hers."

I could see the mental picture before Brenda finished the story.

"The judge needs fifteen stitches." She laughed.

"And the secretary?" I inquired.

"She lost her front teeth." Brenda laughed louder.

I chuckled with her, but I felt embarrassed and uncomfortable. Revealing this kind of information was an unethical violation of the patient's right to privacy. Again, the internal grapevine kept no secrets.

Our unit, like the rest of the hospital, spent the rest of the night talking about the incident. The gossip continued as the day shift poured in. By the time I clocked out at 8:00 a.m. the entire city knew about the judge.

Karen was practically vibrating when I got back to the apartment.

"Joyce, Joyce—" She held out her left hand. A round-cut diamond on the third finger picked up every bit of light in the room.

"Oh, Karen!" I hugged her tightly. "I'm so glad! It's wonderful."

"He's wonderful," she sighed.

"And so are you. *He's* lucky."

"Joyce, you'll be my maid of honor, won't you?"

"Of course. I'd be hurt if you hadn't asked me."

"Oh God, I'm—I'm—flying!"

We chatted happily for about an hour. Naturally, I wished Paul would present me with a ring soon. After this past weekend, I thought maybe he would.

Suddenly I glanced over at the books piled in the corner. I hated to interrupt our joy but a test date loomed. "Listen, Karen, not to be a downer, but—are you ready for Boards?"

"You would ruin a good time. Well . . . I guess so," she said, grimacing. "And you?"

I wasn't and I told her so. We both agreed to make an attempt at last minute studying.

I put my energy in psych, since that was a weak area for me. Karen reviewed nutrition and microbiology. We ate an early dinner and laid out our clothes for the morning. We had to be at the exam site by 8:00 a.m. The testing began promptly at 8:30 a.m., with no admissions after 8:15 a.m.

John called Karen twice. She spent an hour on the phone with him before bed. I was sure that Paul was trying to reach me, but only getting a busy signal.

When the alarm rang at 6:00 a.m. I realized that I had slept all night. I also realized that Paul had not called. The front page of the newspaper lay open on the coffee table. Our well-known patient the judge had suddenly resigned and left town.

SEVEN

One of the better prospects of having to take Boards was seeing our old friends from training. "Hello, you bums," rang out the familiar voice of Leslie, a former roommate. Leslie was working on Long Island. She lived with Karen and me the first year. In the second year we moved our quarters upstairs.

"Joan," Leslie yelled, running past us to embrace her. "How the hell have you been? How is the army treating you?" Leslie gleefully asked.

Karen and I stood by watching the old roommates hug and shriek. I had always liked Joan. She seemed more dedicated than the rest of us. We all knew she was going into the service after graduation.

"Did you finish basic?" I asked, intentionally interrupting.

"I sure did, Strom. Boy, it was rough."

"Where do you go now?" Karen asked.

There had been times when we had all discussed the service and the romance of travelling.

"I put in for Germany," Joan replied. "I think I have a shot at it."

"Oh, Joan, you look terrific," Leslie cooed. Joan nodded and threw a telling glance at Leslie. Joan was quite open about her sexual preference. Leslie liked both sexes, but we knew that she and Joan had been having a relationship.

"Let's all have dinner together tonight," Karen piped up. "We have so much to talk about."

I agreed. "Who knows when we will see each other again."

The first day of exams was intense. We took the Fundamentals of Nursing exam in the morning. The proctors gave us one and a half hours for lunch. In the afternoon we took Psychiatric Nursing. I was drained by 4:00. I walked out of the large hall feeling dejected.

"I just know I failed," I announced to Karen, Joan, and Leslie.

"No, you didn't. You did fine."

I shook my head. "No. I failed psych and I'll have to repeat it."

"Put it out of your mind," Leslie said.

We drove off to a local cafeteria-style restaurant. Everyone filled her tray with her favorite food. Karen led the way to a corner table. I put my tray down and asked Joan, "Seriously, what is the army like?"

"I love it," Joan stated, chewing a pork chop covered with gravy. Her voluptuous hips reflected her love for food. "It's rough. You have to answer to some pretty tough people, but I'm going to be a sergeant before you know it."

Leslie asked what neither Karen or I had the guts to. "How many are like us?"

Joan roared. "Enough. I'm in my glory. In fact, you know how I love to kiss asses!"

I blushed. Karen, too, looked down at her plate and twirled the string beans with her fork. Leslie grimaced with obvious jealousy.

"How's the Island kid?" Joan inquired of her old roommate, changing the subject.

"I like it. I guess. I work a medical floor with mostly old people, which is frustrating and depressing. We spend half our time trying to ship them off to a nursing home. The other half we make rounds changing diapers. But," Leslie hesitantly added, "the fringe benefits are good."

"What fringe benefits?" Joan asked. She looked jealous now.

"The tips," replied Leslie.

"What do you mean by tips?" I asked.

It was Joan's turn to speak out. "The kind a waitress gets for services rendered. We have the same thing too in some army hospitals."

"Not money?" I was shocked.

"Of course," Leslie answered. "If the patients and their families want good quality care like an extra bedpan, or water, or anything else, they tip us. I've made as much as five dollars for giving an extra bedpan."

"Leslie! What are you saying?" Karen, too, was shocked. "It's against the professional ethics of nurses to accept or demand a monetary tip from a patient before or after giving any personal care."

"So it is." Joan jumped to Leslie's defense. "But I'll tell you that if you want to work in some of these places and starve to death on your varicose veins, that's okay. Me, I want to make money. Nursing doesn't pay us enough, so what's wrong with a gratis here and there?"

Karen and I looked at each other. Tipping was forbidden. It has always been acceptable for a patient to give a gift like candy, perfume, or other food, but never money. We were both uncomfortable and sorry that we had insisted on having Joan and Leslie join us.

"Where does this kind of tipping take place?" I asked, losing interest in my dinner.

"All over," came Joan's instant reply.

Leslie agreed. "Sure. It is an accepted fact in many hospitals right here in the city. For heaven's sake! Why are the two of you looking at us like that?" Leslie asked. "I see nothing wrong with it."

"But what about the patient who can't afford to tip

or can't pay the equivalent of some others?" Karen asked, still stunned.

"Oh, they get their patient care, too," Joan replied. "But maybe just not as quickly as the good tippers. We just leave them until last, that's all."

"That's not right." I was getting angry. "It is just not right."

Karen added, "Patient care doesn't exclude anyone. Tipping for care is just plain awful."

"It's no worse than bitching about some patient you don't like, or leaving them until the end for care. We all do that too. You were no different in training about that than I was," Joan stated emphatically.

Leslie agreed again with Joan. I couldn't believe my ears and I didn't want to hear anymore. I changed the subject to Paul, and Karen talked about John and her upcoming wedding.

It soon became clear that Joan and Leslie wanted to be alone. We parted company, promising to see each other again.

On the way back to our apartment, Karen and I agreed that we didn't care if we *ever* saw Joan or Leslie again.

Wednesday's Boards consisted of maternity in the morning and pediatrics in the afternoon. Karen and I drove home in silence, grateful that Boards were over but apprehensive about the results. It would be ninety days before we would know.

I went looking for Paul on Friday evening. He still hadn't called, not even to ask about my Boards. I was hurt and disappointed. I didn't have to clock in until 11:00 p.m. July was half over and so were nights, I hoped.

I asked two interns I saw in the lobby if they knew Dr. Thompson.

"Sure," one of them replied.

"Is he on duty tonight?"

"I think he is somewhere around. The last I knew he was in the ER. Try there."

I thanked them, walking in the direction of the Emergency Room. "Have you see Dr. Thompson?" I asked the ward clerk behind the glass window in the ER waiting room.

She nodded. "He was just here, but I heard him say he would be in the cafeteria with Dr. Kim."

"Thanks." I took the elevator to the basement where the cafeteria was hidden at the opposite end of the morgue and labs. I looked around the cafeteria, but couldn't see any sign of either man. It was 10:46 p.m. I was running out of time.

I could page him, but I didn't want to interrupt him. I decided to swing by the ER one more time.

The clerk looked up as I approached. "He just came back. An emergency." She pointed in the direction of the cubicles and small rooms with closed doors. I walked down the familiar hallway looking up and down the corridor in every direction. Then, I heard sounds coming from a small room. The door was slightly ajar. I recognized Paul's voice.

". . . We've got an OD of demerol . . . BP not palpable . . ."

Suddenly, Dr. Jackson, the anesthesiologist, boomed out, "pupils fully dilated and blown . . . respirations down to 4 . . ."

I heard another voice. "You know, she is one of ours. A nurse from the Critical Care Unit."

Curious, I approached the door and looked in. Nurses were running around injecting medications into IV lines. Paul screamed for the cart. I looked up at the monitor. Her respiration had gone from V-tach into ventricular fibrillation.

The zap of the paddles on her chest and the jumping of her body made me freeze in my tracks. I wondered who she was and what had happened to her.

The electrical charge worked. Her heart rate reverted to a sinus rhythm. It wasn't normal, but she was back from the brink of death. They began to intubate her and connect her to an MA1. Paul was angry. So were two of the nurses.

He bellowed out orders and reprimanded one of the nurses as though she were a child. The room looked more like an operating arena. Finally, the patient stabilized and they prepared to transfer her to the unit for observation.

When I heard them mention the unit I came back to reality. My watch said 10:58 p.m. I had to leave without talking to Paul, but I knew he would probably follow this patient up.

I just made the time clock at 11:00 to punch in.

"We've got one coming up from the ER," I announced, grabbing my assignment off the patient board.

"I know," Brenda said. "An overdose. One of ours, I hear."

I nodded. Report went on, although Bob Morgan was asked to leave to admit his patient to bed ten. He had the ER patient. My curiosity was overwhelming. I also wanted desperately to see Paul.

Finally, report ended. Entering the unit, I saw Bob and Paul talking at the bedside. I walked over. I recognized the patient as a CCU nurse I had seen occasionally but didn't personally know.

"What happened?" I asked.

"An overdose," Bob answered. "Stupid nurse has been stealing demerol and injecting herself with it."

I was horrified. "Taking demerol? What for?"

"It makes the pain go away," Paul replied. "Stealing drugs is a big problem today among health professionals."

Bob agreed. "She apparently was injecting demerol into her thigh in the nurses' bathroom when she arrested. She is damn lucky someone found her. She nearly died."

Dazed, I began my patients' assessments. Tips for services rendered. Stealing drugs and taking them. Was there some sort of pattern?

Paul never came back to talk to me. Somehow it didn't matter. Bob and I met and talked on our break about his patient.

"Bob, I feel confused. Why would a nurse steal drugs?"

Bob sighed. "Addictions are a problem among all phases of life. For nurses it is easy. Steal them and take them."

"But how do they steal them?"

"One way is to simply draw up the solution and inject part of it in themselves and the remaining in the patient. For example, 75mg of demerol is 2 cc's in a syringe. I have seen nurses take half of that dose and inject the other half in the patient."

"Are they that desperate?" I asked gloomily.

He nodded. "Or, they cut off the bottom of the vials, empty the contents into another bottle, and replace the vial's contents with sterile water. They then glue the bottom back on."

"Wait a minute," I exclaimed. "I found a vial like that when I first began working here. In the nurses' bathroom."

"In this unit?" Bob asked.

"Yes."

"What did you do with it?"

"I took it home." I racked my brain to remember where I had placed the vial at home. I really had forgotten all about it.

"Did you tell anybody about it?" he asked.

"No. I really was confused about it and then I forgot."

"I think it would be better if we kept this between us," he said.

"Why?" I asked.

"Don't ask any questions, Joyce. Just keep it to yourself for your own well being."

I was being warned again. But Bob didn't want to pursue it. I had no choice but to let it drop.

Mr. Williams died at 7:30 a.m., while the day shift nurses were in report. I turned off the monitors and covered him up to his head. I then let his family, still waiting in the ER, come in to say goodbye. I stood by, helplessly watching the family cry, scream, and mourn the loss of their loved one. Silently, I was grateful. He had lived for almost four weeks, but the quality of his life and death was nil.

Tina had been originally assigned to him. While she began her a.m. care I did his post-mortem care. It was 8:30 a.m. when I clocked out of the unit.

The parking lot was full, as usual. My car was in the back under the only tree around. I had intentionally parked there to keep my car cool. The days were hot long before noon. The intense summer sun baked my black interior all too quickly.

As I put my key into the door lock, I heard a strange sound. My heart began to race. Fear suddenly came over me. I heard it again: a low moan, coming from the bushes in front of my car. A chill ran up and down my spine. I looked around for the security guards. Robbery and rapes had occurred in the parking lot. Security was supposed to be around to prevent more problems.

I heard it again. Low. Louder. Intermittent. I knew instinctively that I had to check. I unlocked the car and grabbed my umbrella. If it was an attacker I could jab him with the point.

I moved slowly toward the bushes. The sound came again. Suddenly I tripped over a large root of a tree protruding up through the undergrowth. Falling on my knees, face forward, I landed on a large body. I screamed. Blood oozed from the man's right temple.

He had been shot in the temple and the chest. The temple shot looked like a graze. He was semi-conscious and just barely breathing. He was also all too familiar to me. It was Bob Morgan.

Racing up the hill back into the building and into the ER I screamed for help. A security guard came running. "What's the matter, lady?"

I was out of breath. Speechless. In shock. "Help me,"

I pleaded, calling to the ward clerk for emergency assistance.

"What happened?" a nurse yelled as she ran out of a cubicle.

"Shot—" I huffed. "He's been shot."

Everyone followed me out the door and down the hill. I found myself praying that Bob would not die.

He was where I found him. The guard lifted him onto a gurney. They began CPR and emergency measures. They raced him back up the hill into the ER. I followed, sobbing hysterically. By now the police had arrived.

I felt faint as we entered the ER corridor. Watching the staff wheel the body into a small room I began to pray, "Oh, Bob, who did this to you and why?"

Two hours later, after police interrogation and Bob Morgan's preparation for surgery I went home, exhausted, upset and frightened.

"Did you hear the news?" Shelly asked me as I walked through the door later that night.

I didn't care about any news other than knowing about Bob. "How is Bob Morgan?" I asked, looking at the patient board and seeing his name. He was in bed seven. Dr. Carter had been assigned to him.

"You know that Bob Morgan was brought in with gunshot wounds to both the chest and temple?"

"I'm the one who found him," I replied.

"I thought I heard that. Well, the police think he was involved in selling drugs. Cocaine. And, they think it was a drug deal that went sour."

"How could Bob Morgan be involved in drugs?" I asked. I suddenly remembered the conversation between Carol and Marilyn I had overheard. I also remembered Bob's and my conversation, only last night, about nurses stealing demerol.

"Rumor has it that he has been selling drugs for a

long time. Frankly, I was surprised too. I would never have suspected him. He just doesn't seem to be the kind."

As I walked off to report I wondered about that. And I wondered if he was also using drugs or just selling. I still could not be sure when someone really was under the influence.

The bullet had punctured Bob's right lung. He was comatose and on a respirator. The right temple wound was deeper than I had originally thought. His pupils were fully blown and dilated. I figured, from report, that in all likelihood he was brain dead.

Bob's bed was assigned to Carol. I felt tears well up in my eyes whenever I looked over at his bedside. The lifeless body was unresponsive to deep stimuli. The chest tubes were milked hourly and drained into a bottle below the bedside. His foley catheter contained blood-tinged urine. Tubing ran in and out of his body. Only the hissing of the respirator and the beeping of the cardiac monitor signified life.

Paul came into the unit about 3:00 a.m. to check on one of his fresh post-ops. "How are you?" he asked with a twinkle in his blue eyes.

I melted on the spot. "I'm fine. And you?" I tried to act nonchalant while continuing my hourly vitals. I didn't know he was on his twenty-four rotation.

"Okay. Sorry I haven't had time to call you. I've been super busy. Twenty-four and forty-eight hour rotations are rough on the body."

"I know." I *did* know. The residents, like the nurses, kept the hospital going. They worked around the clock trying to catch some sleep in the on-call. Usually, the sleep was never enough. I marvelled at how well they functioned in making life-and-death decisions. I knew I could never do it.

"I'm off next weekend. A long one at that. Three days. Can we get together?" he asked.

I came alive at his question. "I would love to. I have Friday night off, but I'm working the weekend."

"Swell. I'll call you and we'll make plans for Friday."
He walked away from the bedside. I noticed that his fresh
post-op was Shelly's patient. I envied her.

On the coffee break Shelly asked me about Paul. "I'm
not blind, you know," she said.

I sat and smiled. I knew better than to talk about a
relationship before it began. I really liked Paul and I didn't
want to scare him away.

Shelly realized I wasn't going to talk. She changed
the subject. "This patient of mine had a terrible surgical
procedure. I sure hope your Paul isn't responsible."

"What do you mean?"

"He is a seventy-two-year-old who had a prostatec-
tomy, but it is the worst incision I have ever seen. His
ureters are connected to an ostomy bag because, according to the OR notes, his right ureter was accidentally cut."

The ureters are the very fine, thin tubing that con-
nects the kidneys to the bladder. We learned in nursing
school that a ureter is as small as the tip of a pencil.

"How could that happen?"

Shelly went on, "I don't know, but Dr. Peter Bordan
was the attending surgeon." Shelly paused to light another cigarette. "Of course it had to be Bordan. Rumor
has it that he uses drugs."

Drugs again. "Drugs? What kind?"

"Demerol. Dilaudid. Morphine. You name it."

"Shelly, do you know this for a fact?"

"Not really. Just rumor. Frankly, I never see him so I
don't know for sure."

"Shelly, how do you know if someone uses drugs? I
really can't tell."

"I really can't either, Joyce. I do recognize the people
on alcohol. Raymonds abuses alcohol."

Dr. Raymonds was a surgeon I never liked. When I
was a student I once saw the OR nurses sober him up for
a colostomy repair. His work was sloppy.

"And so does Lois," Shelly went on.

"What do you mean, Shelly?"

"Lois drinks. Didn't you know that, Strom?"

"No, I didn't," I confessed, wondering how Shelly knew so much more than I did about what went on in the unit.

"She always comes on duty with red, bloodshot eyes," Shelly whispered, not wanting gossip to be overheard.

"Bloodshot eyes don't mean much to me. I am not a morning person, so I just never thought much of it."

"She has all the signs of a chronic alcoholic, Strom. Red cheeks. Poor skin pallor. A slight jaundice color."

I thought about what Shelly was saying. I really didn't know much more about alcoholism than I'd learned in nursing school, and our studies had centered on Wernecke's disease, which was a final stage of the disease process. Early signs and symptoms still eluded me.

"She also has been called in for emergencies on both the evening and night shift and has reeked of wine. Wine is her thing apparently," Shelly offered as additional information.

I shook my head negatively. "Maybe that is why she was so cruel to me when I first began working here," I considered gloomily. As an afterthought I asked, "Does Marilyn drink too?"

"No. Marilyn does social drugs. Pot. A little cocaine. Quaaludes. She and her boyfriend are into that scene."

"I thought she and Dr. Vorhees were having an affair." I was stunned. "Who is her boyfriend?" I asked, suddenly feeling quite naive.

Shelly's eyes crinkled at the corners. "Terry, the good looking respiratory therapist. They live together." Shelly smiled knowingly. "Do you mean you really didn't know any of this?"

"No. I guess I'm pretty dumb, huh?"

"Listen, Strom. The razzing you got was not unique to you. We all got it. Every new nurse is on the receiving end. The rationale is to weed out the novices and keep good critical care nurses in here. But there is more to it than that."

Now I was thoroughly confused. The shocked look on my face was enough to prompt Shelly to continue.

"I'm going to give you a few facts, but just for your own well being." Shelly's voice lowered to a barely audible point. "Bob was shot because of drugs. A lot of funny things go on around here. Patients complain of pain after being medicated. Dr. Vorhees is always having closed-door conferences with Lois, Marilyn, Carol, Tina, and a few select others, including Terry. I don't know what is going on, but I have my suspicions."

My curiosity overwhelmed me. "Like what, Shel?"

"Well, I think our unit staff is part of a drug ring."

"A drug ring?" I wiped the beads of sweat forming on my forehead. "I know pushers are selling cocaine and buying drugs on the streetcorner."

"Yeah," her eyes flashed with anger, "but what if our nurses and doctors are selling those drugs to the streetcorner."

"Why?"

"Strom, are you really that naive?" Shelly's tone was almost mocking.

"Look, here's some facts. A 30cc bottle of Demerol costs our patients about ten dollars, but on the street that same bottle can bring in five thousand dollars."

"Are you serious?" I didn't ask who would want Demerol. I could figure that out.

Shelly answered the question I didn't ask. "Any junkie shooting up will gladly take demerol. Amphetamines cost six cents to twelve cents per capsule, but the street value is four dollars to twelve dollars apiece. Methaqualone tablets, better known as Quaaludes, cost ten cents to thirteen cents each. On the street they sell for five dollars to twelve dollars each."

I had never heard of a Quaalude until recently. Apparently methaqualones were common sleepers. Sleepers were the barbituates and sedatives like placidyl, choral hydrate, dalmane, and luminal.

Shelly continued. "Talwin and tuinal also sell for five

dollars to fifteen dollars. They only cost pennies to patients from the pharmacy, and cost even less to produce."

"Shel," I asked incredulously, "where did you learn all of this?"

"I've been in nursing for twenty years. I come in and do my job and go home. But I have watched a lot of good nurses come and go in this unit. As I warned you, I keep my eyes and ears open and my mouth shut."

Shelly took a long pause letting a deep breath expel slowly. Her motherly eyes softened. "I only told you all of this because I like you and I think you are a good and caring nurse. If anything, you care too much and you probably would do better working in psych. But, I am warning you now. Keep your mouth shut. Just watch and listen. They don't like you or trust you. Word has it they think you are a narc."

"What the heck is a narc? I keep hearing this word." I felt agitated and uncomfortable.

Shelly shrugged. "Someone employed by Nursing Service or the local police to investigate and squeal on them."

"You have got to be kidding. Me? A narc?" Not in my wildest dreams could I imagine such a role for myself. I wasn't the brave and daring kind of person who could take such risks.

"They don't know. They are simply cautious. You be careful too, and be careful of your resident friend, Paul. He does drugs too." Shelly concluded and walked away from me without another word.

I was dazed. Did Paul do drugs? What and how, I wondered. Throughout the rest of the night my mind raced with all she had told me. I thought about Bob. Maybe he was the narc, if such a person really did exist. I immediately wanted to defend myself and run to Lois or Marilyn saying I was not who they thought I was. I knew better, however. Shelly was right. I had to keep my eyes and ears open.

During the night I remembered, again, that vial of

demerol I had found in the nurses' bathroom some time ago. The one with the bottom filed off and then glued back on. Obviously someone had filed the bottom off to empty it, just as Bob said. By cutting the vial the top would be intact and no one would know the drug had been stolen. I wondered what the drug would be replaced with, and then I answered my question. Normal saline would have been a good choice, or plain old sterile water.

And what of Paul? I had a throbbing headache by the time I went off duty. I looked closely at Lois, trying to observe her at 7:00 a.m. Her eyes were bloodshot and she looked worn and tired. Marilyn didn't look any different. I avoided both of them and left the unit quietly at 8:00 a.m.

My sleep was restless. My dreams were filled with images of pills, alcohol and Paul. Either awake or asleep, I was thoroughly confused.

Bob died five days after his unit admission. He never regained consciousness. The police began an open investigation on his death. They talked to all of us. They were not confident that they would ever find his murderers.

EIGHT

The next three months flew by. In late October I went to the mailbox looking for birthday cards. I was turning twenty-three on the twenty-fifth of October. I wondered if Paul would do anything special for my day. I wondered if he would remember to be free.

Flipping through the mail my eyes immediately noticed the return address on two envelopes. The State Board of Nursing. My heart pounded and blood rushed to my head. I was holding the results of Karen's and my fate.

We had been taught in nursing school that a thin letter meant we had passed, while a thick envelope meant we had failed. The thick envelope would contain the proper forms for refiling.

I could hardly contain my excitement. Both envelopes were thin. I raced into the apartment and woke Karen, who was sleeping later than usual. She and John were spending long hours together preparing for their wedding.

"Wake up Karen. They're here," I exclaimed.

She was groggy as she sat upright rubbing her eyes. "What's here?"

"Our board results."

Karen screamed, grabbing the envelope from me. We ripped them open simultaneously and began sobbing and hugging each other. We had both passed. We held our temporary licenses in our hands, along with our score reports on the subtests. Later, after phone calls to my mother and brother, I read my scores more closely. Psych was my highest grade. Almost perfect. I couldn't believe it.

I raced excitedly into the unit to receive Congratulations from my co-workers and friends. Lois said she would assign me to take the medication course on the next time sheet.

By November, I was enrolled in the medication course. I was being trained to make quick decisions in regard to administering critical medication like dopamine, potassium chloride, lasix, and manitol.

I was struck by how important morphine and valium could be for respiratory control of patients hovering between life and death. I had thought these drugs were only used to rid patients of pain, along with pavulon to anesthetize muscles. Doctors have a tremendous amount of responsibility for life-death decisions. So do interns and residents but, often, it is the bedside nurse who advises them about dosage regulation and medications to order, and who then administers them.

I was anxious about the test for the course, but I managed to pass it. Lois still had not assigned me to giving meds in the unit. When I asked her about it, she told me to wait until the holidays were over.

Every time I saw Paul I watched him closely for signs and symptoms of drug usage. It was hard even with my new training to make a definite diagnosis. He usually looked tired with bloodshot eyes. But, he was on surgical on-call for as long as forty-eight hours. Sometimes he never had any sleep during that time. I wanted to talk to him about Shelly's rumor, yet the opportunity never arose. Even our dinner date was superficial. The chemistry, for me, was dwindling due to my fears. Paul ordered a dry red wine with our Italian meal. Neither of us drank more than a glass or two. The bottle was left half full. If drinking was a problem for him he didn't show it.

But Paul's sinuses seemed always to be bothering him. His nose was red and inflamed. In response to my questions about it, he told me that he had been an allergic child since infancy.

A notice for a Christmas party at Marilyn's house was posted near the time sheet. I was scheduled to work that evening. Shelly told me to come when I got off duty.

"You really should go, Joyce. They have eased off of you in the past few weeks, so go and see what really goes on." She then added, "Especially since you are going to be giving meds here soon."

Reluctantly, I agreed with her. Now that I had passed my State Boards and was a Registered Nurse, Lois had been forced to sign me up for the medication course. Taking the course and giving meds were two different things. I might have the textbook knowledge, but I still wondered when I would have the opportunity to use it.

I had been watching everyone for weeks. Not since that fateful night with Shelly had I spoken about drugs or alcohol to anyone, including Karen, whom I rarely saw as our shifts passed each other. When one of us was working, the other was sleeping.

A week before the Christmas party, I was working evenings. My primary patient was a retired French chef who had a bilateral hernia repair. The OR sent him to the unit on an MA-1 respirator set at 2 with 40% oxygen. He also weighed over 550 pounds. His body quite literally, flowed up the sides of the bedrails and over the top of them. Two OR stretchers had brought him into the unit. I was frustrated at my inability to turn, cough and deep breathe him, much less change his sheets. All of the nurses joked about him while refusing to give me any assistance. His incisions were both over fifteen inches long and held together with the largest metal staples I had ever seen. The heart monitor beeped out a normal sinus rhythm. He was there for post-op observation to avoid respiratory or cardiac arrest due to his weight.

Pierre LaFount tried to be cooperative. His pain, however, was real. I asked Carol, who was the med nurse, to give him his prn order of demerol 75 mg. Dr. Buffs had ordered the demerol to be given every four to six hours as needed.

Carol seemed to move very slowly. I looked up, silently reprimanding her. Finally, she brought the syringe over and injected the pain killer into his main fluid IV. I watched to see his reaction to the pain meds and assess how comfortable they made him feel. When twenty minutes had gone by and he still thrashed about, clearly agitated, I called to Carol, "The medications aren't working. I'll chart the effects."

"He'll just have to hang in there for another three and a half hours," she growled abruptly. "If the guy would lose weight, he could feel the effects of the demerol."

"Maybe 75 mg. is too low a dose for someone his size," I offered empathically. "Can't you call Dr. Buffs and ask for a medication change?"

Carol didn't answer immediately. She was filling IV bags with antibiotics for different patients and adding manitol to the IV bag for a neuro patient. When she finally walked over to me, she stated curtly, "I'll call Dr. Buffs when I have a chance."

I walked away feeling defeated. I didn't like Mr. La-Fount's weight either, but that didn't justify treating him with anything less than dignity. His pain continued until the end of the shift. Mary, the night charge nurse, who also gave meds on nights, medicated Mr. LaFount at 11:30 p.m. I left his bedside ten minutes later. He was sleeping soundly. Glancing at Mary's nurses notes, I saw she had given 75 mg. IV of demerol. I wondered why the medication worked this time, but not at 7:30 p.m.

My locker was in the back of the nurses' locker room. I removed my dirty scrubs. Someone was in the bathroom. I could see her white shoes beneath the stall. I waited impatiently. Nearly ten minutes later, Carol came out. I nodded to her as I walked briskly in. Looking down at the floor, I gasped. Fresh, bright drops of blood left a trail to the sink. At first I thought that Carol might be having her period until I noticed a vial on the floor near the trash can. Instinctively, I leaned over and picked it up. The vial said: "Demerol 100 mg." The top had been removed and so had the bottom. I rifled through the trash can. Unwrapping a wadded-up paper towel, I found an empty 5cc syringe. A 22 gauge syringe was wrapped in another.

Discarding the evidence, I hurriedly left the bathroom. Carol had changed and was leaving. I quickly called out to her wondering what I would say.

"Hey, Carol. Wait up."

She turned and looked at me strangely. Her usual scowl had been replaced with a smile. Her eyes, however, were glassy. "Hi, Strom. Are you going to the Christmas party?"

"Sure, I'd love to," I murmured. Before I could think of anything else to say Carol rambled on.

"It will be a fun party. Lots of food, wine, and happy choices. It's a good thing you are working evenings. You can get stoned or drunk afterwards. Are you on duty the next day?"

"Yes. Evenings again," I replied gloomily.

She shrugged. "No sweat. The downers will help. You'll be in great shape."

Carol and I entered the elevator but did not speak again since we were not alone. Walking to our cars in the parking lot I bravely suggested, "You know, Carol, I would like to get to know you better."

Carol brightened. "Sure, Strom. You seem to be okay after all. We didn't trust you for a long time, but once Lois discovered that Bob was the narc, the pressure on you eased off. Be one of us and you'll have a great time." She entered her car.

As I watched Carol drive off, her words about Bob stung. Who was responsible for his death. Could it be someone in our unit? I felt I had to find out. I knew I couldn't do drugs. I was too frightened of them. But, I decided I would have to pretend in order to find out what was really happening.

I wasn't sure what I would do with the information I was seeking, but I knew I had to help save my profession and the human beings who worked in it, as well as the patients who put themselves in our care.

Marilyn's apartment was only a few blocks from the hospital. A two-bedroom, one-and-a-half-bath, located on the ground floor. There was a small patio that let onto a fenced-in court yard. I entered the open door. The room was filled with the usual blue haze. My eyes began to water at the burning sensation of smoke. Cigarettes and pot burned everywhere. Beer bottles were stewn all over the floor.

Marilyn lay on the floor with her head in Terry's lap. Both of them seemed dazed, staring at the ceiling. I made my way into the smoke-filled room, amazed at the faces I saw. Suddenly I bumped into Dr. Vorhees, who was busy inhaling a white powder being handed to him by another doctor I'd seen before, Dr. Jackson, the anesthesiologist. "Excuse me," I said, feeling embarrassed. Paul stood close by. Then I noticed he was doing the same. He didn't even look up. I was in a state of shock.

In the corner I saw Carol drinking a beer and talking to some nurses I recognized from the OR. I walked over to her.

"Hi, Strom. What's your poison?" Her speech was slurred and her eyes were half closed.

"Wine, I think." I tried to sound normal, but my heart raced.

"The bar is over there." She pointed in the direction of the patio. "Coke is over there," she nodded turning her head in the direction of Paul. "I'm sure Paul will be glad to see you. And anything else you want is floating around. Just grab a lude before you leave since you're working tomorrow."

I thanked her and headed off for a glass of wine. My embarrassment at approaching Paul was obvious only to me. The tap on my shoulder caused me to spin around in a hurry.

"Hi stranger. Glad you made it." Paul looked wonderful. But his voice was slurred. I stared into those beautiful blue eyes, the pupils dilated.

"I'm glad I did, too," I said quickly. My head ached. I was lightheaded, having never seen anyone use cocaine before except in the movies. Why was Paul doing cocaine? Needing to make small talk I added, "it looks like it's a nice party."

"Sure is." He shook his head mischievously. "I'll introduce you around."

Paul knew everyone. Being with him made them accept me. The introduction to Dr. Vorhees really surprised me.

"It's nice to meet you. Want to do a line?"

"A line of what?" I asked naively.

Both doctors began to laugh at me. "Coke, of course."

I nodded and said, "No, thank you."

"Well, there's plenty of stuff around," Dr. Vorhees stated. "Nice meeting you." He walked away, putting his arm around a pretty young OR nurse. Her name was Betsy. Only a week ago there had been a hospital rumor that Betsy and Dr. Vorhees were caught making love in OR number 6 by the evening superintendent. OR 6 was kept open for the trauma team. I watched the doctor's hands roaming all over her body. They began to kiss passionately while his hands cradled her buttocks. Unable to look away, I just stood there.

Paul grabbed my arm. "It is really nice to see you here," he whispered guiding me into a corner. "I want to ask you something."

"Sure." I felt numb and nauseous. The odor of the pot made my head spin and throb.

"I am going to take a three-day trip to Miami next Friday. How would you like to come with me?" His dilated pupils twinked. "We really haven't had any time to get to know one another."

I shook my head negatively. "I don't think I can get Friday off. I only have the weekend."

"If I can arrange it, will you go?"

I brooded unhappily. Even if he was on drugs, I really cared about Paul. I didn't want him to go with someone else. Why not? Three days with Paul would be wonderful. "Sure. But why Miami?"

"Just a little business and pleasure." He smiled mysteriously. "You have to travel as my wife, though. Would you mind?"

Remembering our love-making, I had no objections. "No problem," I said, taking a deep breath.

"Good." He stroked my shoulder. "We leave on the 7:00 a.m. non-stop. I'll have your tickets and I will get you the time off."

I sipped at my wine, feeling light-headed. The smoke of the pot filled my brain cells. I began to care only about the moment. I prayed it would go on indefinitely.

Our flight was smooth. The lights of Miami twinked from the sky. It looked exciting. With Paul next to me I forgot about the unit, my co-workers and my problems. I didn't know how Paul pulled it off, but Marilyn changed the schedule. I was free to leave for a three-day weekend.

Paul and I took a taxi cab to our hotel. The Croton House was located only a few blocks from the Port of Miami. I was disappointed that we were not on the ocean, only Biscayne Bay. But the large swimming pool made up for it.

Our room was lovely. A floral bedspread covered the

king-size bed. Colored tv and standard radio with an air conditioner blowing. The scenery was so different from our drab city. I looked out the window. Even the sky was a clear blue. I was in love with both Paul and the deep South. I denied the reality that he used cocaine.

"Why don't you go to the pool for awhile. I have to go out for a few hours, but I'll be back for dinner." Paul smiled at me, nibbling the back of my neck.

"Do you want me to go with you?"

"No. Just enjoy the sun." He explained further. "Business before pleasure." He kissed me again quickly and ran off.

I languished on the beach, reading the novel I had brought with me.

Paul returned four hours later. His meeting had gone well. We had the rest of the weekend to ourselves.

That evening we decided to eat at a local restaurant. Paul was tired and kept yawning through our meal of bar-b-que ribs and wine at Tony Roma's. Walking back to the hotel, I could tell by his mood that he was preoccupied.

The moon over Miami was a bright orange circle. Looking into the dark sky I felt I could reach out and touch it. Romance and love filled my heart. I gazed up at Paul and noticed the moon beams dance across his dark hair. "Is anything wrong?" I asked.

Paul was silent for a long time. "No," he finally said shaking his head, but he looked anxious and tense.

I didn't push it. I was eager to go to our room and make love, but he had other ideas.

"Let's stop in the bar for a drink," he said as we entered the lobby of the large hotel.

Walking past the gift shops, still open for tourist business, we entered the lounge where a strobe light illuminated the floor in front of a loud disco band. I had expected our evening to be softer and more romantic.

Paul ordered more wine. I had no desire to drink or dance. We sat in the noisy lounge, in silence, watching couples move rapidly across the dance floor.

By his third drink, I was sure something was wrong, but he would not talk. "Paul, how can I help you?" I asked. "I know something is wrong."

He looked at me sadly. He seemed dejected. Suddenly he forced a smile on his lips and attempted to reassure me. "Sorry," he began, "I guess I am just real tired after the trip and all of the stress from the hospital. I am not being very fair to you. Do you want to call it a night?"

I looked at my watch. It was 11:30 p.m. "Well," I said, trying to choose my words carefully, "I had hoped we could spend some time alone together."

Paul said nothing. He finished his drink and paid the bill. In silence we walked to our room.

"I'm going to take a shower," I announced, which was my normal nightly routine.

Paul nodded. He began to undress and lay down on the bed in his jockey shorts. He looked so very handsome and desirable to me. He flipped on the tv and seemed to be a little more relaxed.

I took a quick shower. All I could think about was climbing into bed with this man and making love with him. As I toweled myself and entered our room again, I was shocked and disappointed to find Paul asleep.

I touched his shoulder, pulled back the covers and slid into the bed. Running my hand along his chest, down his thigh, and finally to his groin I found no response. Paul was in a deep sleep. Sadly, I rolled over and silently cried myself to sleep.

Saturday morning arrived quickly. Somehow I had slept, even though I was still feeling rejected. I looked over at Paul's side of the bed, but heard him in the shower.

"Good morning," he announced in a matter-of-fact tone as he came out of the shower. "Did you sleep well?"

I wanted to tell him, "No, I didn't sleep well. I wanted to make love to you and you let me down." But what I

really said was, "Yes, thank you," as I reprimanded myself
for not being open and honest.

On Saturday we were at the pool early. After lunch
we went shopping in downtown Miami, an area now pop-
ulated largely by Cubans. Although the lure of summer
clothing was exciting, in one shop Paul found two large
Chinese figurines, a man and a woman dressed in oriental
clothing.

"Would you like these?" he asked as we stood admir-
ing them together.

I liked Chinese decor; the things in my apartment
were Oriental. "I hope to have a house filled with black
lacquer furniture someday."

His blue eyes sparkled. "Please. I want to give them
to you."

"They are beautiful, Paul, but I can't accept anything
like this."

He insisted. Finally I nodded in agreement. The figurines were wrapped, and Paul carried them back to the
hotel.

That night we ate in the main restaurant of the hotel.
Sitting by the river, we watched the moon rise as boats
travelled up and down the waterway. I was in a romantic
mood, determined that Paul & I would not spend another
night together simply sleeping.

Paul looked over the table at me after the waiter
brought our wine and took our orders. "You look delicious," he murmured, "and you are turning everyone on
in this room."

"Everyone?" I inquired demurely looking at his eyes.
"I am only interested in one person in this room." I moved
my left leg closer to his and began to brush my stocking
calf along his trousers.

"You are driving me crazy," he whispered.

"I certainly hope so," I cooed. "You owe me."

There was a glint in his eye. "I owe you?" he asked
innocently.

"Uh huh. You fell asleep on me last night," I traced his lips with my fingertip.

"Lady, if you don't stop I am afraid I don't know what I'll do," he begged.

I could feel Paul's eyes on me. While the food was delicious, I took more delight in being close to Paul. He couldn't concentrate on his dinner and I didn't want him to. I was relieved when he declined both coffee and dessert. He ordered a bottle of red wine to be sent up to our room.

Kicking off my heels, I began to undress him. Letting his shirt and tie fall away I nibbled at his chest and pulled his hair with my tongue and lips. Paul began to moan softly.

I removed his belt and unzipped his pants. Letting them fall to the floor I slid down with his pants and probed him with my mouth. Desire filled my body and his.

He made the attempt to undress me, but I pushed him gently back on the bed and began to take my clothing off slowly and sensuously.

Again he begged, "Why are you doing this to me?"

I smiled, delighted that I had all his attention. Having never teased anyone before, I was finding the experience exciting.

We kissed and touched, rolling over and over on the huge bed. Suddenly, Paul pushed me on my back and held my arms over my head. He lay on top of me teasing me with his mouth and body. I begged him to stop.

"How do you like it, lady?" he asked, happy to have me in the submissive position.

I groaned and begged him to enter me.

"Not yet," he murmured.

I thrashed against his body, but he held me firm with his weight.

"I am going to tease you as you teased me," he stated with a twinkle in his eyes.

I wanted to reach out and touch him. To run my

fingers through his silky hair, but he held my hands together. "I don't think so," he said.

Suddenly, he got up, moved towards his suitcase and proceeded to remove four silk scarves.

"What is that?" I asked, watching him approach me.

He smiled again. He took my left hand and stretched it over my head, tying it to the head board. Then, he did the same to my right hand. While the scarves were not tight, my range of motion was limited. He tied my feet outstretched in the same manner.

I couldn't believe what was happening. I longed for him desperately.

He stood staring at me and then began to laugh as he laid his body on mine once again. Again I begged, "Oh, please, please . . ."

Paul continued to laugh. "How do you like it, lady? How do you like being teased?"

"Please, please," I moaned, thrashing against the scarves. "I want you so much," I begged.

The foreplay was intense. Exciting. And well worth waiting for. We had never made love this way before. I had never made love with anyone like this before. There was a time when I would have been embarrassed or uncomfortable, but Paul brought out desires in me that I never knew existed.

Finally, after what seemed like hours, we culminated our lovemaking. When our breathing returned to normal Paul untied my hands and feet. I kissed him as passionately as I could. "I adore you," I said. He smiled. We fell asleep in each other's arms.

When we made love again in the early morning hours it was wonderful, but without the intensity of the night before. I wondered if what I felt was an addiction similar to what people felt when they used drugs or alcohol. Was I truly addicted to Paul and to sex with him? I wanted nothing more than to make love to him over and over again.

Reluctantly, I climbed out of bed and showered. We

had breakfast and checked out of our hotel room. Then we had a few hours in the sun before our flight left at 4:00 p.m. I was sad driving to the airport. I wanted to stay in Miami and in bed with Paul forever. I was also a little depressed thinking about the unit on Monday. At least, I was on evenings.

"Can you carry your figurines?" Paul asked as the cab door opened in front of Eastern Air Lines.

"Sure." I picked up the box by its rope and carefully held the treasure close to me.

Placing my weekender and purse on the airport metal detector I gently put the box on the electric runner. "Please be careful with these," I said to the heavy set middle-aged woman sitting on a stool scanning the X-ray machine. She didn't answer. She only nodded to let me know she had heard.

I watched the box slide through, grabbing it quickly on the other side of the machine. This gift meant a lot to me. It was my first present from Paul, and would always be a reminder of our trip.

Paul slid the box gently under my seat in the plane. We talked all the way home about our wonderful weekend. We even made plans to take a trip together again. I was euphoric and happy.

Back in the city we walked to his car in the long-term parking lot. Paul drove me home. He brought my luggage up to the apartment. "Can you stay for a little while?" I asked, not wanting the bliss to end.

"No. I have to check in at the hospital and see when I'm on call again." He leaned over and kissed me gently. "It has been wonderful. Thank you."

I walked him to the door and sadly watched him

leave. As I began to unpack my suitcase I looked around for the box. I couldn't find it. Then I realized that Paul had forgotten to bring it in from his car. I telephoned him, but only got his answering machine.

"Hi. It's me," I said happily. "We had a wonderful time, didn't we? Listen, I left my gift in your car. Just wanted you to know. Could you drop it off tomorrow? And, thanks again." Click. The machine ended.

Walking into the unit Monday afternoon I found that nothing had changed. A few names over the beds were different. But, the hissing of machines and the normal mixture of pungent odors were still the same. I met Paul, accidentally, in the cafeteria on my dinner break.

"Sorry about the figurines," he said. "I'll drop them by your unit. Okay?"

"Sure. I wasn't worried," I said contentedly. I sat down next to him, and we ate in silence. Suddenly Paul's beeper sounded. He never got to finish his dinner.

"See you later," he called over his shoulder racing out.

I felt like the luckiest woman alive. I still didn't know where our relationship was going, but, for now, it felt good.

Paul dropped the box off to me at 8:00 just as evening visiting hours were beginning. "I have to run," he said, handing me the box carefully. "The ER just paged me."

"Thanks again!" I called out to him as he ran out the doors while visitors began to pour in.

Evening visiting hours flew by quickly. I watched, depressed, as relatives cried and pleaded with their loved ones to live a little longer. One critically ill teenager really bothered me. Jim was only seventeen and the star of his high school football team. The day before he entered the unit he'd complained of a headache. By the time he saw his family doctor his neck was rigid and he was losing consciousness. He was admitted to ICU five hours later, unconscious and unresponsive to deep stimuli. His body was rigid and numb. He had encephalitis. The prognosis was poor. He was not responding to antibiotic therapy or manitol.

We all hoped and prayed that a miracle would occur and Jim would get well. His parents cried and pleaded with him. They looked as helpless as we felt. But deep down we all felt it was just a matter of time.

I left my patients to take my figures into the locker room. I still guarded the box carefully. As I approached, I noticed the bathroom door was slightly open. Light streamed out. The fan whirred. Someone must have forgotten to shut it off. Moving closer, I saw that the bathroom was not empty.

Through the crack in the door I peered into the mirror. I immediately recognized the reflection. Sitting on the closed toilet lid was Carol. A tourniquet was wrapped tightly around her left arm. Between her teeth was the cap of a syringe. She held the syringe in her right hand. As I watched she injected the syringe into a vein in her left arm. I saw her draw back on the syringe, and blood flowed into the tubex. Then, slowly, she injected the clear liquid mixed with her blood back into her body.

I stood rooted to the spot as I watched her body begin to twitch and rock.

She pulled the syringe out and untied the tourniquet, letting it fall from her arm onto the floor. She reached over to the sink and grabbed a cotton ball. I jumped back into the shadows, fearing she would see me. Still clutching my box I quietly left the locker room. A few minutes later, Carol came out and returned to the medicine counter. I watched her from my patient's bedside. She didn't really look any different. I don't know what I expected.

Ten minutes later I took my box into the locker room and locked it away. I entered the empty bathroom. Locking the door I picked up the wastepaper basket and began rummaging through it. My hand found the wrapped parcels. Two of them. Brown paper toweling covered them. I opened each carefully. There was a syringe in one. The other contained a vial. Using a fresh tissue, I picked the vial up. "Demerol 100 mg." It was empty. I wrapped the vial in tissue and hid the syringe, again, among the paper towels in the basket. I hid the vial in my purse in my locker.

I watched Carol the rest of the evening. She seemed calmer. She didn't move any faster when she was asked for control meds, but she didn't snap at us either. At one point I looked directly into her eyes. Was it my imagination or were her pupils larger than normal?

Jim died at 10:05 p.m. Post mortem care and his emotional family distracted me for a while. I helped Shelly give him his last bath, since she was his nurse. I also fought back my own tears of sadness. Jim was the same age as my brother.

Mary, the night charge nurse, relieved Carol on medications. They were still counting narcotics when I left the locker room carrying my box and the vial in my purse.

Karen was working nights, so the apartment was dark and empty. I missed her, but I needed some time to think about what I had seen. I untied the box and carefully unwrapped my Chinese figurines. Putting them on the fireplace mantle, I thought about my trip to Miami with Paul. How happy I had been. I looked at the figurines and moved them farther apart.

Lifting the man first I noticed white powder on the ledge. "That's strange," I mumbled under my breath. I lifted the porcelain to see if it was broken. For the first time I noticed that the figurine was hollow with an opening the size of a tennis ball on the bottom. I peered inside. The piece was smooth. I shook it from side to side. More white dust fell from around the hole.

Then, I picked up the female. The same thing happened. Almost without thinking, I went to get some saran wrap. I brushed the white powder into it and folded the packet carefully. Then I washed the figurines out and placed them back on the mantle.

Suddenly, the identity of that white powder hit me—

cocaine. Shaking, I sat down, putting my head in my hands. It throbbed.

I was in deep trouble and I knew it. After all, it was I who had carried those figurines through the radar detector. If caught, it was I who would have been arrested. I tried to calm myself, to think rationally about what to do next. John, Karen's fiancé, was a law clerk, and I decided I would call in the morning and request an appointment to see him.

I thought again about my trip with Paul to Miami and breathed heavily. The trip was a buy. I was just as guilty as Paul. I had allowed him to register me as his wife. I shook my head weakly. Marilyn, Lois, and Dr. Vorhees were definitely a part of this scheme. Carol was a user. All at once, I was sure that patients were not getting their pain killers but receiving sterile water instead. Bob Morgan was a narc who was killed while on their trail. Where they had once suspected and avoided me, they now used me. I shuddered. I was trapped.

NINE

"How can I help you, Joyce?" John asked, seating himself behind his desk. I liked John. He was about 5'10" with sandy hair, brown eyes, and a soft voice. John was always polite to me and very sensitive to Karen's needs. They made a nice couple.

I told John the entire story from the beginning. "So, now I'm an unwilling accomplice to a crime. I feel so trapped, John. Can you help?"

John leaned back in his chair and looked pensive for a moment before answering. "You do have a handle on your dilemma. And you are right. You would be considered a co-conspirator. You could plea bargain and testify against Paul, but you really don't have that much proof."

"I have the vial that Carol used and I have this packet of powder I saved." I opened my bag and offered both to him.

"The problem is twofold," he stated. "You didn't see Carol dispose of this vial and, if this powder is cocaine, you didn't see it in Paul's hands."

"But I wrapped the vial in tissue and didn't touch it, so you could get fingerprints off it." I had probably read too many detective stories.

"Carol was the medication nurse that day. It would

be your word against hers that she gave that demerol to a patient." He paused, shaking his head. "No, Joyce. You just don't have enough proof. And, the cocaine, if that is what this is, is out of your hands now. That incident is not relevant."

I said feelingly, "Can you have a lab see if this is cocaine?"

"Sure." He shrugged. "It probably is. I think your theroy is right. You and Paul flew to Miami for a pickup. He bought the figurines and filled them. You carried them on board. You're lucky you were not caught. Paul intentionally kept them until he could empty them."

My voice choked, the words dispirited. "Oh, John. I am so hurt. I can't believe that Paul would do this." I was stunned and confused. I had wanted to believe that Paul and I had something special, that he cared for me.

"Drugs and drug money make people do strange things," John gently tried to explain.

'What do I do?" I asked, hoping that John would have the answers I didn't. I wanted to find any solution that would make my pain go away.

Speaking quietly and rationally, John said, "As I see it, Joyce, you should do nothing unless you really want to get involved and obtain proof."

"Be a narc, you mean." The idea made me shiver. Saying it out loud was even more frightening.

John sighed before saying, "Well, I don't like that term. But, I have a friend in the Drug Enforcement Agency who might be able to help. Do you want me to call him?"

A resurgence of fear swept over me. I shook it off. "John, I feel like I'm in over my head. I have to do something. I cannot sit still and wait for the bomb to drop." I was silent for a moment, then I leaned forward thoughtfully. "Go ahead. Call him."

One hour later Detective Al Thurston joined us in the attorney's office. John called in one of the senior partners, since he was still clerking. He told both men my story while I sat quietly in the corner.

Al spoke to me first.

"Your first name is Joyce, isn't it?"

I nodded.

"Look, I know this must be difficult for you."

"Very difficult," I said feelingly.

"Joyce, Trinity is only one of the hospitals we have been watching."

I was visibly shaken.

He continued. "We have known for some time that drugs are stolen, traded, sold, and used by medical professionals. Unfortunately, we never get enough proof to submit to a Grand Jury." The room grew quiet.

Trying to reassure myself, I scrutinized Al Thurston more closely. He didn't look like my image of a drug enforcement detective. He was a man in his early fifties with a stomach pouch firmly hanging over his belt. His ruddy cheeks with thick darkening stubble, and gray, thinning hair, contrasted. I wondered how he could possibly chase after a criminal without having difficulty in breathing. The humor of my vision calmed me. Suddenly, a picture of Bob Morgan passed through my mind.

"Was Bob Morgan one of yours?" I broke the silence.

"He was. We had him in there with the support of Sister Theresa. I have a proposal for you, Joyce," the agent went on. "You do have the right to refuse," he added emphatically.

"We could use the help of someone inside the hospital who isn't a suspect. I know it sounds dangerous, but I promise you that we will be by your side constantly. You will be wired and always within our reach."

"That sounds like the movies," I said, "but this is real." I felt scared. I could be killed. With that realization I asked, "Besides Bob Morgan, has anyone else been harmed that you know of?"

Al paused for what seemed a long time before answering. "As I recall there was a nurse, a Marie Constanza, who died under very strange circumstances. She didn't work for us. Apparently she was trying to help a union get into the hospital. Her death was never ruled as a homicide, because there wasn't enough evidence."

I shuddered. "How did she die?" I thought I had heard something about this nurse, but I was not absolutely certain.

"A drug overdose. Cocaine." Al paused again. He stared at the floor which made me more uncomfortable. Then he added, "It seemed strange because the union fight was pretty intense when she died. After her death the union quietly pulled out." Al lifted his head and finally looked me in the eye. "Look, I can understand why you would refuse. And, you would have every right to." I drew back, and he quickly interjected, "But you are already in over your head, you participated in a buy in Miami."

Was he trying to intimidate me? I couldn't be sure, but even if he was I knew he was right. I chose to go with Paul. I chose to call on John for help. If I didn't like the options, that was my fault. I didn't want to put my life on the line. I also didn't want to see patients suffer from watered-down medications, or because some nurse was too high on drugs to make a sound judgment.

I owed patients that much, and I also owed the help to nurses. This was my profession. My mother's profession. We had made commitments to care for others. I felt them intensely. "I'll help you," I replied timidly.

John interjected, "She'll help you if you will waive all charges against her and allow her to be a state's witness."

Al agreed. John further added, "And if she needs the witness protection program, you will also comply. Put that in writing and she'll sign it."

I nodded affirmatively.

The agent looked at me again.

"Can we begin now? I am on duty at 3:00 again today." It was close to noon, and I was hungry.

"We need a few hours. When is your day off?" Al asked, looking at his watch.

"Thursday."

"Fine. Here is my business card. Meet me at the court

house at 9:00 a.m. and we will begin. I'm in Room 606. In the meantime, if you have any questions call me. Use a pay phone," he said soberly.

The gravity of my position was seeping into my mind. I took the card, slowly turning it over in my hand. Thanking John, I left the office for another two days on duty.

The next two days were a blur. I saw little of Paul. Every time Dr. Vorhees's name was mentioned I shuddered. Working evenings I didn't see him. Lois put the new time sheet up. I was assigned to giving medication on evenings starting the following month, but what should have been a thrilling responsibility now filled me with dread.

Lois came up behind me. "Are you ready to take the responsibility?"

I jumped. "Ah, yes. Thank you," I murmured, trying to stay calm. I turned towards her.

"You passed the course," Lois said cheerfully, "so I'll start you on evenings working with the charge nurse. After six months you can be trained for evening and night charge."

"Thank you." I smiled in return, realizing Lois now trusted me.

"You have been a surprise to all of us, Strom. Personally, I never thought you would last this long. Looks are deceiving. You really do have a backbone." Swiftly she walked away without giving me the chance to reply. I realized that was her way of staying in control.

At least I had something to look forward to besides meeting with Al Thurston on Thursday morning, which I dreaded. And which arrived too quickly.

W alking into the Federal court house at 8:50 a.m., I found myself looking over my shoulder, convinced I was being followed. Detective Thurston, who eagerly awaited me, ushered me into a nearby room.

"Have a seat," he nodded toward a large, over-stuffed leather chair. As I walked over, the ink marks and dirty stains I saw made me cringe. I wondered how many criminals had sat there.

Three other people were sitting in the room. "Let me introduce you." The State Attorney, Leonard Elliott, was on my immediate right. I was familiar with his name from the press. A short man, compared to the others, he held out his hand and briskly shook mine.

Detective Mark Gibson was introduced to me next. He was Al's immediate supervisor, a striking black man whose age was hard for me to guess. Again, the actual image of these real law enforcement agents confounded me. There was nothing that signalled them out. They tended to blend into society. Later, I would learn that was one of the ideas.

Finally, I met Sister Theresa, the Mother Superior of the Religious Order at Trinity. I had seen the Sister, but never officially met her. She was present at our graduation like many other social functions. But she was aloof and apart from us. Sister Theresa was a Registered Nurse. She had earned all of the nursing degrees, including a very rare Doctorate in the Science of Nursing. She spoke softly. "It is a pleasure to meet you, Miss Strom. I want to personally thank you for offering to help us."

If I had any doubts up to that point, seeing Mother Superior there erased them. I felt honored. Perhaps it was my Catholic upbringing. "Thank you, Sister," was my response to nearly everything she said.

We talked for three hours. Then we went to lunch. In the afternoon, I was introduced to wire taps and tape recorders, and taught how to look for clues. The vial I had left with John had been evaluated by the laboratory. Carol's fingerprints were on it along with three others. The contents were demerol. No surprise there. Next time I was told to confiscate the syringe and needles.

Since I was not trained for law enforcement, I was given quick instructions on how to defend myself. Basic maneuvers to avoid holds, unless a weapon was being used. I was grateful I would not be given a weapon. Guns made me nervous.

By the end of the day I was becoming adjusted to my new routine. No major changes. I would just listen and observe everything carefully and I would record everything in a small log book I was to leave at home. I was allowed to jot notes to myself, but not to carry the book. Most importantly, I was not to act as if anything was different. If Paul approached me again to go on another trip I was to agree. Only this time, we would be followed.

I drove quickly home. It was already dark. I parked nearby. Thoughts of the meeting flashed ominously through my mind as I got out of the car. "I have to relax," I mumbled to myself. Half running across the street, I raced into my building and collided with a husky, brown-haired man carrying a bunch of brown paper packages. He helped me up. I cradled my right arm. It must have been struck by one of the sharp-edged packages.

"You all right?" he said in a muffled tone, hurriedly walking away. I didn't even have time to say "Excuse me" before he was out the front door.

Sitting in my bathtub later that evening, I let the tension of the day and preceding days drain out of my body. Pictures of Carol injecting demerol flashed before my eyes. I recalled my excitement at Paul's gift in Miami. I remembered the Christmas party: Paul inhaling cocaine; Marilyn and Terry high on drugs; Carol telling me to take 'ludes in order to work the next day. I thought about nameless patients with faces still showing pain because they have been given sterile water. I remembered Dr. Vorhees's behavior and Lois's drinking problem which often interfered with our nursing care.

I thought about the nights with Paul. My feelings for him and addiction to him. I thought of how much I was beginning to love him. Then, I began to cry, at first for my loss and then in self pity. I cried until my eyes were red and puffy and my nose so plugged that I couldn't breathe.

I sat in the tub for a long time thinking about my life and vowing to make some major changes, including my relationship with Paul.

It was medical treason. But the realization that a disease affected Carol, Lois, Marilyn, Dr. Vorhees and even Paul was also obvious to me. Nursing was filled with stresses— low pay, shortages in staffing and over-worked hours were significant problems. But drugs and alcohol would not solve them. Creating havoc among ourselves would not solve them either. Perhaps the personality of each of us contributed. Nature seemed to have designated us caretakers and rescuers. But who takes care of and rescues us, if not ourselves? The question echoed in my mind as I got ready for bed and fell into a troubled sleep.

Somewhere, off in the far distance, a loud bell was ringing. Wandering through a dark, narrow hallway, I reached for the sound. It was out of reach and kept moving away from my drifting body. It seemed to be floating. The ringing bell stopped. A voice slowly drifted into my eardrums, but I couldn't understand it. There was a shadow of a man. I couldn't distinguish his features. His mouth seemed to be moving rapidly, but no sounds came out. The feeling was euphoric. I never wanted to wake up.

The man leaned over me. His open mouth seemed to be screaming at me. A syringe loomed in the air filled with a clear fluid. I saw the needle as it approached my arm, noticing the exaggerated length and width of the instrument. I never felt my skin pierced or the injection of the fluid.

The man stood there. Then a second man appeared. The men talked in low whispers. I couldn't hear them.

My fitful, dream-filled sleep was suddenly broken: my

abdomen wretched violently. Nausea and vomiting took over, and I began to awaken. The two men lifted me from the bed, and dragged me to the bathroom. I leaned over the toilet clinging to their arms. Then water pulsated on my back and brought me fully awake. My head throbbed. My whole body ached. My stomach felt queasy. Finally, I was able to recognize the male visitors.

Al Thurston spoke first. "Thank God you are all right, Joyce. How do you feel now?"

"Better," I said in a shaky voice I hardly recognized as my own.

The second voice spoke. "She'll be okay now, I think. I still feel that she should go to the hospital though," it said.

Al shook his head. "Sorry, doctor. You have to take care of her here. The hospital is not any safer. In fact, we think it is more dangerous for her right now."

Their words seemed mumbled to me. I felt groggy, unsure where I was or what had happened. Finally I asked Al, "What happened?"

"You gave us quite a scare, young lady," Al replied. "When you didn't show up for your appointment today I got worried. You didn't answer the phone and we couldn't hear you on your microphone. You probably would have died if we had not found you."

"Died?" I asked in a panic.

"That's right," interjected the doctor's voice. "You had enough cocaine in you to kill you."

"Cocaine?" I mumbled again trying to remember where I had been and how I would have cocaine in me. "I don't do drugs," I protested.

"Yes, we know." Al shifted his body. His mouth worked nervously. I fought to stay awake and make out what he was saying. "This is Dr. Bill Monroe." I nodded sleepily. "He is the police department's personal physician and he is the one you should credit with saving your life."

"Thank you," I stated meekly.

"It's okay, Joyce." He laughed, a hollow sound that reverberated in my ears. "Now, let's get some clear fluids into you. Can you sip some water?"

I nodded again. The doctor held a glass to my lips. My lips were dry, cracked. I sipped the metallic-tasting water. 'How did I get cocaine into me?" I asked, my anxiety rising.

"Slow down," Bill called to me. "One question at a time, Joyce. First, I called in sick for you today. I telephoned Sister Theresa directly and told her what happened. Secondly, all we know is that you were injected with cocaine. We're hoping you can remember something." He looked at my vacant facial expression. "Can you tell us anything at all?" he asked.

My head throbbed. "No, nothing," I said huskily. "Except for the man I collided with when I got home last night."

Al was excited. "What man?"

"I don't know. Really. He was carrying a bunch of packages and I was in a hurry to get inside my apartment. Could he have slipped me something?"

Al mused, "Maybe narcan or another street drug."

I nodded. I had seen narcan ordered for heroin addiction overdoses in the unit. It made people feel very ill. "This is worse than the flu," I said, feeling nauseous.

The doctor agreed. Al continued his questioning. "Now, tell me everything you remember about that man."

"Not much, I am afraid. It was dark. He was there when I came home. Dark-haired, chunky looking, but I don't remember much else. God, my mouth is dry. Can I have another sip of water?" I asked.

"Of course," the doctor replied, lifting the glass to my mouth.

"I thought you guys were going to keep an eye on me?" I suddenly asked Al angrily.

"Well, we have been," he apologized, adding, "I will find out who was on duty last night. I can promise you that."

"Do you feel like trying to stand and walk?" the doctor asked. "We should get you moving around while we hydrate you."

I nodded. "I'll try."

The two men lifted me to my feet. I felt my knees buckle. My head was swimming. Nausea rose. "Maybe we can get some soda from the kitchen," I said hoarsely. I seemed to have pins and needles in my feet, especially my right one, as I worked my way to the refrigerator. I thought if I could find some of Karen's Coke to drink it might help the nausea while hydrating me. In the hospital we always used warm coke syrup to help nausea and vomiting.

I opened the door and let out an ear-piercing shriek. The men pushed me aside and peered inside the refrigerator.

Al turned ashen. A huge, dead rat had been strategically placed on one of our poultry platters. The head, severed, was sitting alongside the body. Bill took the carcass to the trash room down the hall. Later, he told me he had wrapped it in a plastic bag and sent it to the police lab for testing in the hopes of finding any signs of evidence.

Al called his supervisor, Mark Gibson. I collapsed in a chair and cried hysterically. The rat was a message, along with the cocaine in my body. I was deathly frightened.

When Mark arrived he tried to comfort me. "Sorry this got so rough. We never expected anything like this to happen so soon."

"So soon," I repeated brokenly. Images of Bob Morgan's death flashed before me. "Tell me more about Bob Morgan," I said harshly. "I feel like I am walking in his footsteps."

Mark began talking. "Bob Morgan was not only an undercover RN working as a narcotics informant in your unit, he was also an undercover agent in Viet Nam." Slowly I learned that Bob was aware of some of the major drug pilferers in Trinity and he thought he had a lead on their outside source for disposing of the drugs. "He telephoned us from a pay phone the morning you found him in the parking lot." Mark paused for a moment. "Joyce, did Bob tell you anything at all before he died?"

I shook my head. "No. He was unconscious when I found him."

"My guess," Mark continued, "is that whoever killed him knows you found him and is afraid he may have said something to you. This was a warning, meant to scare you."

"It did a great job!" I exclaimed. "Do you think the man I saw standing outside last night might be the one?"

"We can't be sure," Al said slowly, "but my theory is he was waiting for you when you got home. He may have given you something on the street when he brushed against you. Then after you were asleep he came in here and finished the job."

Al nodded.

"Where's Karen?" I asked, suddenly frightened.

Al answered. "Karen is working the day shift. We have already checked with Trinity. Sister Theresa said she is on duty and she is fine. You both have separate rooms, don't you?"

"Yes. We also each have windows in our rooms. Mine overlooks the alley. Karen's is on the street."

They began to look around carefully. The doorbell rang. I jumped. Dr. Monroe slowly packed his bag. I watched his hands, shaking. A team of officers entered. One of them was there to specially "dust" our apartment. "Stay where you are," he called to me.

Several minutes later, Al and Mark came back into the living room. "He got in here, all right," Al announced. "Through an open window."

"I like some fresh air when I sleep," I said lamely.

"Well, that is how our man got in," Mark said.

"Why didn't I hear him?" I asked. "I would have heard him."

"He probably gave you narcan in the street and then he used this." Al held up a clean white linen handkerchief.

The kind my father used to carry. "We found this under your bed. It has ether on it."

"Ether? We haven't used ether in ages."

"It still works," Mark contributed, "and we see it often. Apparently, you were woozy when he crept in, then our assailant covered your face with this handkerchief. You were unconscious before you knew what happened."

The doctor, who was about to leave, was scrutinizing me. "Do you hurt any place in particular?" he asked me.

I shook my head, "no," but as I thought about it, though all of my muscles ached, my arm ached particularly and one of my feet had felt tender when I walked on it to the kitchen.

"Let me stand up," I said. Putting full weight bearing on my right foot the ball of my foot was tender. "Ouch." I jumped back and sat down.

"Does it hurt here?" The doctor bent down and looked at my foot. He poked the spot with his finger.

"*Yes.*"

"Well, that's how he made his final impact," Dr. Monroe said. "He injected her in the ball of the foot."

The case was taking a new twist. Al and Mark discussed the possibility that my intruder probably had intended to scare me off, because if he wanted me dead he had the perfect opportunity.

Mark interjected, "Maybe he just wanted her addicted."

"That might be his idea," Al said soberly, "and if it is he'll be back. One dose wouldn't do it."

I considered their idea for a moment. If he did want me addicted, what would he do next? I ached with a sense of foreboding. After all, it made sense to me that they would want to keep me in the inner circle and make me drug-dependent if they could.

"It makes sense to me," Al said, "but I hope you don't consider pretending that you are."

"No, of course not," I laughed. It was my first laugh

of the day. It seemed to take tension off all of us. Then I reconsidered. "I could pretend I do drugs."

"That might involve you in another scene like tonight, or you may have to pretend around other people, which means you might have to show you're a user. They'd want to make sure," Mark replied. "And I don't like either idea. Drugs are addicting, especially cocaine."

"This whole idea is dangerous," I replied slowly, "but I am in this knee deep now."

"Well, I think you had better move out of this apartment," Al suddenly announced.

"Why?" I asked gloomily. "If I leave they'll know something is up. No," I shook my head, "I have to stay here." Reluctantly they agreed. "But I think Karen should leave. I don't want her in any danger. She doesn't know about any of this."

Al and Mark shook their heads. "We'll call John Bivens and tell him what happened. He can handle Karen."

Dr. Monroe gave a further piece of advice. "I don't think you should work for the next three days," he said, watching me intently. "Take the time off and allow the drugs to get out of your system. Your liver is going to be working overtime. Here, take my card," he offered, "it has my home number on it too. Call me if you need me."

"Thank you, Dr. Monroe," I mumbled, taking the police card with his name, title, and phone numbers. "I will be fine."

He agreed. "Yes, with some rest." He smiled at me again. "You are in good physical shape. By the way," he inquired, "do you work out or something?"

I laughed again. "Aerobics, and weight lifting in between."

"Well, you'd better rest for the next week," he admonished, and began packing his instruments. "Take care," he said seriously. He left with the other officers following him.

Mark and Al talked to each other, finally deciding that I should spend the next three days at Al's apartment for my own safety. Later, I would learn that Karen was staying with John. He didn't tell her where I was, "just away." Busy with wedding plans, she accepted his words at face value.

Al's spacious apartment lay nestled on the north side of the city among a series of brownstones. The place had belonged to him for over twenty years.

Between Al and Mark, they had cleared my time off with Sister Theresa. I tried to relax. At least this call-in was legitimate. I didn't have to feel guilty.

My sleep was sound and peaceful. Awaking as the noon sunlight streamed through the window, I felt more refreshed than the day before, although I still felt hung over, probably because I had taken sleeping pills. I could hear Al moving around in his small kitchen. The aromatic smell of bacon and coffee brought me to my senses.

Standing in front of the door mirror, I removed my nightgown and put on a tee shirt and jeans. In my own home I would walk around half naked, but not in the home of a man I barely knew. I looked at myself. The exercise was paying off. I liked my firm, rounded breasts and my stomach, flat from hundreds of sit-ups. Even my cheeks looked rosy pink again. Only my hair was dull and lifeless.

"I need a trim again," I thought to myself. "When was my last one?" Then I remembered—the night of my first date with Paul. I grimaced. "Where are you now, Paul?" I questioned mentally. "And what are you involved in?" Taking a deep breath, I realized I still loved Paul. I wasn't sure I still liked him, however.

Some pictures on the dresser caught my eye. A double frame with the eyes of two beaming school children. The boy looked like Al. He was probably ten years old. The little girl was younger, maybe eight. I wondered if she resembled her mother.

. Suddenly my musings were disturbed. "Well, good morning, sleepy head. I hope you feel better now. You certainly did sleep. I didn't disturb you, did I?"

I liked his kindness. The gentle smile. His brown eyes looked concerned and chagrined.

I shook my head. "You didn't disturb me. I hope I didn't oversleep." I paused to look at the sizzling bacon. "That sure smells good."

"I hope you like bacon and eggs," he said, adding, "and fresh orange juice, bagels, lox, and coffee."

I laughed, thinking of Karen. "I'll skip the lox, but I love those nitrates and cholesterol!"

We both chuckled. "Are those pictures of your children in my room?" I asked.

"Yup . . . Al, Junior, is eleven. Tracey is seven. They live with their mother just a few blocks from here."

"It must be hard for you," I said, spreading cream cheese on a bagel.

"Sometimes, but having a cop for a husband is not an easy life for some wives. Cathy and I love each other. She just can't live with the fear that I might get killed out there. We parted as friends, and we share the custody of our children."

I looked up, seeing him as a person for the first time. "It must be tough to be separated from your kids."

He nodded. "Yeah, but the kids and I enjoy our quality time. Unfortunately, they worry, too, about something happening to me."

"Your work is dangerous," I mused between bites.

He nodded and sat down across from me, giving me my breakfast plate. "And, you are in danger now, too. But you handle it real well. Maybe when all of this is over you will join the force."

I grimaced, shaking my head. "No, I don't think so. I love nursing. When all of this is over I just want to go on with my life and my career."

Al cautioned me. "You won't be able to in this town, you know."

I did know, too. "I have been thinking about that. I don't have a future with Paul and," I took a deep breath, "I am not even sure I want to stay in critical care."

"What do you want to do?" His voice softened.

"Well," I considered, "my highest grade on State Boards was in psychiatry. I am beginning to think that maybe I should change my field and go into that area."

"There are problems there, too," he said, scrutinizing me.

I looked him fully in the face and sighed. "I know, but I think I would like to try it. Maybe I'll go back to school and get a Master's degree."

The discussion was getting very heavy. I changed the subject. "Breakfast is delicious. Could I make dinner?"

Al readily agreed. "We can shop for what you need."

I smiled in reply. "Fine. I make great Swedish meatballs."

"Sounds wonderful," he chuckled.

We headed off for the local supermarket, shopping list in hand, after I had surveyed his kitchen to see what ingredients he had on hand. I felt safe and secure with Al. I forgot about the danger I was in or the possibility that I was being tailed. I relaxed and felt comfortable.

The three days flew by fast. I felt better and stronger daily. Dr. Monroe visited me two more times, just to check on my health. "You're doing fine," he commended on the last visit. "I guess you can go back to work."

"Great," I said, caught up in the bubble again. "I am ready. Can I go home?"

"Sure," Al answered. He knew I needed to be home. I wanted to be alone again among my personal possessions. "Your windows are now bugged and you have an alarm system in your apartment, compliments of the local police." He laughed.

I looked at the doctor. "When can I leave?"

"Now. Call me if you need me."

Al teased me. "Bored with my hospitality already."

I teased him back. Just as he was preparing to help me load my car with my clothes, the telephone rang.

"Hi, Mark. Yeah. She is still here, but just leaving." Pause. "You did?" Another pause.

I waited, wondering about the conversation.

"Okay. I'll tell her," he said soberly. "Thanks."

"So what did Mark want to tell you?" I asked, watching his face intently.

"They found fingerprints on the serving plate on which we found the rat. They belong to a man by the name of Harry Cappuzzio, a local strong-arm hit man."

"The Mafia?"

He nodded. "Perhaps."

"Do you really think the Mafia could be involved in this?" I was getting nervous again. My stomach began churning. I wondered if I really should go home.

His eyes met mine. "It wouldn't surprise us, Joyce. There is big money in drugs. All kinds, as you know. Street drugs have to be smuggled in from other countries and across borders. A lot get through, but some don't. Prescription drugs are already here. Some are made in basements and garages, while others are stolen and sold on the street."

"Al, I'm beginning to get scared again." I felt pretty dumb, but I wanted to tell him how I felt.

He considered for a moment and then went on. "Do you still want to go through with it?"

I shook my head. "I have no choice. If this Harry Cappuzzio could harm me once, he will try again. I want him caught." I was getting angry.

Al said morosely, "Okay. We have bugged your apartment. Your car, too. Wear the microphone on you. Our officers will surround you at all times and keep you under surveillance."

I breathed in heavily. "LIke the night Harry broke into my window?"

He drew back, looking upset. "We know what happened. Our officer on duty was knocked out by Harry. Probably that same ether you got. When he came to he called us immediately." He wiped the beads of sweat forming on his forehead. "Of course we knew immediately you might be in trouble, especially when you didn't telephone us about meeting with us."

I watched him closely. "What's to stop that from happening again?" I no longer had doubts they had screwed up.

He chose his words carefully. "The officers will work in teams. And, in squad cars. Unmarked, of course. This time we won't lose you."

Al and I drove back to my apartment. I noticed a dark car up the street and felt panic. "Al, I see a husky man in a dark car over there." I took one hand off the wheel to show him where. "Should I just drive by?"

He leaned forward to scrutinize the strange car. "It's okay, Joyce. It's one of ours."

Suddenly a man's voice penetrated our car over the radio. "This is Officer Branden. My partner is Detective Barnes." He continued, "The apartment is empty and safe."

I stared at Al, feeling upset, my voice quavering. "What about my privacy?"

"What about your life?" Al said calmly and rationally.

"They have keys too?" I asked as Al walked me into my building.

"Yes," he nodded. "And, before I forget, here is your alarm key. Karen already has hers."

My mood of depression persisted. "Speaking of Karen, isn't she asking what is going on?"

He made his tone official and businesslike. "John told her that someone broke into the apartment while you were asleep. He also told her you took three days off to go away, because you were frightened. Karen thinks John put the alarm system in. To protect her."

"Okay," I said, knowing I sounded sulky and defiant. "I guess the alarm key turns the internal system off." Al nodded and showed me how to work the unit night and day.

We walked to my front door. I turned the key. Once inside I surveyed my apartment. It felt good to be home.

The light on my answering machine was blinking. I walked over and turned on the message tape. My mother had called. Some of my friends. Several calls were for Karen. Paul had not called. Somehow, I felt disappointed.

Al left me alone. At first I felt uneasy until I realized that I was not alone. Police officers were listening to my every move. I called the hospital to see when I was working. Marilyn had transferred me to the day shift for the first two weeks of the month. For a moment I wondered why. Then I decided. She wanted to keep an eye on me and see how I felt. I hoped I could convey the message that I was using drugs. I also hoped I would be believed.

TEN

The morning shift was slow. I had a patient who broke my heart. Janice Dexter was only twenty-six years old. She had just given birth to her second child, a boy, only three months earlier. Her other child, a little girl, was only two. Janice's husband, Herb, who visited her all the time, was a kind man. Tall, thin, soft-spoken, he worked as a high school math teacher. He was very religious and devoted to the Catholic church. He was also devoted to his wife.

According to the nurses' notes, she and her husband were moving the living room furniture when she began to complain of a headache. She then began to vomit excessively. Mr. Dexter thought she had eaten something that disagreed with her, but when her vomiting stopped he found she was not fully conscious. In a panic, he telephoned the paramedics.

The medics found her unconscious and unresponsive to all but deep substernal stimuli. Racing her to the emergency room of Trinity, she became lifeless and was immediately intubated. Her pupils were fixed and fully blown. Watching her, we all knew she was neurologically brain-dead.

Mr. Dexter sat in the waiting room with swollen, red

eyes. I noticed him whenever I walked by. He kept peering into the unit. And he was asking all the nurses, "How is my wife doing?"

Mrs. Dexter had a ruptured aneurysm. A small balloon-like bulge in one of her cerebral arteries had expanded and then exploded inside her head. There was no warning other than the severe headache she felt, and the vomiting.

Aneurysms can occur anywhere at any time and at any age, but cerebral aneurysms seem to be more common among young women. They also tend to run in families. Because she was so young we were all depressed.

Janice Dexter's two sisters visited her frequently. Sara, the older, was thirty-four. Sharon, the younger, was twenty-two. Each woman asked about their own prognosis and that of their children. We just didn't have the answers.

The microphone taped to my chest made me feel both secure and uncomfortable. Sometimes, I forgot about it as I went on about my work, and, at others, I was acutely aware I wore it. Sally was working days with me along with Tina, Marilyn, and a new nurse I didn't know, Annette.

Sally called me over. "Could you check these two patients with me," she asked in a worried tone.

Sally's two patients were dialysis patients. One had an arterial shunt placed in the artery so that an exchange of blood through the dialysis machine could be done. I checked the shunt in his left wrist. It was important for the shunt to function correctly so that hemodialysis, the removal of the body's wastes and toxins, could be accomplished. His kidneys weren't functioning. He was being transferred to the dialysis unit at 10:00 a.m. for detoxification, so that his body could be cleansed of wastes and poisons. He had this procedure every other day. Her second patient had endocarditis. We were both worried about him. He had an inflamation around the pericardium sac, the membrane lining on the outside of the heart. His electrolytes, which indicated the body's normal chemical balance, were way off. Sally and I both watched him intently—because he was exhibiting ICU psychoses (the mental confusion exhibited by a patient who has not had enough sleep or whose electrolytes are too high or too low in the blood system) and becoming very violent.

I tried to reassure her that we were doing all we could and then walked over to my second patient. He was an elderly man with a pulmonary wedge line, a line into the pulmonary artery connecting the heart and lungs, that I had to read every thirty minutes. Only a few days before, exploratory surgery had indicated that he had rapidly spreading cancer. The surgeons decided not to remove any of the malignant tissue. He was also not a good candidate for chemotherapy. At least, not until he gained some strength. We were taking life-saving measures in order to prevent cardiac complications.

I continued my morning care. Once in a while I looked over at Sally, only to find she was still having a difficult time with her two patients. Finally, her first patient left for his treatment. The endocarditis patient, Mr. Johnson, was in four-point restraint to protect himself, keep his IV lines in, and to protect the staff. Still, he thrashed about trying to fee himself or accost the staff members, whom he blamed for imprisoning him.

Sally still had not spoken to me about the incident with the overdose of potassium chloride. My work was complete, as were my vitals. I again offered to give her a hand.

"Thanks, Strom. I can use it. This one has me rattled."

I prepared the washbasin, filling it with warm water, and brought two sets of towels and washcloths for us. "I'll begin on his left side, you do the right," I said wearily. She nodded her approval.

I left Mr. Johnson's hand tied, feeling I didn't need to remove it until she was ready. "We have to untie his hands one at a time to remove his patient gown and replace it with a fresh one," Sally sighed. "Okay, I'm ready." She carefully untied his right hand and leaned over the side rail.

His hand lashed out and smashed across the left side of her face. It flung her body halfway across the room. Sally landed on the floor, hitting her head against a chair. She was stunned and seemed to be unconscious momentarily. I reached over and grabbed Mr. Johnson's hand, restraining it again. Then I rushed to Sally's side. Annette and Marilyn followed.

Sally held her face. Annette put an ice pack on it, but I could see the swelling and beginning of a bruise around her left eye and cheek bone. She began to sob hysterically, rocking back and forth on the floor.

Annette spoke soothingly, "Let us help you," and knelt beside her. Sally pushed her away, curling up in a fetal ball.

One of the male respiratory therapists came over and picked her up. He carried her to a stretcher. Marilyn, Annette and I ran over. "Put the side rails into place," he said firmly. Sally continued to rock and cry.

"Better telephone nursing service and call for an attending physician," he ordered Marilyn. She obeyed. Paul came running through the door, his beeper still calling him to report to ICU for an emergency.

I told him quickly what happened. He began checking Sally's face and trying to reassure her. "Let's do a skull series. That ought to detect any abnormalities," he ordered, "and start an IV with Ringer's lactate."

Marilyn brought the IV needle tray over and immediately stuck Sally on the first try. Blood from Sally's left hand vein filled the syringe.

A hospital transporter arrived to push the stretcher out the doorway and down towards X ray. Sally was still sobbing and rocking.

Annette and I agreed to each take one of her patients. I got Mr. Johnson. I decided that his clean gown and clean sheets could wait until his electrolytes were in better balance. He was scheduled to begin peritoneal dialysis at noon.

The day was busy. I assisted the surgeon as he placed the IV tubing in Mr. Johnson's abdomen, hanging a 2000 cc bottle of saline and allowing it to flow into Mr. Johnson's abdomen for fifteen minutes. Then we clamped the tubing for forty-five minutes, waiting for osmosis so that the exchange of salt water for circulatory contaminates which would normally be excreted through the kidneys could occur. The last fifteen minutes the fluid drained out.

Peritoneal dialysis lasts twenty-four hours. We tried to make Mr. Johnson comfortable while the procedure took place. Janice Dexter was unresponsive. Each time her family and husband came back to the bedside, they cried. I was teary-eyed myself.

Paul came back into the unit at 2:30 p.m. to check on his patients and give us a report on Sally. "She has a hair line fracture in her left jaw bone. We transferred her to the psychiatric unit for both medical and psychiatric treatment," Paul said somberly. "She keeps talking about some patient she had killed." Paul thought she was hallucinating. No one told him differently.

Walking back to my patients, I watched him talking to Annette and Marilyn. Finally, he sauntered over to Mrs. Dexter's bed. I went with him. "Sorry we keep missing each other," he said. "I heard you were out sick."

"Just the flu. Nothing serious," I added. "I think I partied a little too much."

"Can you make it over around 6:00?"

"Sure. Can I bring anything?"

Paul reached around and pinched my rear end. "Just bring this," he joked. I felt the pulsing race through me.

As he walked away I whispered, 'Did you hear that?" Then, I laughed.

Leaving the unit I nearly wiped out a young woman I had never seen before. "Excuse me," I offered after grabbing the door before it hit her in the head. One accident for the day was enough.

"Oh, thank you," she said.

"Are you new here?" I asked, noticing her name tag.

"Yes. Dr. Heather Lear. Third year resident. This is my first day at Trinity. I just came over from General."

"Welcome," I said.

I noticed how young and pretty she looked. She was approximately 5'4" with short, blonde hair. Unlike many blondes, her hair looked natural. And, I noticed, she was pregnant.

"You look so young," I commented, introducing myself to her.

"Twenty-five," she replied. Patting her abdomen, she told me this was her first. I was right about the gestation. "Six months," she answered.

There was something about her I instantly liked. Female physicians have the same difficulties that male nurses do. I wanted to be her friend and I told her so.

"I would love that," she exclaimed. "I really don't have any friends. It is tough on my husband, too."

"Is he a doctor also?" I inquired.

"No. He sells computers, but he's wonderful anyway," she insisted.

I laughed at my own bias in favor of attractive doctors. Nurses and doctors think medicine is the only career.

"Well, I had better let you go. Here is my phone number." I pressed it in her hand.

She took the piece of paper and thanked me. "I spend so much time in the hospital. Coffee—or lunch—will be fun," she said.

"Fine. Maybe Friday or Monday. I'm on days."

"Me too."

"Let's meet at noon Friday in the cafeteria." I looked forward to getting to know her better.

"**W**hy don't you go to medical school?" Heather Lear asked me over lunch Friday.

I laughed. "I just barely made it through nursing school." What I didn't tell Heather was that I really had never considered medical school. My family couldn't afford the tuition, and since my mother was a nurse there had never been any pressure for me to achieve beyond her degree.

Heather twirled the cafeteria spaghetti on her fork. No matter what we did to it the food was just barely edible. "You could be anything you wanted, Joyce," she stated encouragingly.

"Why did you decide to become a doctor?" I inquired.

"Because no one in my family ever obtained any education beyond high school. I thought about becoming a nurse when I was younger, but when I discovered that doctors really had the power I knew that was for me."

I was curious to know more about her thinking and her motivation. "How do you endure the years of study and long hours on call?"

"You just get used to it," she said.

"I could never get used to it," I announced. "I am probably the only girl at a high school pajama party who fell asleep."

Heather laughed. "You're kidding."

I shook my head "no" in embarrassment. "It gets worse," I confided. "I would tell my dates to bring me home by 11:00 p.m. just so I could go to bed."

Heather laughed uproariously. "I presume you mean to sleep."

My face turned beet red. "I am afraid so," I answered meekly. Momentarily my mind left our conversation. I closed my eyes and saw Paul and me in Miami. As I daydreamed about him, I lifted my hand to my face and was surprised to feel it hot and fevered.

Heather was silent as she apparently sat observing me. When I finally looked back at her she asked, "So where were you?"

"Don't ask," I chuckled.

"Joyce, I know what love and passion are and I see them all over your face."

I was beginning to fidget. "Does it show that much?"

"Uh huh. I felt that way when I met my husband, Dan."

This was a perfect opportunity to change the subject. "Tell me about Dan."

It worked. "Dan is sweet. A computer salesman, as I told you. We met last summer when I was on my rotation at Memorial."

"How did you meet?" I asked, becoming genuinely interested.

Heather laughed again. "He was a patient of mine. He had pneumonia. I cured him and we began to date."

"Doctor," I exclaimed in a joking fashion, "that is grounds for a malpractice suit."

"Only if you don't marry them," she replied with a twinkle in her eye.

I could see that she really loved her husband. She spoke of him with admiration and pride. "Does it bother him that you are a doctor?" I inquired. I knew some men have difficulty in accepting the professional status of their wives, other men feel competitive.

"No, he is very proud. He tells everyone that I will eventually support him in the style to which he is unaccustomed."

We both broke into deep laughter. I liked Heather and didn't think of her as being in a different class than I was. The old doctor-nurse gap line did not seem to affect our communication or friendship.

Reluctantly we left the cafeteria. Our assigned thirty-minute lunch break was over, but we agreed to meet again the next week for lunch.

"I don't have many friends, Joyce," Heather said as we walked towards the elevator.

"Why not?" I asked, genuinely surprised.

"I am a threat to both sexes. The nurses look at me like a doctor and treat me differently, while the doctors look at me as a woman and send the message that I should be a nurse. I am not welcomed in any area."

I felt empathy for what she must be going through. I realized for the first time what problems a woman doctor faced from her perspective instead of mine. Heather and I spoke by phone a few days later and had lunch the next week. We even began to share some of our intimate secrets and fears. I told her more about Paul and our Miami experience.

"Scarves?" she asked, this time blushing herself.

"Do you believe it?" I half questioned. "I still don't believe it, but it was fantastic."

"Joyce, you are not the prude I thought you were."

"Well, would you ever try it?" I asked, not wanting to feel like I was some kind of sexual deviate.

"If I do, I promise I will tell you."

We both laughed together like two school girls."

Leaving the hospital that afternoon, I breathed the cool, brisk air and heaved a sigh of relief. I was no longer living in fear of my life. Nothing had happened all week. No one approached me. Although I kept the alarm on at all times, I felt safe and secure in my apartment, and I felt excited about seeing Paul that evening despite my trepidation about him.

Al and I had discussed my tape recording device. He instructed me to keep it in my purse with my purse open and in close proximity to Paul and me at all times. I gave him Paul's address. He assured me that the apartment was staked out, too.

Karen had decided to have her bridesmaids wear light pink and mauve. We went shopping, and found a dress for me. John and his party were wearing gray, pin-striped tuxedos with mauve cummerbunds. She wanted to carry mauve and pink roses. I had never heard of "lavender" roses, as she called them. But, seeing them in the florist shop I had to agree they were beautiful. Our bouquets would contain pink carnations with some pink roses. The streamers were mauve.

Karen and I were both excited as we entered the salon of a large department store where she had her wedding gown on lay-away. "Isn't it beautiful," she swooned, floating out of the dressing room.

The white gown was covered with beautiful hand-sewn-on beads. Clusters of tiny pearls covered the top of the gown in the shape of a V down to the waist. The layers of chiffon were filled with delicate lace and pearls sprinkled down the front and across the bottom of the gown.

A long train fell from the back of the dress. "My flower girls are going to carry my train," she gleefully announced, pirouetting in front of the mirrors.

Her veil had seed pearls sewn in a circle covered with two layers of netting. The first flowed to the bottom of her train. The second, shoulder length, was to be put over her face as she walked down the aisle. She would be married at St. Mary's Church, a lovely, old Roman Catholic church in the heart of the city. As I watched her in the mirror, I fantasized that it was Paul and I who would walk down the aisle, I who was wearing the glistening two-carat diamond which soon would be joined by a diamond-studded wedding band.

The wedding was only one month away. My gown had to be altered. I needed the waist taken in and lowered. Karen's other bridesmaids, friends of hers from high school, had already tried their gowns on the week before. We were each paying for our dresses. I told the saleslady I would try mine on and pick it up the following week. I got paid then, which made it easier.

"So, what are you doing tonight?" Karen asked as we got into the car to drive home, still talking about the wedding and her future.

"I'm seeing Paul," I said excitedly.

Her eyes met mine. "Is anything coming of that? You and Paul, I mean."

I looked away. "I don't think so," I replied. "I think we just enjoy each other's company when we can get together."

Karen nodded slowly. "Have you decided who will be your roommate when I move out?" she asked.

I hadn't thought about it. Our lease was not up until May 31st. "No. Maybe I will just spend the six weeks alone and then think about moving," I told her.

"It's not fair of me to leave you like this, Joyce. John and I both decided that I will still pay my share of the rent for April and May."

"That's very kind of you, Karen. Thank you."

"I'll miss you, my friend," she said tearfully. "I'm happy about getting married, but I will miss you."

I felt tearful too. "I know. I will miss you, too. We have been through a lot together. Nursing school. State Boards. Our first apartment."

"I am not leaving, Joyce. I'll still be at Trinity."

"I know. Until you get pregnant, anyhow."

Karen nodded. She and John did want a family and talked about it. "After John passes the bar, we will decide where he'll go and when to have a family. I do look forward to the day when I can retire from nursing for a while."

"That is one of the benefits of nursing," I stated. "We can work when we want, as often as we want, and always have a career."

I dropped Karen at the apartment. My overnight bag was in the car. Nervously, and excitedly, I drove off for Paul's apartment. I spoke into the microphone in my car. "Guys, I'm about to embarrass us both."

Paul looked radiant and wonderful. This time I brought the bottle of wine, a dry Cabernet Sauvignon.

Paul pulled me into his apartment. Kissing him, I felt comfortable and at home. Looking around the room where we had first made love brought back flashes of memory.

Paul was a super cook. He grilled a rare filet mignon with Bernaise sauce, and fixed a Caesar's salad and baked

potatoes. Fresh strawberries and cream completed the
dinner. We sat back in his dining room, sipping our wine
and allowing the candles to melt. Talking with Paul was
so easy. I really forgot about the microphone and my role
as an undercover agent.

I rambled on about Karen's wedding. Paul sat quietly
listening.

He reached his hand across the table. "I want to make
love to you," he stated, brushing my babbling aside.

I blushed, then I nodded. Out of embarrassment, and
desire.

Paul moved away from the table and walked over to
me. Pulling my chair out he took my hand and pulled me
to my feet. I felt nervous and unsteady as he guided me
down the hall to the large bedroom.

"Excuse me for a moment," he said, smiling. "Nature
calls." He moved away toward the bathroom. I looked
around for a place to stash the microphone. Not seeing
anything convenient, I pulled it out and pushed it under
the bed.

We sat close together on the side of the bed. I felt the
thick, velvety comforter beneath my body. The bed felt
soft. Smooth. Memories flashed through my mind of the
last time we made love in this room. I trembled in excitement.

Slowly, sensuously, he lingered on each button until
my blouse fell away. He unzipped my skirt and let it fall
to the floor. Tenderly, he kissed me and then looked at me
as he removed my bra and panties. I felt exposed. Vulnerable. Aroused. I lusted for him to be as naked as I.

Paul unzipped his own pants, letting them fall somewhere near my clothes. He seemed to fly out of his remaining clothes. Socks. Underwear. Our bodies entwined clinging to each other. His soft, warm, smooth skin felt
wonderful on top of me. We made love in a passionate
fury—all too fast. Then, he fell on his side and held me in
his arms.

As good as I felt, I was also disappointed. I think Paul

sensed it. He had been too eager. We had not spent enough time on the foreplay. I was still aroused and barely unable to contain myself.

"I didn't satisfy you in my own greed, did I?" he quietly asked, much to my surprise.

As embarrassed as I was, I couldn't lie to him. "No. It was too fast for me, Paul. I need time."

"I know. I was just too greedy, but I'll make it up to you."

I lay on the bed quietly allowing my body to ebb back to normal. I told my body to relax, promising it that we would still seek the needed relief and pleasure I so longed for.

Paul moved over to his nightstand. He opened the drawer and removed a small, dark brown glass bottle. The bottle looked like the kind angina patients carry with their valued nitroglycerine tablets which they place under their tongues when they are having an attack.

I stared at him, wondering if Paul had angina attacks. Although he was young, I realized angina could strike anyone. He unscrewed the bottle top.

He didn't exhibit the usual signs and symptoms of someone in pain. He was not grabbing at his chest, or turning red, or gasping for air. But I was beginning to panic, fearful he was having one.

Instead, he laughed. "No. This is butyl nitrite," he replied. "I am just going to inhale it and then I will satisfy you in ways you never dreamed."

I felt afraid but excited. "I don't understand."

He laughed again. "That's what I like about you . . . your innocence."

He paused. "Butyl nitrite is like amyl nitrite. It is a vasodilator. It will make me erect again, in a hurry. I'll be able to make love to you for hours."

I could smell the slightest whiff of a sweet, fruity odor as Paul passed the bottle under his nose. "Is this stuff legal?" I asked, suddenly remembering that somewhere, outside on the street, this entire conversation and scene was being recorded by strangers.

"Anyone can buy butyl nitrite in any sex shop." Paul's face flushed. His skin looked warm and red. And his erection was both sudden and intense.

"It works that fast?" I asked, unable to take my eyes off his male parts. He looked bigger than I had ever felt or noticed before.

He nodded, letting his head fall back on the pillow and apparently feeling the heightened experience of the inhalant. "Why don't you try it?" he asked, handing the bottle to me. "We can only use it this one time."

I hesitated. My heart pounded. I wished I could put this whole scene on "hold" and talk to Al. There was a big difference between my mental decision to "fake" using drugs and this. This entire sequence was being recorded. If we ever went to court I could be declared an unfit witness. Moreover, I had never tried any drugs and was scared to death of them. My mind flashed back to the night of the apparent cocaine injection and my violent reaction. Suddenly I felt tremendously frightened. Paul's behavior had made me quite sure that my denial about his use was as thick as his probable denial. If I used butyl nitrite this time, was I in danger of becoming addicted, of wanting more drugs? All of these confusing thoughts and questions raced through my mind.

Suddenly, the decision was no longer mine. Paul had gone from asking me to placing the bottle under my nose. Although I didn't inhale deeply, the sweet fruity aroma, almost like fermented apples, filled my nostrils. Blood raced to my head. I was glad I was lying down. My legs and arms tingled. Passion arose in me quickly and intensely.

Paul reached over me to put the bottle on my side of the bed, and then moved back to kiss me, a long, hard passionate kiss with his tongue probing me. I was aroused to a depth and level I had never known before. The foreplay lasted for what seemed like hours. My body throbbed. I longed for him to penetrate me. The intensity went on and on; we moved together thrashing and moaning.

I felt I would either die or faint as we finally climaxed together. I felt faint. Blood and pleasurable sensations rushed through my body.

We talked for a little while after. "So, did you like the jac-blaster?" he asked.

"Jac-blaster?" I inquired.

Again, he laughed. "One of the street names for butyl nitrite. We call it jac-blaster or rush."

"I don't think I should ever do it again," I mumbled, frightened.

"Why?" he asked.

I lied in what I hoped was a convincing voice. "I have just recently tried some drugs, Paul, like cocaine and now this. I like the way I feel, but I am afraid of becoming addicted to them."

Paul was serious. "I know. I am afraid of the same thing, but if we use them with care, we should have no problem."

My mind flashed back to the party at which I'd seen him snorting coke.

"I don't believe we are immune to addictions," I interjected.

"Oh, Joyce. I am a doctor. I can handle it. And you are a nurse. You can handle it, too."

I wanted to scream out that Carol wasn't handling anything with her demerol dependency, nor was he with his multi-drug use, but I knew that my purpose was to let the microphone incriminate him.

Suddenly, I didn't want to spend the night with him, but I wasn't sure how to tell him. "Paul, I am so tired right now," I said hesitantly.

He pulled me close, kissing me tenderly. "Of course you are. The rush of the blood flow and excitement causes exhaustion." He smiled, his blue eyes crinkling. "Let's get some sleep."

Sleep hit suddenly. Even if I could have found a way

not to spend the night with him, there was no way I could lift my heavy, spent body out of his bed.

"How do you feel, lady?" he asked, rolling over to greet me as the sun rose towards a high noon.

I was groggy. "I'm not sure," I replied. "I think I feel like something mowed me down."

"That's pretty normal," he replied as he threw his covers off and stood up to greet the daylight. Again, I couldn't help but admire his beautiful body. It was lithe; firm; strong; supple. I wanted to pull him back into bed and make love to him again. The desire was mental. Physically, I had no stamina.

I wondered how Paul and I would part at this point, or if we would just continue to stay together for the day. As he went into the closet to get his robe, I reached under the bed quickly, scooping up the microphone and covering it with my tee shirt. I jumped out of bed. "I'm going to take a shower," I called, scampering from the room.

I emerged from his bathroom, my hair washed, my makeup on, my body more relaxed than I could ever imagine. Breakfast was on the table. Paul had used his guest bathroom to clean up in. He, too, was dressed.

"I have some bad news," he announced, pouring steaming coffee for both of us.

I looked at him, unable to respond.

"I have to go into work today," he stated. "One of the residents has the flu and I have to cover for him."

I nodded, feeling glum. "Sure. I understand," I murmured.

"I hope you're not too disappointed," he said, reaching over to squeeze my hand. "I know I am."

"Of course I am, but things like this happen to doctors and nurses," I grimaced. "We knew it would."

"I love the fact that you are so understanding." He stroked my cheek slowly. I was vacillating between denial and love for him. He looked so innocent, yet he was so manipulative.

"How much time do we have?" I asked.

"Just enough for breakfast, I am afraid," he said stoically.

We ate in silence. We never discussed the previous night or my disclosure about having tried cocaine. We never talked about the butyl nitrite or our sexual encounter.

We parted with a soft, tender kiss. Paul held me close offering his apologies again. "I'll make it up to you," he promised, walking me to my car.

"I'll hold you to that," I said seriously, unlocking the door and entering my car.

Driving away, I looked in the rear view mirror at Paul, his long legs striding towards his car. Tears filled my eyes. I felt intensely and passionately in love with him, yet he was a man who could hurt me, not only emotionally, but physically. I wondered how I could care for him so deeply.

"Y ou did well," Al said sitting with me in his parked car at a shopping center on the outskirts of the city. I had phoned him from a pay phone after leaving Paul's house. I needed to talk to him and to be reassured. "We have everything on tape," he said soberly.

I blushed. "Al, I can't believe how I felt when he gave me that butyl nitrite. How much I wished we were really alone and he was sincere."

Al seemed to sympathize. "I know. Making love should be a personal experience without Big Brother watching over your shoulder."

"I am ashamed, too, Al. I really liked the stuff and the way it made me feel at the time."

"I have tried it, Joyce. I know." His eyes met mine.

"I don't think I should do it again," I told him.

He nodded. "I can understand that also. I felt the same way."

He patted my hand; I drew it back, suddenly realizing that we had become quite close, perhaps too close.

"Al, Paul said that anyone can buy that stuff in any sex shop," I interjected.

He drummed his fingers on the windowpane. "Joyce, there are all kinds of drugs, legal and illegal. Amyl nitrite and butyl nitrite are legal prescriptions, but butyl nitrite seems to have missed something in the legislation and can be sold in stores. A lot of people are using it: gays, high school kids, college students."

I shook my head. "Al, how can I have taken the hospital medication course, graduated from nursing school, where pharmacology is a major part of our training, yet no one ever taught us about the illicit interactions and misuses of drugs?"

"Would you consider going to an AA meeting?" he said suddenly. "You could learn a great deal."

"An AA meeting is for someone who uses and abuses alcohol," I said, annoyed. "I can't see myself there telling strangers that I have a problem when I don't."

"I wasn't referring to your going to say you had a problem," Al said, flushing. "What I meant is, if you were to go to an AA or NA meeting (Alcoholics Anonymous or Narcotics Anonymous), you would hear the truth about what happens to people on drugs, and you would be able to pick up the AA literature."

Al was right. I needed to know more about drugs. I nodded. "You're right. Where do these meetings take place?" I asked.

"I'll take you to one," he offered, "if you wouldn't mind the company."

His eyes met mine. Again I looked away.

"I would be very grateful," I replied. I felt as nervous as I had been trying the butyl nitrite the night before. I was glad Al was there for emotional support.

He found an NA meeting located in a warehouse in the south end of the city. Coffee and cigarettes were everywhere. I looked at the faces sitting in the circle, clutching their styrofoam cups. Hands were shaking, my own included. Al and I sat close together. I had agreed to follow his lead.

The group began with each person introducing himself and being welcomed by the others, and then allowing the individual to tell his or her story. By the time the group reached Al we had heard every kind of tale imaginable, from one woman's guilt over stealing family possessions to buy crack cocaine, to one man losing his wife, children, home and job to his heroin addiction. The horror stories frightened me. Many of the people in this circle looked like skid row bums, but others were obviously upper middle class in Bill Blass and Pierre Cardin suits.

The group came to Al. "Hi. My name is Al," he said.

"Hi, Al," the group yelled all together, as they had done for each preceding introduction.

"I am addicted to narcotics," Al continued.

I looked at him in shock.

"I used to use pot, heroin, and uppers," he continued. Then he told about his divorce, his wife, and his children. When he was done, he thanked the group for listening.

I was still shaken, but it was my turn. "Hi. My name is Joyce."

"Hello, Joyce," they all yelled together again.

"Well, ah . . ." I paused, coughing and feeling embarrassed. "I am new to this."

"That's okay," the man opposite me said. "We all had to get started too. Take your time."

I looked at him. He smiled back. "I have just begun using drugs," I finally said. Fabricating a story and lying was foreign to me, so I decided to be as honest as I could in my disclosure and not add to everything. "I tried cocaine and, last night, I tried butyl nitrite." I paused to survey the room. All eyes, including Al's, were on me. "I am here today because I liked them, especially the butyl and I am afraid I might become dependent."

The same man spoke first. "Good for you, Joyce. We're here to help you. Now, tell us, how did you feel?"

Feelings were apparently an important part of the program. I had already heard confrontations of feelings by group members towards others. "Well, when I used the butyl nitrite last night, I felt intensely aroused and excited," I replied.

The group laughed. "That's not what we meant," another man said, "but we do appreciate your honesty."

I realized what they meant. "I felt, and feel today, embarrassed, vulnerable, and ashamed." That was what they wanted to hear. But was it the truth? Did I feel that way?

The meeting continued. It was important that I continue to attend meetings and find a sponsor. They handed me a white chip for coming forward the first time. I could earn a thirty-day chip the following month. They commended me for seeking treatment so soon after my initial use. Then they moved on to the woman next to me. I felt relieved to have my story over with. Al nodded at me.

After the meeting the first man who had encouraged me approached. "I don't know if you remember me," he said, "my name is Gary. I hope you will come back."

"I think I will," I replied.

He added, "I would like to get to know you better." He winked and then handed me his business card.

After he walked away I looked at his card and noticed his name. Gary Feinberg, Ph.D., Clinical Psychologist.

I purchased the packet of AA/NA books for $15.00 from the group leader and took them with me back to Al's car. "I was a nervous wreck," I said as we drove out of the alley way.

"You were super," he said admiringly.

"And so were you. I really believed you."

He laughed. "I did sound convincing, didn't I? Well, you were also convincing. Apparently to the point of being invited out by someone."

I produced the business card. "Can you imagine," I asked, "a psychologist going to these meetings?"

"Joyce, all kinds of people go. Your doctor friend probably is also a Viet Nam vet. A lot of those men began abusing drugs in Viet Nam, and many of them are highly respected business professionals today who are still living with their nightmares."

"Were you in Viet Nam, Al?" I asked.

"Yes. For thirteen months. It was hell. I don't like to talk about it."

"Did you do drugs over there?"

He nodded slowly. "Joyce, now you know something about me that I want kept secret. Yes, I did heroin over there, and I was addicted for many years after my return. I belong to NA. The meeting I took you to today is one of my regular meetings."

"No wonder you sounded so convincing."

"I am not ashamed of it, Joyce, but please respect my privacy."

"Of course, Al. I don't think any less of you. Besides, what I said today, I meant. And I did like the meeting."

"You are welcome to come with me anytime," he added. "Now, go home and read all of those books you just bought."

I did, too. By nightfall I knew the twelve steps and the problems of ACOA's, who are adult children of alcoholic parents. I had read about the AA philosophy and began the book on drug data.

Besides alcohol, cocaine, LSD, PCP and inhalants, I read about the addictive qualities of caffeine, tobacco, amphetamines, barbiturates, and the benzodiazepams like Librium and Valium, which relieve anxiety short term but often cause depression when used over a long period of time.

Lying in bed, so overtired I could not sleep, I realized that in the past twenty-four hours I'd learned more about legal and illegal drugs and their effects than I ever dreamed. I thought about how nursing school ought to prepare us to confront and handle the real problems of alcohol and drug misuse, especially among ourselves.

I thought about Paul—our sexual encounter, the way I had felt. I vowed never to try butyl nitrite again. My feelings were too intense, but I also realized that the very intensity of those feelings might indicate that I too could easily become addicted if I let down my guard.

ELEVEN

Spring was finally in the air with red, yellow, and orange tulips poking their heads through the ground. The little snow which fell was mixed with rain. The March wind had an ice-cream chill rather than the biting cold of winter. I looked forward to leaving my boots and heavy winter coat home.

I was also looking forward to Karen's wedding. My dress hung over the closet door on the chair. Nearby I had placed my matching shoes and hat. Looking at the festive dress, I remembered my initial excitement when it was my uniform and white shoes and cap hanging together there for my first day on duty. That was nearly a year ago. In that time I had grown from being a novice nurse living in a world of innocence to a professional living in a world where experiences of disillusionment and heroism were daily happenings. I was exposed to life and death. I was also acting as an undercover agent spying on my friends and co-workers. It was difficult trying to ascertain to whom I owed allegiance.

The responsibility and pressures were both exciting and overwhelming. A side of me seemed to thrive on the crisis state. I learned to make quicker decisions and I learned how to be in control. I liked making nursing

155

diagnoses and then following through on them. I also liked feeling useful to society as I did with Al, who seemed to need my help. I began to think that I just might want to get more involved in law enforcement, although I didn't know to what degree.

The first part of the week went slowly. Our patient census in the unit was low. For the first time in months, staffing was decreased. Lois told me that I could begin giving meds on the evening shift the week before Karen's wedding, since I had the three-day weekend of the twelfth off.

Heather Lear and I went out for coffee a few times. I felt worried that she might be drinking too much caffeine. "It's not good for the baby," I admonished.

She laughed good-naturedly. "Who's the doctor?" Then her face took on a more serious look. "Don't worry, Joyce. I wouldn't do anything to injure this little guy—or girl." She patted her stomach. "Dan and I are really looking forward to our new parental roles. I just don't believe in treating all these new medical admonitions so seriously. After all, babies have been born since time immemorial, and all those scare tactics haven't changed the procedure much."

I frowned. I didn't agree; infant mortality was a serious problem, and most of the new research pointed to caffeine as a substance pregnant women should avoid. Still, I didn't want to offend Heather. After all, she was right, she was the doctor.

"Well, you ought to be careful," I said, trying to make my tone lighthearted.

"I will," she promised.

Paul and I passed in the hospital. We spoke by phone several times. Each time he asked me if I was looking forward to our next encounter. More than he knew or I admitted, I did. I only prayed that somehow I would discover he was innocent and I had made a mistake about his drug use before we met again. I longed to make love to him, but I didn't want to try butyl nitrite again ever.

On Thursday, April third, when I came on duty at the day shift, I found that I was being assigned to observe open heart surgery. When the unit was slow, nurses were floated from one unit to another. Every nurse dreads being floated. We hate to work in an area we don't know with patients and staff with whom we are not familiar. Many nurses also hate to work the floors. I was no different. I lived in fear of being asked to float, although during this first year I had done my fair share of it.

Lois and Marilyn felt we should all have the chance to observe an open heart surgery and other major surgical cases. They felt we should spend time in the cardiac catheter lab too. The hospital was beginning to take the position that departments should swap jobs with each other, or, at least, observe each other. Stress management was beginning to become a reality along with the first nursing shortage impacts.

The surgery was intricate and interesting. The patient's mitral valve was not working adequately and had to be replaced. A plastic cup with a stainless steel ball was sutured directly into the heart.

I watched intently as Dr. Jackson, the anesthesiologist, painstakingly monitored the patient's vital signs, his dedication evident as sweat poured down his forehead. Somberly he called out the numbers indicative of dropping blood pressure. Pictures of him snorting coke with Paul at Marilyn's party flashed through my mind. I shook them off and tried to concentrate on the intricate surgical techniques being used. But with the blood and numerous staff surrounding the patient, it was difficult to see.

The surgery lasted five hours. I felt exhausted. My legs hurt from standing in one place for so long. We were not allowed to leave the OR during the surgery. I had been warned not to drink anything before entering the OR. I hadn't, but my bladder was ready to burst. I had a whole new respect for circulating and scrub nurses.

I also saw how nasty and angry surgeons could act. Every time the doctors tried to remove the patient from the bypass pump, his pressure would bottom out and he would have to be put back on the pump. One of the surgeons became so anxious and frustrated that he began to scream obscenities at everyone in the room. He threw one of the surgical trays and acted like an irate child. The OR staff was intimidated.

Finally, the patient's mean arterial pressure came up, and he was transferred to the recovery room. In the nurses' lounge, I removed my green scrubs gratefully. As the nurses gossiped about the tenseness of the surgery and the doctor's anger, I listened.

"I wish we could do what five North does," the first one named Donna said to the other.

"What's that?" Andrea, the other, asked. She was the scrub nurse.

I watched Andrea rubbing her neck and massaging her shoulders. I also listened quietly as they talked.

"The head nurse on five North has developed a great program that works. Her nurses got tired of being intimidated by angry doctors, so now, whenever a doctor tries to chastise a nurse she calls a 'Code Pink.'"

I was interested. "What is a Code Pink?" I asked.

The two nurses included me in their conversation. Donna asked the same question.

"A Code Pink brings all of the nurses out, just like any emergency code. The nurses surround the doctor and nurse he is accosting in a circle. They stand silently, but obviously, in support of their co-worker."

"I like their spirit," I exclaimed.

Donna nodded. "Yup. And it works. The doctor is the one who is embarrassed."

"All nurses should support each other that way," Donna stated.

I agreed. "What a great way to defuse a negative situation," I commented.

Andrea continued. "All of the physicians know they should be careful when they go on that nurse's floor. I just wish we could implement something similar here."

I was eager to tell Karen about the Code Pink concept. She was working days, so I hoped to catch her by the end of the shift. I had to return to the unit to see if I was needed and to clock out. It was 2:30 and my shift was not quite over.

Returning to the unit, I expected to find everything still quiet. Instead, I walked in on a Code. Instinctively, I knew the Code was on Janice Dexter. She had never responded to any of our life-saving measures. We all knew it was a matter of time.

I watched the Code in silence. The pressure and tension grew thick in the unit. Everyone, including the few remaining patients, seemed to have put their lives and feelings on hold. When the Code ended, and Janice Dexter was officially pronounced deceased, we all stood in solemn quiet. Tears filled my eyes. I noticed everyone else was also crying.

Janice's death reminded us all that life is very short. There really is not much time between those two transitions called birth and death. I felt more vulnerable. The pressures in my life seemed unimportant as I watched the family enter the unit to tearfully say goodbye to their beloved wife, daughter, and sister.

"This is the worst," Lisa, my team nurse on the unit, commented as she walked beside me to the nurses' lounge.

"I know," I agreed wearily. "Dealing with untimely death is the most stressful part of critical care nursing."

Lisa nodded, adding, "and dealing with doctors is the second most stressful."

I decided to share the Code Pink concept with her. She seemed receptive to the idea. Lisa laughed. "I like that!" she enthusiastically exclaimed. And that took some of the tension off of Mrs. Dexter's death.

"Why don't you share it with some of the other nurses," I suggested.

"Yeah, I will." Then her face darkened. "I have to begin the post mortem care." I offered to help her.

We both talked about everything but the death which

had just occurred. When we returned to the unit we shared the task of preparing Janice Dexter's body and literally blocked out the fact that we were washing the cold, empty remains of a very attractive, once vital, young woman.

Her body was taken to the morgue by the transport personnel. I clocked out feeing weary and beaten. Just as I was getting ready to walk out the door the ward clerk called me.

"Joyce. You have a phone call." She left the receiver on the desk and moved over to another counter.

My heart skipped a beat. All of us hated to get calls in the unit. They were usually emergencies. I wondered if it could be Paul or Al. "Hello," I said, holding the receiver to my ear.

"Joyce, this is Karen. I need your help."

"What's wrong?" I asked, concerned by her voice. She sounded frantic.

"Heather Lear was admitted to our unit five hours ago. She is having an unproductive labor and is probably going to lose her baby. We can't find her husband. Apparently, he travels quite a bit and is out of town. Anyhow, she said you were the only one she knew at the hospital. She needs help, Joyce."

"Karen, I'll be right there."

I ran out of the unit and towards the stairwell. Heather and I had just started to become friends. I was both surprised and pleased that she felt she could rely on me. I thought about the hospital drama of the day as I took the steps two at a time: an open heart surgery patient who faced life and death; a young woman who died from an aneurysm. And now, a doctor aborting her baby. I wanted to weep.

I rushed into maternity. Karen was waiting for me by the door.

"Here, put these scrubs on," she said. Her hands shook as she gave me the folded white dress.

I changed quickly. Leaving my clothes in the locker room, Karen waited outside to take me to the private room assigned to Heather Lear. When we walked in she was in the middle of an intense contraction. Her face was cortorted in pain. She held onto her stomach, crying out.

Karen whispered to me, "Let her know you're here. Then meet me at the nurses' station. I need to share something with you."

I nodded my head. Walking over to the bed, with its siderails up, I took Heather's hand. The contraction had subsided.

"Joyce. Thanks for coming. I'm so scared."

"I know, Heather. I'll stay with you." I stood by the bedside holding her hand. Suddenly she squeezed my hand tightly and began to moan. I could see her stomach tightening again. She was having another contraction. Instinctively, I looked at my watch and counted the seconds. This one lasted twenty-five. I glanced at the nurses' notes and saw she was having contractions every two minutes. She was five centimeters dilated.

Because the baby was so small at six and a half months, I knew she probably would not have to wait until she reached ten centimeters to deliver. A precip or unsterile delivery was quite possible. I had seen one when I was a student in L & D (Labor and Delivery). A young, black woman had delivered a six-month-in-gestation baby girl in bed. The baby weighed 1 lb. 14 oz. The woman had been only six centimeters dilated when she suddenly grunted and pushed the baby out. To everyone's surprise and pleasure, the baby survived and did well. The attending pediatrician told us that black, female babies had the highest survival rate of any preemie.

I prayed that Heather would be as fortunate. After the contraction subsided, I leaned over her, whispering gently. "Heather, I have to talk to Karen for a minute, but I will be right back."

She nodded, too much in pain to speak.

I left the room and quickly walked to the nurses' station. Karen was waiting for me. "We need to talk," she said, guiding me to a quiet corner.

"What's wrong?" I asked.

She sighed. "Dr. Lear is losing her baby because she does drugs."

Shock hit me like a bolt of lightning. "What?"

"We did a routine urine to see if she had toxemia or pre-eclampsia. Her urine is filled with drugs: demerol, talwin, vistaril, even dilaudid."

"Dear God," I gasped, "I can hardly believe it. Does she know what you found out?"

Karen shook her head wearily. "No. Not yet. And there's more. She has terrible injections because of the talwin. There are injection sites all over her hips. They are as deep as craters."

This news came so swiftly and was so surprising that I felt overcome and sat down in the nearest chair. "She has been giving herself injections in her own hips?" I echoed almost unbelievingly.

"Apparently. Anyhow, this fetus is probably addicted to drugs. It would be a blessing if it didn't survive."

"What can I do to help her?" I asked as my head cleared. I liked Heather. I also felt sorry for her.

"Can you stay with her while she delivers? I'm too angry. I feel like she killed her own baby. But I know she still needs emotional support and help."

"It's all right, Karen," I said. "I can understand why you could feel that way, but I feel differently. I can stay with her," I said softly. "What about when this is over. She needs treatment."

Karen looked up bitterly. "What you say to her is your choice." She leaned toward me, her face tightening. "I think it is really sad that we don't have any programs to help these doctors."

"It's not just doctors, Karen. It's nurses, too. And all kinds of other people."

"I know," she said, "but medical professionals have

more access to legal drugs than any other group. Doctors are the worst. I know nurses steal drugs, Joyce. But doctors can use their samples or write prescriptions for themselves."

"It's a mess."

She nodded. I rose. "I'd better go back. She's going to need someone."

Her contractions were getting closer. After fifteen minutes, Karen followed. She examined Heather vaginally.

"She's almost six centimeters. I think we had better move her to the delivery room to avoid a precip. I'll buzz her gynecologist."

"Heather," I said, "we're going to take you to delivery just in case."

She moaned. "Please. I can't stand this pain. Can't I have something for it?"

Karen and I looked at each other. Neither one of us wanted to tell her that she already had far too many painkillers in her body. Karen finally pulled herself together and spoke in a quiet but authoritative tone. "I'm sorry, Dr. Lear. We don't want to harm the baby. It is already far too small and may not survive."

Heather nodded weakly. We wheeled her bed down to the delivery room and lifted her on the table. Her attending gynecologist came down the hall.

"Is she ready?" he asked, preparing to scrub and put on his sterile gown.

Karen replied, "She's six centimeters. We thought we would avoid a precip."

"Fine." He turned and entered the room to scrub in. Reentering the delivery room, Karen helped him into a sterile gown and sterile rubber gloves.

Heather's legs were in the stirrups. I sat next to her, holding her hand, and trying to calm her. My heart pounded.

The doctor seated himself in front of her legs. "Here it comes," he announced. "Heather, push hard."

I instructed her to take a deep breath and bear down. She panted and pushed. I could see the head of the tiny infant just beginning to push through her labia.

"Push again," her doctor ordered.

Again, she pushed and panted. She began screaming, "Oh, it hurts so badly." She still had pain as she was still dilating.

Finally the tiny infant shot through. The doctor held it up. "It's a boy," he commented. We didn't feel joy, only fear.

He suctioned the tiny infant who barely whimpered. The baby looked so small and frail. His color was poor. The skin terger was as thin as an onion skin.

Gently Karen lifted him into an incubator. A neonatal nurse began to use emergency techniques similar to the ones we used on ICU patients. The baby was attached to monitors. An anesthesiologist intubated his tiny lungs and connected him to a respirator.

"How is my baby?" Heather asked. Her head strained to see the incubator.

I tried to reassure her. "They are doing everything they can, Heather. He is very tiny."

He was tiny, too. 1 lb. 15 oz. The group whisked him off to neonatal ICU.

Heather didn't need too many sutures to her episiotomy. I stayed with her while the doctor finished. Karen monitored her blood pressure and vitals. The room grew quiet. There was a deep sadness unlike the thrill of most deliveries.

Heather was finally taken to her private room on the maternity floor. I was exhausted and left her when she fell asleep. It was 5:30 p.m. I was as hungry as I was tired.

Karen and I checked on the baby before leaving the hospital. The prognosis was not good. He was going through withdrawal. He was too small, too sickly, and would require intense care for some time, if he managed to survive the first several hours. Then, there was the genuine concern for brain damage or other functional losses.

Karen and I talked about Heather and the baby over dinner at home. We both felt depressed. At 10:00 p.m. she called the unit to see how both Heather and the baby were.

Heather was still sleeping. The baby had died.

The next time I stopped by Heather's room, she was withdrawn and depressed. I visited her several more times; we never talked abut how or why the baby died. No one confronted her about her drug usage. Everyone seemed to be playing the games of cover-up and protection, though we all knew they were dangerous pastimes dealing with patients' lives. Heather requested a leave of absence based upon the loss of her baby. The hospital administrator gave it to her. She didn't return to hospital service. I never saw her again or found out her fate.

The long-awaited day when I could give medications alone grew near. I had been giving them with the assistance of Annette for three days. On the fourth evening, Lois notified me that I was to be on my own. My spirits lifted. I really was moving ahead. The unit was slow. Only six beds were filled. The open heart post-op wing where eight patients could be cared for simultaneously had recently been opened. Open heart was another critical care course in which I needed special training. Lois and Marilyn were preoccupied with this new area and pretty much left us alone.

I concentrated on dispensing meds, feeling proud and conspicuous. No one seemed to notice my awkwardness. After the evening meds and visiting hours, I felt bored. I looked around for something to do, a lesson we'd learned in nursing school. Closets could always be cleaned. Supplies could be filled. The crash cart could be checked for outdated drugs. There were only four of us on duty. Mary was in charge. Shelly was reading "Reader's Digest." Melanie was studying for a midterm at the University. I decided to clean the medication cupboard.

Sitting on the floor cross-legged, I pulled all of the IV bottles, bags, and tubing out from under the medication counter. I washed the cabinet out, feeling like I was doing some constructive spring cleaning. With my compulsive tendency to do things well, I literally climbed head first into the cabinet to wash the back wall. The unit was quiet as patients slept. Only the sound of respirators hissing and monitors beeping could be heard.

As I pulled out of the cabinet I hit my head on top so hard that it made me breathless. I sat on the floor holding my sore head and rubbing it. As the dizziness passed, I wondered what I had hit. The overhead lights were dim so that patients could sleep. Adjusting my eyes to the even darker interior, I peered in. There was nothing but empty space. I looked up towards the underside of the cabinet. Suddenly, I saw it. A metal box with sharp corners, one of which had struck me, was protruding from the underside of the counter.

"That's strange," I mumbled to myself. I began to palpate the box. It didn't move. It was screwed into the counter with small, heavy bolts in all corners. I felt around it trying to find an opening. The thing seemed solid.

I stood up to survey the unit. Mary was on the phone. Shelly and Melanie were sitting in the corner quietly involved in their reading. Using a sponge I began to wash the counter top, trying to look inconspicuous. At the same time I carefully felt around the top of the box with the tips of my fingers.

Finally, I felt a crack. Wedging my nails in it, I pried the top open. Suddenly it sprung back with a whine. My head snapped around, afraid I would be discovered. No one was paying attention. Seating myself on the floor again, I surveyed the box, studying how it worked. It slipped forward from metal grooves. Gently and quietly I got up and pulled the box towards me once again, laying it inside the cabinet. It was not empty.

I peered in. Small, unopened vials and ampoules of demerol, vistaril, morphine, valium, and even thorazine were loaded inside. I continued looking. Sealed packages of nembutal, seconal, dalmane, and halcion were also there. Astonished, I quickly replaced the box, afraid someone would discover me with it. My heart pounded rapidly.

I wondered who had placed the box there. And how many other departments had similar boxes in their med cabinets.

I replaced the IV bottles and packages, acting as if nothing had happened. Then, I put IV bottles on the counter top to prepare the night meds for nurses. Lining the bottles up along the front of the counter, I was able to build a discreet area for checking out the hidden slot again. Probing gently, the counter top gave way with the same small clearance. I knew that medications meant for patients were hidden away here. Where did they go and who removed them? I wondered silently.

At 10:00 p.m. I went over to Mary and said, "If you don't mind, I think I will run these requisitions to the pharmacy now."

"Sure, Strom," she nodded as she transcribed doctors' orders from charts to the kardex. "It's quiet in here. Take your time."

I took the elevator to the basement and left the requisition slips in the pharmacy night box. Back on the elevator I pressed the button for the sixth floor. I decided to check out the OR.

I knew it was time to tell Al what I was doing, and I was finally in a safe place. "Al, or whomever is out there right now," I whispered in the microphone in the center of my chest, "I have just stumbled on where the drugs are hidden in the unit. I am going to the OR to see if I can find something similar. I will keep you advised."

The elevator doors opened. I stepped out into the dark hallway. Fortunately, no one was around. No emergency surgeries were being done. The medication room was located in the center of the hallway, adjacent to the operating suites. The counter top was similar to ours in the unit. I opened the cabinet door and groped in the dark, feeling the underside of the cabinet. My heart raced. I could feel a box. I felt around it. It was the same size as the one I'd found in my unit. I looked inside. It was empty, except for some crushed pastel powders. I pressed them on my fingertips and brought them up to my mouth. Their bitter drug taste was familiar. I knew what the box was used for. I slid the box back into its hiding place. Feeling the counter top as I had done before, I soon found my fingers pushing the same narrow opening. I quickly closed the top and ran out of the room.

"It's here, too," I announced to my chest again. "I found the same thing in the OR as in the unit. I'll contact you when I go off duty."

Pausing to call the elevator, suddenly I didn't feel safe. How would I explain to anyone what I was doing up there? I spied the stairway at the opposite end of the hall. My breathing became short and irregular. Perspiration rolled down my face and neck. I tried to walk as softly as I could. Suddenly I heard voices. Stopping short I turned. OR Number Six had a light on in the back. Two men were talking. Afraid of being seen through the glass window, I pressed myself against the wall.

I strained to hear them. "Look, you're behind on your quota for the month, doc," a hoarse voice protested.

"I know," a second deep voice said, "but the census is low. We are doing the best we can."

"It's not good enough."

Although both voices were muffled, one seemed familiar to me. I racked my mind. Where had I heard it before?

"Look, I promise. We will have a supply by next Friday. Our nurses are wasting as much as they can."

"You're not up with St. John's or General, Doc. But, you've been a good account. So, we'll let it go."

"How about the cocaine? Do you have any?"

I dared not breathe or move, afraid they would see me. The doctor's voice was becoming clearer. Dr. Jackson. An anesthesiologist for most of the major surgical cases. I had observed him in OR during the valve surgery just today.

"Sure." The other man's voice was throaty. Harsh. He could have had a cold or perhaps some surgery done on his larynx. "Say," he continued, "how about sending someone on another run to Miami? We have a big shipment coming in next Tuesday."

Dr. Jackson replied, "That should be no problem. We take turns with the residents and nurses. I know just the couple."

Would Paul try to foist another buy on me, I wondered. The sudden scraping movement of their shoes jarred me back into reality. I looked around the hall wondering where I could hide. Reaching my hand behind me, I felt the door on OR Four. Quietly, I turned the handle, sliding inside just as OR Six opened.

My back was against the wall. I held my breath, mostly out of fear. What if they had heard me?

"Take care, Doc. I'll see you next week."

"Use the stairs," Dr. Jackson whispered.

I listened for their footsteps to die as they distanced themselves from my hiding spot. The glow from my watch reminded me that I had been out of the unit for over thirty minutes. Since I was the medication nurse it was my responsibility to be available. Critical patients' conditions can turn quickly. In spite of this, I was too frightened to leave the safe, dark corner of OR Four.

I let several more minutes pass. Then, not hearing anything, I opened the door carefully. Peeking up and down the hall I saw all was dark and quiet. I tiptoed out quietly, pushing the door shut. Fearing being discovered on the elevator I opted, once again, for the stairwell. At

least I could make it to the fifth floor where Karen worked
on maternity. She would be my cover if necessary.

The heavy metal door clanked behind me. Holding
the handrail I raced down the metal steps hearing my
footsteps echo throughout the stairwell. Just as I got to
the fifth floor and began to pull the door open I looked
down. Dr. Jackson looked up at me at that exact moment.
Our eyes met. Panic filled me. Did he know who I was?
Did he know I had just come from the sixth floor?

Swinging the door open, I wondered what story I
could make up. Fear enveloped me. I ran for the elevator
and jumped on quickly with the door closing fast. I was
not alone. A tall, heavyset man with large, hairy hands
and dark, protruding eyes stood silently at the back of the
elevator. Instinctively I knew he was the other man.

At the third floor I raced out, running back into the
unit.

"Where have you been, Joyce?" Mary asked angrily.
She was standing next to the medication counter drawing
up morphine. Before I could reply she continued, "We
have a new patient in bed four from the ER. Auto accident.
Head trauma. I'm giving him morphine and I already
hung the mannitol."

"Sorry, Mary," I puffed, adding, "I didn't mean to be
gone so long. I detoured by the fifth floor to see Karen. We
started talking about her wedding and I lost track of the
hour."

Mary was calmer and no longer angry with me.
"That's okay. I did tell you to take your time. It's just that
all hell broke loose ten minutes ago. The OR was called in
too. Another ER patient is on their way for an exploratory
lap (laparotomy—exploring the abdomen).

Taking over on the ER physician's orders, I carefully
prepared the next bottle of saline solution and added the
mannitol for our new patient. I knew I could be giving
critical medication. I forced myself to focus on my work.
My mind raced. My heart pounded. Had Dr. Jackson seen
me? Did he know who I was? When could I tell Al about

the medication counters and the conversation I overheard? What if I got caught?

Minutes ticked by rapidly. At 11:00 p.m. Tina came on duty. We counted meds together. She took the keys while I departed from the unit as quickly as I could. Once outside, I paused to look up at the hospital. The large red brick building bustled with activity, even this late at night. Lights in the student nurses' quarters lickered on and off.

The lobby—always open—with its aged doorman standing outside, glowed. Scattered lights in the rooms and hallways made the building's shadows loom even bigger and more dramatically.

I loved hospitals: the smell; the thrill of adrenaline flowing; life and death filling the halls. I loved nursing— not the nursing my mother did, dressed in a long sleeve uniform with a perfectly starched cap on her head, standing by the bed of a mildly ill patient, but the nursing of my era where critical procedures, responsibility, and decisions were made by us. I was lucky to live in a time when our nursing judgment helped a client live or die.

Looking up at the large building I noticed the entire sixth floor lit up. Emergency surgery from the auto accident victims, I thought. My feelings of excitement at my drug discovery in both the unit and OR suddenly gave way. I saw a face peering down at me from an OR window. There was no doubt in my mind. The face was Dr. Jackson's.

I drove to a pay phone and telephoned Al's private number. "What did you find?" he asked, telling me he had been informed of my dialogue through the hidden microphone.

"I found out how the drugs are stolen in the unit and in the OR. There is a little crack built into the counter top where the drugs are slid through. A metal box catches them underneath. Someone apparently empties those boxes."

I felt proud of my accomplishment. "What do we do now?"

"We," Al answered, "do nothing right now. You go home and get some sleep. We will meet in the morning and talk about everything. Okay?" he asked ruefully.

"Fine, Al. I'll see you tomorrow."

"You did great, once again, Joyce. Thank you."

I hung up the receiver and headed home.

Detective Al Thurston listened pensively. I left out no details including Dr. Jackson's observation of me as I left the hospital. Telling the agent helped to relieve some tension, but, I still felt very frightened.

At the conclusion of my story he leaned forward saying, "You did a great job, Joyce. And those boxes— that's more than anyone else has ever found for us before." Al paused for a moment in silence. Then, nodding his head, he went on, "Yes, sir." He mumbled almost under his breath, "What a great find."

"What do I do now?" I asked, interrupting his thoughts.

Al immediately looked me in the eye. I had his full attention again. "With the bug we have on you we can monitor your every move. If anyone attempts to harm you we will be only seconds away."

"I'm not sure I believe that anymore," I said shakily.

"You can," Al said calmly. "We'll use Sister Theresa's office inside the hospital. Your telephone line is already bugged."

"You're kidding. When did you do that?"

Al flushed. "The day we first met you and you agreed to help us."

"What else do I do?" I still felt alone and isolated.

"Just keep watching for us. Only this time, if you

want to talk to us, you can. Anything you see or suspect, just whisper it. We can tape record everything. That is how close to you we are."

I shuddered, thinking about the invasion of my privacy. Again, Al knew what I was thinking. "Turn us off whenever you desire, only tell us first," he said, his voice softer and more friendly, "and be careful."

When I finally left the federal building I tried to feel safe: I had more telephone numbers, including Al's home number. But driving off to work for the evening shift I felt conspicuous and unprotected. I was also very frightened of running into Dr. Jackson.

Report was exceptionally long. We didn't get into the unit until 4:00 p.m. The automobile accident the night before had brought in three DOA's—dead on arrival. The unit had four patients, all of whom were in very critical condition. I was assigned to two of them.

Stephen Weiderman, an accident victim, was nineteen years old. He had compound fractures of his right tibia, fibula, and femur. His pelvis had been broken six times. Emergency surgery had been performed to set his fractures and remove his ruptured spleen. Although he was still unconscious he was intubated and connected to a respirator. If Stephen needed help in breathing the machine automatically took over. He was in bed four.

My patient in bed three had also been involved in the accident. Eleanor Terry was a fifty-five-year-old woman who had been a passenger in one of the cars. She did not have her seat belt on. Her head went through the windshield. She had multiple lacerations of her face, neck, and chest. Her right temporal lobe was compressed, leaving her paralyzed on the left side of her body. Her right arm was broken in several places. She had a lacerated liver, a collapsed right lung, and had gone into cardiac arrest at the scene of the accident. I walked over to scrutinize her more closely. Though her eyes were wide open, her pupils were fully blown and dilated. "She's in a coma," I murmured half to myself, watching the respirator breathing for her. I looked up. The cardiac monitor beeped out irregular heartbeats. Her heart had already gone into V-tach. The day nurse had given her lidocaine to regulate the beat. She was on morphine to slow her respirations and allow her body the chance to recover. But we knew from report and her diagnoses that she was apparently brain dead, due either to the head trauma, the cardiac arrest, or both.

Having completed my vital signs and IV flow rates, I walked back to Stephen's bedside to review the nurses' notes. I looked around, trying unobtrusively to see if any of the other patients were restless or in pain, which might indicate that their medications had been stolen or swapped. I wanted to ascertain whether a pattern was emerging. Lost in thought, calculating the hours, I never heard Paul approach.

"The son of a bitch," he mumbled. I looked up, startled.

"You scared me; I didn't hear you sneak up."

Paul apologized. "I didn't mean to scare you. I am just angry as hell with this bastard." He pointed towards Stephen.

"I don't understand," I said confused. "Do you know him?"

Paul grew flushed. Angrier than I had ever seen him. "Not personally, but I'd like to be the one who could pull the switch on his electric chair."

I was thoroughly mystified. "Paul, I don't understand."

He looked at me in surprise. "Didn't they tell you in report?"

"Tell me what?"

"This is the bastard who was driving last night and caused that accident. This young punk was so high on drugs and alcohol that he should never have been behind the wheel of a car. He killed three people. Of the other three he injured none of them may make it, like Mrs. Terry over there." Paul paused to take a breath and nod in the direction of my other patient. He was so angry that his face was beet red and sweat formed on his brow.

"This bastard will survive. Can you imagine that?" he asked.

I could only shake my head, "no." It stunned me that Paul was so angry at Stephen when he himself was a drug user. I had seen him snort cocaine. And, there was our trip to Miami. I wanted to ask him how many drugged drivers were using the stuff he brought back and ask him if he didn't understand that he too could cause an accident or death just as Stephen Weiderman had. Could Paul be schizophrenic? Didn't he realize that although he was a doctor who saved lives, he was also a drug user who endangered them?

But I kept quiet. I guessed that in his own mind he divided his private from his professional responsibility. Paul broke into my thoughts. "This guy deserves to fry. He should have died instead of all of those innocent people. One of them was a ten-year-old girl. Damn." Again, he paused to take a deep breath and continue his diatribe. "The worst part of it is we will have to fix him up. Then the courts will give him a ridiculous sentence like five years for manslaughter. He'll serve one year of that sentence if he is lucky. Then, he will be out driving again. He was driving on a revoked license for DWI." Paul looked at me.

"I am sorry, Paul," I murmured, wondering what I was sorry about. All at once, I had mixed emotions about the quality of care Stephen deserved. Taking care of someone who had been the cause of such a severe fatality was difficult. Nurses and doctors can sabotage the care they give patients. It is a form of revenge or punishment. I wanted to keep my head on straight and not play that game with Stephen.

"I've ordered nubaine for him," Paul said to me with a malicious smile.

"What is nubaine?" I asked naively.

Paul chuckled. "Nubaine, Joyce, is a wonderful synthetic narcotic like demerol. It will control pain nicely unless the patient uses drugs. It has the opposite effect on drug-users. It works like antibuse."

I knew what Paul was getting at. Antibuse is given to alcoholics to help them mentally and physically from taking a drink. It does nothing to their bodies unless they consume some alcohol. Alcohol makes them violently ill with flu-like symptoms of nausea, vomiting, and severe stomach pains. Nubaine, from what Paul was telling me, would do the same thing. It would send Stephen into withdrawal.

I flipped through the bedside notes looking for the lab slips from his admission. Finding them I read his urine screen. "Cannabinoids (marijuana) positive by screening procedure along with cocaine, percocet, benzodiazepines, and alcohol." Stephen was on pot, cocaine, valium, and alcohol at the time of the accident. His blood alcohol level was 2.1, twice as high as the illegal rate for driving a vehicle. Nubaine would make him feel even sicker than he felt now.

"He can have nubaine 100 mg. every four to six hours as needed," Paul wrote while telling me. "When he wakes up let him suffer."

"Paul, I don't think you ought to do that."

"You're the nurse, I'm the doctor. These are my orders. Follow them."

"Thanks, Paul." My tone was sarcastic.

To allow a nauseated accident victim to have the kind of pain Stephen would have was sadistic. Rather than challenge Paul I decided to say nothing. When the situation occurred, I would have Carol call another physician for a pain medication order.

Paul and I both turned around simultaneously hearing heavy footsteps approach us. I found myself face to face with Dr. Jackson. The panic on my face almost gave me away.

Dr. Jackson spoke to Paul while looking directly at me with his dark, piercing eyes. "How's the patient?"

Dr. Jackson's eyes met mine. "Still unconscious, but I've ordered nubaine 100 mg. when he does wake up."

"Good," the anesthesiologist nodded, still looking at me.

"Haven't you two met?" Paul asked.

"We haven't had the pleasure," Dr. Jackson replied in a low-pitched monotone that made my skin crawl.

"This is Joyce Strom. She is a critical care nurse here." Paul looked at me, adding, "Joyce, this is Dr. Leslie Jackson."

I stuck my hand out to shake his. When he didn't extend his I let mine fall limply to my side. "It is a pleasure to meet you, Dr. Jackson," I said, trying to regain my composure. "I've seen you in OR several times and I saw you last night when this accident came in."

The doctor stood his ground, trying to stare me down. "Oh, where?" he asked almost innocently.

"I took the elevator to the fifth floor last night to see my roommate, Karen. She works on maternity. Only, I guess I hit the sixth floor by mistake. I got off and walked down the stairwell to the fifth floor. I noticed you in the stairwell." I wondered if he would believe me. I wondered if I believed myself.

Dr. Jackson stood quietly as if he wanted to hear more. His angry eyes squinted, turning almost pinprick in size.

"I felt so embarrassed," I added, trying to maintain my composure and air of innocence. The silence on his part was making me more nervous. "It's nights like last night that make me think I want to leave nursing."

Seconds of silence finally fell away. "I know the feeling," he smiled. "I hate getting called in for those late night surgeries myself. So, how long have you been here?" he asked.

"Almost a year," I replied.

Paul came to my defense. "Joyce and I date. She is the one I took to Miami." The two men's eyes met sending what I was sure was a silent language of understanding.

"Oh, so this is Joyce." Dr. Jackson turned back to me exhibiting a kinder face. "Well, it is nice to meet you. Paul speaks so highly of you."

"Thank you, sir." I wondered if I was really off the hook. "Well, if you will both excuse me, I must get to work." I replaced Stephen's lab work in the nurses' notes. "It has been a pleasure to meet you, Dr. Jackson." Looking at Paul I said, "I hope I see you later."

"Nice meeting you, young lady."

Paul nodded without replying. Both men walked off together talking in low whispers. I was sure they were talking about me.

Melanie and I went to first dinner at 5:00 p.m., leaving Mary in charge and Carol on meds. We talked about the accident victims. She had the other two injured accident victims, both of whom were not expected to survive. Our conversation turned to the abuse of drugs and alcohol.

"It's getting worse," Melanie said, picking at her chicken. The hospital food left much to be desired. Eating it day in and day out was boring. "Even elementary school kids are using drugs now."

"And selling drugs. And they aren't the only ones," I added, hoping that my statement would open Melanie up to talking more. She did like to gossip.

Melanie picked up my cue. "It's pretty bad among medical people too. The ER had a heavy case come in Sunday night. Apparently one of the X-ray techs used a lot of cocaine intravenously and had a bad migraine. Cocaine does that, you know." She bit off a small morsel of chicken before continuing. "Well, one of the new attendings was on duty. It seems this tech had been going to the ER all weekend and getting demerol IM for the headaches, only this doctor wouldn't give her any. Instead, he told her to take thorazine. The stupid X-ray tech allowed him to give 25 mg. of thorazine IM into each buttock."

I cringed. "But thorazine is a strong anti-psychotic medication, usually given to acute schizophrenics or other psychotically agitated patients."

She nodded. "Not only that, but he gave her the max—25 mg."

"Was she real sick?" I asked, wondering how a non-psychotic person would react to the medication and how the medication would affect narcotic abusers.

"Very," Melanie replied. "You know how thorazine burns and irritates stomach muscles, plus the usual side effects of dilated pupils, swollen tongue and general malaise. She got them all."

I scratched my head thoughtfully. "Why did she allow him to give her those shots?"

"Because she was too embarrassed to say no, get up and leave. She was sure the doctor suspected cocaine and she was afraid leaving would make him think she was guilty."

With drugs one mistake seems to lead to another. People really do crazy things once they're caught in the spider's clutches.

"Strom, chemical dependency is a web of denial. I am not an addictive person, but I am an ACOA so I do know about the denial process and the distrustful personality of addicts."

The conversation suddenly had become confusing. "What is an ACOA?" I asked.

Melanie shrugged. "Oh, an adult child of an alcoholic parent. That's what I am. There are lots of us. A lot of scientists think that addictions are genetic and that fifty percent of all ACOA's are chemically dependent on drugs or alcohol. Apparently, the other fifty percent tend to have passive dependent personalities. Many mistrust and have difficulty in personal relationships. We also tend to rescue others to the detriment of ourselves."

I grimaced. "The description you just gave sounds like a personality profile of nurses."

Melanie nodded in agreement. "Well, it is similar and a lot of nurses are also ACOA's. I am the passive dependent type who rescues others. That is why I chose nursing. And, I married twice." She shook her head. "Never again."

A trifle shyly, I remarked, "I didn't know that about you, Melanie." I was surprised that she shared her personal history with me. I also felt flattered that she trusted me enough to do so.

"Yeah, well I don't talk abut my past much. But, both of my husbands were alcoholics. I go to ACOA and Al-Anon meetings regularly." She grinned. "Thanks to individual therapy and AA, I now understand myself and know I am not ready for an independent relationship. Maybe someday." She sighed theatrically.

I said thoughtfully, "That's why you know so much about drugs and their interactions."

She nodded in agreement, still picking at her dinner.

"Mel, can I ask you something in confidence since you have been so open with me?" I decided to take the risk and get her impressions about drug problems in the unit.

"I'll answer you if I can," she replied.

I took a deep breath. "This is a double question," and a loaded one, I knew. "Do you think any of our nurses use drugs they steal from our patients?"

Melanie looked up at me, dropping her fork. Fumbling for the silverware she whispered, "So, you finally caught on. I knew you would."

"Help me, Mel. I have seen too much. I feel out on a limb alone with this."

She shook her head. "I can't help you, Strom. This is a dangerous game. It's not just drugs for personal use. I know there is something bigger. None of us make a lot of money, as you know, but some of these nurses live extraordinarily well. Haven't you noticed the cars they drive or the jewelry they wear?"

I thought about what she was saying. All at once I remembered Marilyn's knockout diamond earrings and some of the other diamond tennis bracelets. Even gold Rolex watches. Marilyn drove a Porsche. Carol had a Mercedes 450SL. "I thought they came from wealthy families or just had nice gifts given to them."

"Nice gifts is right. And they earn them." Melanie

lowered her head. "I'm tempted to ask you just how much you know, but I'm not sure you're not one of them at this point in time."

I leaned forward in amazement. "Mel, how can you say that? I don't own any expensive jewelry or drive a foreign sports car. I can just barely make the payments on my little Chevette."

"Strom, you hang around with Paul. Grapevine says a lot of negative things about him."

My cheeks flushed with embarrassment. The invisible grapevine. There is always one in every institution. No one knows where it begins, but messages fly around and always begin with the unknown "they." Tears sprang to my eyes. "What is Paul's reputation?"

Melanie answered tersely, without looking directly at me. "Well, I hear he does drugs, buys and sells them." Melanie paused to push the food around her plate. "But," she said, resuming the conversation, "you would know more about that than I would, I think."

I hesitated only momentarily. "I don't know a great deal about Paul. I really fell for him when I first met him. He is very aloof and closed. We don't date all that much."

"Just take trips to Miami," she interrupted.

I wondered if I should pursue this conversation further. Maybe she was trying to narc on me now. Conflicting thoughts swirled within me as I tried to sort out what would be best. "I went to Miami but I think we both found the feelings were just no longer there." I took a deep breath and continued. "I never saw Paul do drugs other than the Christmas party at Marilyn's. At least, he never did them around me."

Melanie nodded empathetically. "Sorry, Strom. I didn't mean to upset you. And be careful who you talk to about all this stuff. It's dangerous."

I nodded. "I know, Mel. And thanks for sharing yourself with me." As an afterthought I asked her, "Do those AA meetings really help?"

"They sure do. It's my lifeline. Group support. I would be lost without them." She pushed her tray away.

"Wouldn't it be nice if nurses had the same kind of support system with nurses' groups?" I started to verbalize an idea I had been turning over in my mind.

"Yes, it would, but I don't think you will ever see the day when nurses will trust each other enough to even get the concept off the ground."

"I hope you're wrong, Mel."

Back in the unit I found Stephen waking up. Carol had medicated him with nubaine just as I arrived. She was leaving for dinner and I knew I was in for a horror show.

It wasn't long before it began. Stephen began thrasing about. Then he started to violently wretch, pulling his NG (nasogastric) tube out before I could get wrist restraints on him. Mary ran over. "What's going on here," she asked. Quickly I told her. She grabbed the nubaine order and immediately called the on-call resident. Dr. Kim answered. I was thankful it wasn't Paul. Kim ordered demerol 75 mg. IM every four to six hours as needed. He gave an order for narcan to counteract the nubaine and drugs in Stephen's system. We couldn't give him the demerol for another three hours. He moaned, groaned, and cried out in severe pain constantly.

As busy as I was I tried to keep my eye on Carol while she prepared meds. At 10:00 p.m. I saw her draw up demerol for Stephen and another patient, a fresh bypass. I couldn't see if she slipped anything into her pocket or in the counter top. IV bottles lined the front of the counter blocking my view.

Instinctively I knew she was not going to give Stephen his demerol, or, if she did it was going to be diluted. When twenty minutes passed and Stephen was still agitated and restless I asked her to give him something else. I was burning with anger, because I wanted to confront her but knew I couldn't.

Carol gave him a 50 mg. injection of vistaril. With

demerol it has an immediate calming effect. But Stephen continued to be agitated until I went off duty. I felt badly turning him over to the night nurse. She was going to be busy until 2:00 a.m. when he could have another shot of demerol. Then he would probably go to sleep.

Leaving the hospital, I felt exhausted. I couldn't sit down even once during my shift because of Stephen. When I got home I found a package waiting on my doorstep addressed to me. Excitement perked me up. I loved surprises, wondering who it was from.

Karen wasn't home. The message light on our answering machine blinked, but I was eager to open the gift. Wrapped in plain brown paper with no return address. I tore the paper off and opened the plain box top. Peering inside I shrieked. A frightened, nauseated scream.

The room began to swim. Nausea swept over me. The last thing I remember seeing before passing out was a rat's head separated from its body, blood oozing out.

TWELVE

Momentarily, I wondered where I was as I opened my eyes. My right elbow hurt. Apparently I had landed on my elbow and shoulder.

But, then I realized why I had fainted. I remembered seeing the animal carcass. I have always hated rats and this one was no exception. The head lay alongside the body. It exuded a disgusting odor. The message this little gift sent was all too frightening.

I pulled myself together and began to clean up the mess. Closing the cover, without looking at it again, I set the box outside to take it to the trash room. Then I thought I really had better leave it for the officers on duty. For the first time I began to think like a criminologist again and wondered if I had tampered with any important finger-prints. I knew mine were on the box now.

I placed a phone call to the police station telling the officer on duty what I had found. He assured me that I would be fine and to leave the box in the hallway. Someone would retrieve it later on the next shift. The shifts were changing.

I turned on the police monitor in our kitchen and the radio receiver Al had left for me. I still had not told Karen of my involvement. I explained the new equipment by stating I had a new hobby. She thought I was crazy, but apparently had accepted my explanation.

The doorknob turned and the door creaked open. I jumped with a start. Then I heard Karen's voice and that of her mother.

"So, Strom," Karen laughed entering the apartment with her mother in tow and carrying several packages. "You're playing with your police radio again." She placed her packages on the cocktail table.

I was relieved to see her. "Here, let me help you," I offered, taking boxes from her and from her mother. Ignoring her statement, I made my own comment. "And, I see you are already learning how to be the perfect wife and spend your husband's money."

Karen's mother laughed at that line. "Not really," she interjected, adding, "although I don't suppose it will take my daughter long to learn how to do that. Actually, this is the rest of her trousseau and some gifts from people who cannot attend the wedding. We brought them with us."

I was slightly embarrassed until I saw Karen head for the door. "Hey, where are you going?" I asked, suspecting she was heading for the awful box.

And, I was right. "Oh, I just saw another box out here," she replied with a coy smile.

I raced to the door. "Forget that one, Karen. It is not a gift."

She was reaching down to lift the box top when I passed her and quickly picked the box up. "This is trash," I called out, adding, "that I forgot to dump, so I'll go do it now."

Karen looked disappointed. I couldn't blame her, but now I had to do something with the awful box. In my arms I could smell the odor again and I could also feel my body and head beginning to swim.

"Deep breaths, Strom," I saiad silently, looking around for a safe place to hide the box. None existed. If I put it in the trash room it might disappear forever.

Finally, I decided to take it back to our door and leave it where I had originally placed it. I felt confident that Karen and her mother were probably in for the night.

Fortunately, when I slipped back into the apartment, I discovered that I was right. Karen's mom was already in bed and Karen was in the shower, singing at the top of her lungs. It was time for me to settle in too, I decided. I turned the police monitor down and headed for a long, hot soak in my bathtub.

Twenty minutes later I left my bathroom only to find the apartment quiet and the lights dimmed. Karen and her mother were fast asleep.

Sliding in, I pondered the box, its contents and its message. I lay awake listening to the silence from the street below and listening to my heart. It was my heart that apparently kept me awake as the pounding and gurgling of the valves forced the life muscle to contract and expand.

I couldn't sleep. Even with the physical exhaustion I felt my mind raced. I lay in the dark for thirty minutes and then I decided to go back into the kitchen and turn both the monitor and radio receiver back on. The solitude and silence were eerie. I needed to sense some reassurance.

I knew that the policeman continued to watch the apartment. He had been ordered to do so. His radio receiver was with him at all times. I had one in the apartment with me. There were times, he had said earlier, when being a policeman was a boring job. I could tell by his voice that he was probably lost in thought, dreaming of his house, and his wife sleeping alone in their massive bed.

It was late, he had announced as he apparently punched the radial watch he wore. He whispered that his watch said 12:15 a.m. The night was still early for him. His relief wouldn't come until 3:00 a.m. I knew that from the shift assignment we had on the kitchen table. The assignment was meant to reassure me.

The streets were quiet and dark. A slight chill was in the warm night air. Again, I knew that the policeman noticed every car as they pulled up and then left the vicinity. Nothing strange was happening. His two-way radio was in the front pocket. Suddenly he reported that he'd noticed a man lurking near the apartment.

I could tell by his quickened breathing coming over the microphone that something was wrong, but I could not call to him. If I made any noise I could blow his cover. My heart pounded as I looked out the window and saw the policeman moving back into the bushes.

Then I heard the police monitor in our apartment flip on. The officer described a possible intruder. I felt panic and fear beyond anything I had ever known.

"His body is tall. Heavyset. Rugged in stature. His hair is dark. Thick. Curly. Appearing to be a man in his early 40's," the officer whispered to someone somewhere in the distant night as he continued to watch. He's looking in the direction of Joyce's apartment.

"I wonder if this man is Harry Cappuzzio," he said.

The officer repeated his earlier plea for assistance.

"Cherokee One . . . this is Cherokee Two . . . do you read me? Over?" The policeman whispered quietly from his hiding place into the small radio. "I have a man . . . early 40's . . . about 6'2" . . . heavyset . . . dark wavy hair . . . in view. He is standing in front of the apartment . . . looking up at their window."

A voice came over the radio. "Okay. We'll send a squad car. Wait until they arrive. Over and out."

I was relieved to hear the other officers' response coming over the radio. My breathing was slowing, coming back to normal. Fear began to leave my body. I was safe. All would be just fine with additional help on the way.

Minutes passed as I stared out the window. Suddenly I heard a car and saw the flashing lights. Then, a big man raced down the alley, in the direction away from the policemen.

The squad car stopped. Two officers jumped out. The

undercover officer ran after the fleeing man. I heard the clang of overturning garbage cans and shouts to stop. Then I heard one of them say that they lost sight of the man.

I began to panic again. My muscles tightened up the back of my neck. I found myself trying to concentrate on my own breathing and allow myself to relax.

"Look, Joyce," I mumbled to myself, "everything is fine. You are safe and they will find this man." The sound of my voice failed to reassure me. I felt terrified and alone. The apartment was dark and empty. I did not dare turn the lights on for fear this possible assailant would find me. The dark seemed safer. I could hide.

All three policemen stood in front of my window panting for breath. "What do we do now?" one of them asked.

"Wait a minute," the first one exclaimed. "What if this whole thing was staged to divert us from the apartment?"

Overhearing their conversation filled me with even more fear. What if this was a diversion, I asked myself. Then I really was in danger. Perhaps more than I knew. I stood frozen to my spot. I could not be out of earshot of the radio receiver for fear I might miss some important piece of information.

I was in the apartment along with Karen and Karen's mother, who had arrived that afternoon for the wedding. The prenuptial dinner was on Friday night, with the wedding scheduled for Saturday afternoon.

But I felt frightened and alone since Karen and her mother were now asleep. Neither knew of the radio receiver or my problems. I had to protect them, just as I had to protect myself. "Let's get upstairs fast," the undercover officer said.

Once again, I was beginning to feel safe. The officers were back on their way.

Then, I heard the window in back of me being forced open. "Oh, God, no," I whispered, grabbing at my chest again. I felt nauseous and certain I was going to be very ill. I saw a man's outline. It matched the description I had heard. Tall. Heavyset. Dark curly hair.

"Please don't hurt me," I moaned in a low whisper.

His face was set. Determined. He moved toward the radio and deliberately switched it off. Large hands with black leather gloves came towards me.

"He is going to smother me," I thought. Momentarily, for a brief second, I accepted my fate. "I'm going to die," I thought.

The man's beady, dark eyes penetrated my entire body. His face was set. Determined. His jaw was rigid. I noticed one of his hands come towards my face. Then I saw the four by four gauze.

Instinctively I knew that I was going to be put to sleep again. The gauze contained some lethal medication that would either kill me or render me unconscious. Again, I silently prayed for help. My heart pounded so rapidly that I wondered why no one heard it.

The man moved closer. I tried to run, but he grabbed me with his left arm. He was strong and clung tightly to me as I attemped to lunge across the kitchen floor. We both heard the police radio and knew the officers were on their way back to our apartment.

The man said nothing. I could only hear his heavy breathing and respirations that sounded as if he had a slight upper respiratory infection. If I lived through this ordeal, I decided, I would need to remember everything about him that I could. After all, I would have to identify this man.

His right arm came around and hit me on the side of my head. The room began to swim as I felt myself lose my balance. My head hurt. The crushing blow had thrown me off my feet, but I regained my balance quickly. Attempting to stand on my feet he grabbed me again and pulled my right arm behind me.

I swung freely with my left arm trying to reach him. He had me in front of him. I kicked, but flung my foot in the air away from his body. How I wished that I faced him because then I could knee him. Perhaps he knew it also; he held me away from his body. He was strong. His hands were powerful.

Then I felt his left hand slap my face with the four by four. The smell was familiar. "Ether," I thought, remembering the horrible odor when I was five years old and had my tonsils removed. Ether was rarely used anymore, but once I smelled the drug I understood that I was to be put to sleep.

I held my breath and pretended to fall into a faint. I was good at faking sleep having learned the trick successfully as a child. Faking sleep allowed me to meet the Easter Bunny and Santa Claus in the same year. Faking sleep also allowed me time out from responsibilities and chores while letting me overhear my parents' conversations.

I let my body relax and fall to the floor. The man believed me or perhaps he was simply in a hurry. He dropped me, allowing my left hip to smash on the tile. I had all I could do to keep from groaning in pain.

I was dazed. Although I had avoided some of the ether fumes there had been enough to disorient me. I seemed to lose consciousness for a few moments. In the distance I could hear the sounds of smashing furniture. I could also hear the sounds of bodies falling and moans, but I could not find my voice to scream out.

Suddenly, he came back for me. I resisted the urge to fight him. Lying on the floor as limply as I could with my eyes closed, I heard him breathing heavily. I could feel the large hands moving closer to me. The smell of the leather gloves was strong. The man had a pungent body odor that I vowed I would never forget.

The large hands reached down and picked up my seemingly unconscious body. I fought the impulse to tighten my muscles. He carried me to the sofa as if I were nothing more than a toy doll. I sensed, from the height I felt myself to be off the floor, that he was probably well over 6'4". I am 5'8" which does not make me a petite china doll to be carried easily. Yet this man did carry me easily, almost gently, at this point, which seemed ludicrous since he had been so rough with me earlier.

He laid me on the sofa and proceeded to tie my hands behind my back with duct tape. The tape hurt as he peeled it around and around my skin. He took another piece and placed it tightly across my mouth. The top part of the tape covered my left nostril. Breathing was fast becoming difficult.

He left me on my stomach with my arms taped behind me. Then he bound my feet together with the same tape. I could hear him panting as he worked rapidly.

As I lay on the sofa pretending to be unconscious, I began to pray silently, once again. I wondered if he was going to shoot me in the head when he finished taping me up. The daily newspaper was filled with similar deaths, especially when drugs were involved. My heart continued to pound and my head began to throb.

Finally, he stopped. I sensed that he was looking down on me. For a few seconds the man stood next to me saying or doing nothing, other than breathing heavily. Then I felt his hand gently slide up the back of my legs and underneath my underwear.

The skimpy little lace set I had on was one of my favorites. Not until this moment had he made any sexual overtures towards me. As I lay on the sofa, face down, dressed in nothing more than a tiny bikini with a teddy to match, I feared rape.

My mind raced, familiar with the horror stories on the news. In my position I was sure it would be sodomy. Chills of terror raced up and down my spine.

But, as my mind raced he simply stood close running his fingers up and down me. At one point a finger pulled at my bikini but suddenly, he pulled back. He patted me gently on the buttocks and then on the head.

We could both hear the police monitor. I knew and he knew that help was fast coming. He didn't touch me again.

Finally, he left our apartment. I thought he had taken something or someone with him. I wasn't sure. My limp body lay on the sofa no longer feeling pain. The state of peacefulness was euphoric. Tension flowed out of me with the relief that he had left me unharmed. Momentarily, I forgot about everything and everyone, including Karen and her mother. I was alive and was basically unhurt. A prayer of thanks rose from deep within my being.

Then I heard voices.

"You two wait here while I check on them," a male voice outside the front door instructed. The officer waited. A long pause.

Minutes seemed to tick by in silence. I could barely hear the police radio in the background.

"They are probably asleep," I finally heard a voice say. Even though he could hear no sounds when he rang the doorbell again apparently he waited. "Someone should answer," he said under his breath. Then I heard him fumble for keys. We had given a set to the officers with our alarm key on it.

Fog continued to pervade my body. The sound of someone turning the key in the lock momentarily revived me. He opened the door cautiously. I knew that he had reached for his service revolver and removed it from the holster inside his coat jacket. Adrenaline surged through my body.

He flipped on the light switch.

"Oh, God," he moaned, noticing my bound and gagged body lying on the open sofa bed. He checked my pulse. I was breathing, but I was only semiconscious.

He pulled his radio out. "Call for an ambulance and backup. Call Al Thurston and Mark Gibson. And one of you get up here now!"

The two officers wasted no time. The tall, lean one raced up the stairs into the apartment while the other phoned dispatch for backup and emergency vehicles.

The room was a shambles. Both men, with drawn police revolvers, began to search the premises just in case someone was still there. Moving down the hall they called out that they had found Karen, unconscious. Her mother, next to her, was bound and tied. Karen had needle marks on the inside of her left elbow.

Paramedics arrived and administered oxygen. They began IV's. One of the paramedics carefully removed the duct tape from my mouth. The tape hurt as he pulled it back. I could feel skin being pulled off and a taste of blood from the left corner of my mouth, but I could also breathe again. For that I was grateful.

"Damn!" yelled the younger officer, bursting back into the room. "The whole thing was a trap. What the hell do we do now?"

The other officer began to chastise himself and talk about how his job was on the line at times like this. "How could I have been so stupid," he cursed himself, mumbling. Al Thurston walked into the apartment. The policeman looked up and blushed.

"It was a trap, sir." He described the man outside of the apartment and how the officers had given chase to him. He prepared for a reprimand.

Al stared at me. His eyes widened. I could see he was worried about me. "I'm okay," I said quietly. The reprimand never came.

"We have to protect her," he finally stated emphatically, pointing at me. "That, not chastising ourselves, is our primary concern."

Then he called to the paramedics. "Where are you taking them?" he questioned, apparently referring to Karen and her mother.

"To General," one answered.

Al went on, "I think I know what happened. They have been drugged, an overdose of cocaine, most probably."

"Okay sir," the paramedic answered. "We'll get them checked out."

"Are they going to be all right?" Al's face was set grimly.

The paramedic met his eyes. "Their vitals are fine. I think they've had enough drugs to scare them, but not kill them."

"I am not sure that wasn't the intent," Al stated sharply. The way he said it made chills run up and down my spine again.

I was now fully awake. All of the duct tape was gone and I could move. The paramedics had rolled me over on my back. Thankfully, they had the dignity to cover my nearly naked body with a blanket. Now that I was alive and safe I was also feeling modest and exposed.

Al leaned over me, brushing my hair back from my forehead. "How are you doing, Joyce?" he asked gently.

I nodded groggily. "Fine. I think. I was really pretty scared for a while there."

"I'm sure you were. What do you remember?"

"Almost everything." I began to tell Al about the man, his smell, his heavy breathing, the way he had first thrown me around and then how I feared being raped. I left out the sodomy fear. That thought was embarrassing enough. Besides, it didn't happen so why bring it up, I decided.

"Did he give you anything other than ether?" Al finally asked when I finished my dialogue.

I shook my head, "no." Then I thought about Karen and her mother. "How are they?" I asked nervously.

Al looked at one of the paramedics. He answered my question. "They've been drugged with something. They are unconscious. Both their pupils are equal and react to light, but the younger one's are sluggish. We need to get them both to the hospital stat."

I began to cry. I had gotten into this knowing the danger, but Karen hadn't. "She is getting married in two days," I exclaimed.

The paramedics ignored my statement. They were too busy doing their work. I watched them first take Karen and then her mother out of the apartment on stretchers with IV tubings attached. Karen's color was very pale. I was frightened that something might happen to her. I also began to feel very guilty for my own fears of rape and sodomy. The intruder had not really harmed me, so why did he hurt Karen?

The paramedics came over to take me. "No, I am fine," I insisted. "Please let me stay here."

Al interjected. "No way. You are going to the hospital to be checked out, too," he said firmly.

"Al, I am fine. Please." I sat up on the sofa. The room began to swim. The blanket fell away from my body, exposing my right breast.

Al was embarrassed. He looked away. I gathered the brief piece of fabric on my teddy and held it close to me to cover myself. "I am not leaving," I said again defiantly.

Al looked back at me. "You are stubborn." His face was angry as his eyes glared at me, but I was determined.

The medics finally told him I was stable and that the hospital would not do anything more than check me out and probably send me back home.

"See," I said proudly, my stubborness showing. After the terror I had been through nothing frightened me now. Not even Al's cold, hard glare.

The paramedics left, taking Karen and her mother. I could hear the sirens wailing up the street. Al looked very worried. I knew he was concerned for Karen, for her mother and for me.

Al began to survey the apartment. "It's a mess," he said grimly. "How did they get past the alarm system?" he questioned one of the officers.

"We don't know that yet," the officer responded.

Al and Mark went down to the basement. I listened to their conversation on the radio. "Here's the answer, Al," Mark said, calling him over. "The wires have been cut."

Al looked further. "Yup. Even the telephone wires."

Everything ws dusted for fingerprints. "I think our man is Harry Cappuzzio," Mark stated while the men sat in the living room waiting.

"I know," Al answered. "What the hell do we have her

into?" He pondered the question. "Mark, something is wrong."

"I know that," Mark said glumly, "but what?"

"Well," Al said, "my gut feelings are always right. And I'm waiting for the clues to surface."

"Any ideas, Al?"

Al sat pensively. He replayed the events. "The wires were cut. The apartment was ransacked. For what?" he exclaimed. He was silent for a minute, then went on questioning himself. "Dr. Leslie Jackson was very concerned about Joyce. Karen and her mother have been overdosed and taken to General. It has to all tie together, but how?"

By now I was fully dressed in blue jeans and a sweatshirt. I had been following Al around, listening to his every word. I forgot about the box by the door and everyone, including me, seemed to ignore it in the chaos.

"I don't know," he finally said. "Let's drive over to General and see if Karen or her mother can tell us anything."

Mark agreed. "You guys finish up here," he said adding, "and lock it up."

"Fine," the officers replied.

"Wait," I yelled, reaching for my purse. "You are not going without me."

There was no argument. Everyone understood that I needed to be with Al and I needed to see Karen. Guilt and fear consumed me. If anything happened to her, I would never forgive myself.

I raced ahead of the officers to the intensive care unit at General. General was not anything like Trinity. It was old, worn, and looked dirty. The tattered floors, walls, and furniture made the facility look like a run-down tenement.

At the unit door I stopped. Al and Mark were close behind. I pushed the door slightly open and peered inside. Lights were dim, but I saw a doctor and a nurse talking. Straining my ears I tried to find out if they were talking about Karen or her mother.

A doctor said he was "looking after the girl personally after his resident's report from the night shift in the ER." Apparently, the resident had given her a dose of narcan at 2:15 a.m., he said, after the blood and urinalysis verified cocaine present in her system. The doctor stated that his trained eyes, as he informed the nurse, had found the needle marks instantly. The resident had ordered a stat drug screen and chemical profile to recheck her electrolytes. Then the doctor instructed the nurse to "call me with the results the minute the lab sends them." The nurse mumbled a reply and he added, "At least her pupils are equal and responding to light."

It seemed to be Karen he was talking about. I wondered why Karen had been given cocaine when I had not. I began to wonder if the intruder had confused Karen for me and vice versa. Or had the intruder known Karen was about to be married and was he planning to rape her just before her wedding night? My heart raced nonstop.

I pressed my ear closer to the door. "The large dose of cocaine in her blood stream could have been lethal," the doctor said. "She's lucky that both she and the other woman had been found and that neither woman needed to be intubated." He went on to say that the anesthesiologist on call was a man he didn't respect. "We both know about his earlier mistakes. Remember that patient who had been intubated into the right lung only. Due to lack of oxygen she became brain dead."

The nurse's voice interrupted. "And then he inserted the wrong size oral endotracheal tube into a woman. He tore her phalanx."

"Of course," the doctor continued, "neither case ever went to court." Human errors were never talked about. Everyone protected their own.

As I stood there eavesdropping, I was fully aware that what I heard was a common theme in many hospitals. We all have our professionals with problems and we all protect one another. But at the same time, I reminded myself that we are all under severe pressure to save lives. I would not want to be an anesthesiologist or nurse anesthetist for anything. It would probably be too easy to make a mistake, especially when one has to make a split second decision in the life-or-death moment of crisis.

Suddenly, the nurse turned towards the door and saw me holding it slightly ajar. The doctor turned and walked away toward a nearby bed. As the nurse marched towards the door I knew it was to reprimand me.

Fortunately for me, however, Al Thurston and Mark Gibson produced their badges. "We would like to see the two women brought in tonight and talk to their doctor," Al said firmly.

The nurse looked at the men and their badges. Then she looked at me. "If you will wait here, I will have Dr. Gensing come out and talk to you." She closed the unit doors leaving the officers and myself in the outside hallway.

Dr. Gensing was Karen's doctor. In my eagerness to see her I opened the unit door again and saw the nurse approach him. Once again, I could overhear the conversation.

"Excuse me, Dr. Gensing," the nurse said walking over to him near the younger woman's bedside. "Two officers and a woman are in the hall. They want to talk to you about these patients."

Dr. Gensing nodded. I quickly shut the door. Both officers were pacing up and down and no longer paying any attention to me and my snooping.

The unit doors swung open. "Can I help you?" he asked, looking at me and then at the officers, adding, "I'm Dr. Gensing."

"Mark Gibson. This is Al Thurston." Both men produced their badges again. Then, almost as an afterthought, they introduced me. "And this is Joyce Strom. She is the roommate of the girl you brought in here."

The doctor nodded, but said nothing. "We would like to ask you about the roommate and the other woman brought in here tonight. We think it was a cocaine over-dose."

"It was," the doctor firmly stated. "But they're both going to be fine even though they are still unconscious."

"We had hoped that we could talk to them," Al said.

"I'll notify you when they wake up," the doctor said briskly.

"Please," replied Mark. He handed the doctor their business cards. "Call us as soon as they are alert."

"Fine." The doctor placed the cards in his shirt pocket and reentered the unit.

I had wanted to speak but I was unable to say anything. I could tell by the way Dr. Gensing looked at me that he probably wondered what we three women had been up to and why the police were involved.

Al and Mark decided to wait in the lounge and have a cup of the metallic coffee provided by a standard machine in the waiting room. I decided that I was not leaving my post by the door. If I was careful I could hear almost everything going on. I knew I couldn't stay by the door all night, but I was determined to stay as long as I could.

I shut the ICU doors frequently and then quietly opened them again. No one seemed to pay any attention to me.

Finally, I saw Dr. Gensing walk up to Karen's bed and I could hear his voice ask, "How are you feeling?"

"Sick," she mumbled. Then she asked, "Where am I?"

"General," came his answer. "You're fine. Do you feel like talking yet?"

Karen sounded foggy. "I guess so," she said.

I was so relieved to know she was alive and talking that I nearly raced through the door. Holding tightly on the door handle I stood my ground to listen some more.

"Well, there are two policemen waiting to see you," he stated. "If you don't feel up to it I won't tell them you are awake yet."

"Policemen?" she asked.

I knew she was confused. Dazed. Karen knew nothing of my dilemma. I wondered if she would still be my friend when she did find out, especially after her close call with death just prior to her wedding.

The doctor nodded.

"Yes," Karen finally said. "I would like to talk to them. I really don't understand anything."

"Okay." He left the bedside and began to walk towards the unit to the large double doors that I was still holding.

I shut the doors quickly and waited for him to exit. As he did so he stared at me. The look held many questions. I had several myself. However, I didn't speak. I simply stood in silence as the doctor approached.

"Al and Mark are in the lounge," I offered. I followed behind the doctor as he approached Al and Mark.

"You can see her now," he announced. "She is awake, but she is as confused as I am."

Al and Mark stood up and threw their coffee cups in the already overflowing wastebasket. Mark butted out his cigarette. I tried to be patient with them, but I was eager to see Karen. "Come on, guys," I nudged.

The doctor led the way. As the three of us approached her bedside I found myself looking at both Karen and her mother in the bed next to her.

"Will they both be all right?" I asked Dr. Gensing in a low voice.

"Yes," he replied, looking at me. "They are both very, very lucky."

"So was I," I added, feeling a need to defend myself. Without his asking I offered the doctor an explanation. "The intruder only used ether on me. I don't know why."

Dr. Gensing looked at me. His eyes were curious, but he nodded his head slowly as if to say he had seen much over the years and that nothing surprised him anymore. Certainly, working at a public hospital like General he would have seen much more violence than any of us at Trinity.

We stopped at Karen's bed. "What happened to me?" she asked, gazing first at me and then at Al and Mark. She looked confused and somewhat disoriented. Then she asked, "What happened?"

"We are not sure ourselves, Karen," Mark answered. "We think you were overdosed."

In the rush of her questions no one introduced Mark and Al. "Karen," I began, "this is Detective Al Thurston and Detective Mark Gibson. They are here to help us."

The officers produced their badges again, but Karen barely noticed. "How is my mother?" she screamed.

"You mother is fine," Dr. Gensing interjected. "She is asleep now in the bed next to you." The doctor pointed to Karen's right.

Karen looked over at her mother and lay back relieved. Then she asked, "Overdosed with what?" It was obvious that she was beginning to panic. "Joyce," she cried, "what the hell is going on?"

"Karen, try to calm yourself," I said mostly to try and calm myself. "It is a very long story. I am so sorry. They wanted me, not you."

Karen was obviously confused. "Who wants you? What is this all about? I am getting married in two days." Before I could answer she cried, "Can I go to my wedding at least?"

"We know you are getting married and, yes, you should be able to go to your wedding," Al replied. Then he realized that perhaps he shouldn't speak for the doctor.

Dr. Gensing stared at all of us. "I can't promise," he finally said, "but if you continue to improve, I don't see why not." He smiled gently and patted Karen's hand.

Karen started to cry. Softly at first and then deep heaving sobs.

I held her hand as tears flowed down my cheeks also. I felt so helpless and angry at the same time. How could someone hurt her, I wondered. It was bad enough they wanted me, but not her. She knew nothing.

When Karen finally stopped crying, Al began to question her. "Look, Karen, what do you remember?"

I knew that he was hoping Karen could provide some detail or insight into the intruder other than what I remembered.

Karen lay shaking her head. "I was asleep. I don't remember anything at all."

I searched my mind. Then it suddenly occurred to me that I had forgotten to tell Al about the box.

"Al, I just remembered something," I said urgently. "Could we go outside?"

"Karen, you get some rest now," Al said patting her on the forehead. "We will talk to you later."

Karen nodded. She rolled over and seemed to fall asleep very quickly.

The three of us turned and walked away from her bedside. I stopped at her mother's bedside and noticed that her vital signs were doing well. Her color was good. She looked as if she were sleeping a normal night's sleep.

When we were no longer where Karen could hear us I leaned towards him and said, "Al, I found a package on the doorstep when I got home and I thought it was a present and opened it." The picture of the rat oozing blood flashed through my mind. Just as it did, I felt nauseated. "I'm going to be sick," I announced, turning away and beginning to retch. The entire sequence of events had been too much for me. I could no longer endure any more traumatic mental images.

From somewhere, someone handed me an emesis basin. Al and Mark looked away, turning green themselves. I gagged, producing nothing but gastric juices. I stood alone with the basin in my hand until finally I could continue.

"The package had a decapitated rat in it," I finally announced.

Al and Mark looked at each other. "Just about the time we think you are safe, you get another message."

Mark's radio went off. He called in over the two-way speaker. I heard the call.

"Someone just came back to the apartment. We're running a make on the car and license plate."

"Did you see anyone else?" Mark asked.

"No sir. Just the car with two men in it."

"Well, we have Joyce with us at General. Karen is here along with her mother. It looks like they will be all right."

"I've called for backup, sir," came the voice over the radio again. "We'll go in as soon as they arrive."

"Fine," Mark answered. "Keep me posted."

"Why would someone want to go back to the apartment?" I asked, wiping my mouth with a tissue. My stomach was still upset, but I felt a little better.

"I wish I knew," Al stated, lost in thought. "Is there anything else you can tell me, Joyce?" he asked again, looking at me.

My knees were shaking. I shook my head. "No. I don't think so." I thought for a moment. "Wait a minute." I paused.

Al and Mark looked at me hoping I could provide them with some additional clues or details.

"I just remembered that there was something funny I heard. I'm not sure," I began carefully, "because I thought all of the background noise I had heard was the police monitor and radio receiver."

I paused, trying to concentrate. Al and Mark were impatient, but they waited in silence.

"I may have been dreaming because I lapsed in and out of consciousness, but I think the man had a radio on him. He was talking to someone."

Al and Mark were excited. "What did he say?"

I shook my head. It had begun to throb. "I just cannot remember."

They understood. "Let's get you to a safe house for some sleep, lady, and we will work on this later."

"I am exhausted,'" I said, grateful to call it a night.

As the three of us left General, it was early morning. The moon I last looked at from my bedroom window was now fading as the sun rose. Morning fog clung to the ground. Birds chirped as they always did.

I fell asleep in the patrol car. They woke me when we arrived at the apartment. As soon as I got inside I threw myself on my bed fully clothed and fell into another deep sleep.

Two officers stayed with me through the night until Al returned the next morning.

Karen and her mother were being discharged that afternoon just in time for the wedding. A dazed, angry, and confused Karen would be coming home from the hospital. Fortunately, John was bringing her, but I knew that when she arrived we had to talk about my situation and her near death. I dreaded it.

"Let's try hypnosis, Joyce," Al offered hoping he could discover some threads of evidence that neither Karen nor I could remember. Her mother had been unable to help either.

"I have never been hypnotized before," I replied adding, "and I am not sure I could be."

Al shook his head. "Well, let's give it a try. Okay?"

I agreed. Within two hours the hypnotist employed by the police department was at our apartment. When the hypnotist arrived he told me that the environment should help trigger blocked memories.

Victor Sullivan had a strong voice and equally strong hands. He also had a sensitivity and gentleness about him that made me immediately relax. As I lay on the sofa in the living room trying not to remember the position I was in on this same sofa the last time, Vic's voice began to soothe me. To my surprise I was beginning to relax and allow the tension to leave my body. I was no longer aware of the tape recorder or Al's presence.

At some point, when I was in between a waking and sleeping state, Vic began to ask me questions.

"Now, tell me what you see, Joyce," he instructed

adding that I would only witness what I described while not feeling any fear or pain.

"She hurts all over. Her body aches. I see large bruises on her legs and arms." I paused before slipping back into the first person of seeing myself. "And, I must have hit my head on something. The right temple throbs."

I didn't know how long I was unconscious. Coming to, I still felt nauseated and disoriented. After what seemed like hours, but was apparently only minutes, I realized what had happened.

The box lay on the floor, its contents still inside. The smell of the decaying carcass filled my nostrils. "What kind of a nightmare is this?" I cried.

I whispered, "Help me." I remembered wondering who would hear me and wondering where I was. Someone was knocking at my door. "Who is there?" I called out.

The door opened. "Get her up on the sofa," one of them ordered.

"Call an ambulance right away," the other screamed, using his walkie talkie and speaking to someone unknown across the air waves.

I felt my motionless body being turned over on my sofa. The room was spinning. One officer turned the lights on, hurting my eyes.

"Oh, my God," he moaned, grabbing his jacket and throwing it over me.

Suddenly the room was filled with policemen dressed in uniforms. The tall, dark man who turned me told one of the officers to check out the rest of the apartment.

"Are you all right?" he asked, ordering the other officer to bring a cool, wet washcloth for me.

"I think so," I mumbled trying to sit up.

"Just lie there," he instructed.

I knew he was right. I was too weak to move. "Where is my roommate?" I screamed. "And her mother?"

"Both Karen and her mother are fine," the officer said. "They are both going to General."

I had been repeating everything Al already knew.

While I was awake and aware of my surroundings I was also feeling foggy. Yet, I wondered if I could possibly remember anything else significant.

"Now, Joyce," Vic's soft voice continued, "try to remember the man who came into the apartment. Can you describe him? Do you remember anything about him?"

The smell of the man immediately returned. I tried to describe it. "English leather," I finally commented. "Maybe it was the leather gloves he wore when he first came in." Then I remembered the way he held me and how he lifted me to the sofa. I also remembered the tape being wrapped around me and the feeling of his glove-lined finger running up and down my leg and under my bikini. I described the events with Vic reassuring me that I was safe and not to feel the panic that was beginning to envelop me.

"Do you remember the man going into Karen's bedroom?" Vic continued on.

I thought for a moment. "Yes, I do." I was surprised at my memory. While lying on the kitchen floor I thought I had passed out, but I could hear the man's footsteps as they walked down the hall.

"Now, Joyce," Vic whispered, "do you remember anything else? Anything at all?"

My mind pushed hard for any images or memories. Suddenly, as if a dam had broken loose, I remembered hearing the moans of someone, probably Karen. Then I realized that I heard the man talking to someone.

Al's voice penetrated my hearing. "Ask her what she heard."

Vic continued with the questioning as my mind raced ahead.

"Someone is saying, 'You stupid son of a bitch. How could you do this?'" I said. "The voice was male and I thought it was coming over some kind of radio."

"Go on," Vic instructed.

Taking a deep breath, I continued.

"It is dark in here, Ralph. How the hell do I know which one is which?" The man's response was nervous.

Ralph apparently spoke again. "Well, what are you going to do about it? I want her taken care of. Do you understand?"

"Look," the intruder said, "I gave one of them an overdose of cocaine. There is an older woman in here. I gave her just a small dose. This is getting complicated, Ralph. I can't tell them apart in the dark. And they have a police monitor I switched off in the kitchen, but there has to be another. The cops think I am here and they are on their way back."

Ralph was livid with anger. "You screwed it up, Harry. I wanted you to bring me the ICU nurse and find out what she knows. She was seen leaving the OR by Leslie Jackson the other night. I don't give a damn what Paul Thompson says, I am not sure she can be trusted." Ralph paused, still mumbling over the radio receiver.

"I have got to get out of here," Harry whispered in a determined voice.

"Yeah," came the reply, "but don't forget to leave the transmitter."

Al was apprehensive and on edge. "Where is the transmitter?" I heard him ask.

Vic didn't need to instruct me. I remembered the man whose name was Harry turning furniture over in the living room. He played with a lamp on the end table. While I continued to lie on the sofa speaking, Al began to check all of the lamps.

"Son of a bitch," he groaned, finding the tiny transmitter in the lamp shade. "We've been had."

I was still in a twilight sleep with flashing images coming at me. I continued to repeat what I had overheard that night, images and words that had been locked deep within my subconscious.

"Boss, the cops are too close. I can't get the transmitter to work."

"Get the hell out of there. Go back later when it is safe," the man on the other end of the receiver instructed.

I didn't hear any more conversation. The man turned off his radio and then approached me, running his finger up an down my leg. I began to shiver.

Vic brought me out of the trance. "Was I really hypnotized?" I asked, feeling somewhat dazed and confused.

"Do you remember everything you said?" Vic queried.

I nodded. "Why didn't I remember all of that the night of the incident?"

"It is not uncommon to block memories from our minds, Joyce," Victor replied. "That is where hypnosis works."

I looked over at Al. "Is that the transmitter?"

He nodded. The look on his face was one of anger and disgust.

"You mean someone knows all about this?"

Al was flushed. "Probably," he said. "At least this explains one thing."

"What is that?" I was frightened.

"Someone came back here at 4:00 a.m. while we were at the hospital."

"The two men you were radioed about," I commented, nodding my head.

Al shook his head in agreement. "Probably to connect this thing."

"Al, is it possible that it isn't working and I'm still safe?" I didn't want all of my work to end now.

"God, I hope so," Al said soberly. Al thanked Vic, as I did. Then he telephoned his station for someone to come and check out the transmitter. In the meantime, Karen and her mother came home from the hospital.

I looked at my friend as she walked through the door with John. I realized she was very angry with me.

Karen sat in a corner chair near the sofa and glared at me. "Do you want to tell me what this is all about?" she asked in an icy tone.

"How are you feeling, Karen?" I said, hoping to stall for time.

"I'm fine," she answered in the same bitter, aloof fashion.

There was a knock at the door and I felt momentarily saved. Mark Gibson entered along with a policeman I had never met. After the introductions and questions about our health one officer moved into a corner with Al and the tiny transmitter. The two men kept their heads together talking softly. I couldn't hear them.

It was Mark who finally offered Karen an explanation when she made the request of me again. "Joyce has been working with us on an important case. It's not safe to tell you about it. But," he added almost cautiously, "John has been closely involved with her and with these men."

Karen was shocked and confused. "What could John possibly be doing with Joyce and these men?"

Mark Gibson introduced himself and then Detective Al Thurston and Lieutenant Bjorn Trinker.

The lieutenant took out a small black bag containing electrodes and began to probe at the transmitter. Al's pensive face broke into a smile. Finally I asked Al, "What does all of this mean?"

"It means that we are getting close to someone who doesn't want us to." Then he added, "We think Harry really screwed everything up. This device doesn't work. Thiat is probably why he came back later, only he couldn't fix it then either."

I let out a sigh of relief. "Then, my cover is not blown. I am still safe."

"As safe as you can possibly be under the circumstances, although I don't call dead rats and attacks on your life safe," Al responded.

Karen was agitated. "What is going on?" she cried. John hugged her and held her close. She began to sob on his shoulder hysterically.

"Honey, look. We have kept you out of this intentionally." John sat holding her and rocking her as if she were only a small infant.

The officers asked Karen if she could remember anything at all about that night. "No. Nothing. My mom went to sleep in the guest room. I went to bed. The next thing I knew I was in the hospital feeling sick." Karen paused. "What did happen?"

"You and your mother were given an injection of cocaine." It was Al who responded to her question. "We have to swear you to secrecy about this, Karen," the lieutenant said.

Karen nodded. "John and I are getting married tomorrow. I am leaving for my honeymoon right after the wedding. I will never speak a word about this incident to anyone."

Karen's mother was confused and very upset. She was concerned about her daughter's safety.

"How could this happen?" she asked her daughter's fiancé.

"I'm sorry, mom. She really wasn't supposed to be involved in this," John said. "It is Joyce they were after. They probably suspect she is an agent."

"Do you think anyone suspects I'm a narc?" I asked Al. I didn't want to explain anything further to Karen. The more she knew the more danger she was in, and I knew John wasn't happy about it. He loved her and wanted to protect her. I wondered if anyone loved me and wanted to protect me. To these officers I was part of the job and their case. Protecting me was a legal duty, not an emotional one.

"Al, can I ask you something?" I whispered, not wanting Karen to hear. He nodded, leaning closer to me. "I have seen a lot of movies. Is this the kind of thing that organized crime might do?" I wondered if I was being overdramatic.

Al confirmed my suspicions. "I'm afraid it could be, Joyce. We have always wondered how prescription drugs stolen in the medical facilities could be sold on the streets."

I really wanted Al to lie, but since he hadn't, I needed to continue the conversation. "Look, Al. You and I both know that nurses, doctors, and probably other medical professionals are stealing drugs and taking them. I have seen Carol injecting herself. I have found the vials with cut-off bottoms glued back on, keeping the sterile pull tabs intact. I know that drugs are hidden in small boxes in the medicine counter tops. But, I don't know who removes them. Or how. Or where they go from the hospital." I paused, gathering my thoughts. "If they are sold, who gets the money?" I thought of my dinner conversation with Melanie about those staff members who had expensive cars and diamond jewelry.

"That's what we have been trying to find out for a long time," he quietly answered. "And you are real close to a lot of answers. We have a lot of suspects, but we still need the proof."

"What else do you need?" I asked wearily.

"We need to know who takes the drugs from the counter tops and how they are transferred out of the hospital."

"How am I going to find that out?"

Al didn't reply immediatley. He seemed to be lost in thought. "Well, our job is to help you, but we need you on the inside to continue being our eyes." Again, he sat silently. "Look, Joyce, I know this is getting dangerous, but I can only try to convince you that we are close at all times."

I nodded slowly. My mind raced on. "Do you think Dr. Jackson had anything to do with this?" I voiced out loud.

"Your guess is as good as mine," he replied. "When are you on duty again?"

"I have the weekend off for the wedding, but I'm back on the schedule on Monday."

Karen came over to me, interrupting our conversation. "John just told me everything, Joyce. I am so scared for you."

Al and John exchanged glances. "I had to tell her, Al," John said. "She will be in danger now too. In fact, I really want her to resign and leave Trinity."

"I agree. She should leave as soon as possible," Al said somberly. It was obvious that he was not happy to have Karen in on my role as an undercover agent. Not when we lived together and worked in the same facility.

Karen's voice quivered. "I agree with John, Joyce. I am going to resign. I am scared." She squeezed my hand. "I don't know how you do it," she exclaimed.

Lieutenant Trinker walked over. "Al, do you need me anymore?"

Al waved him on. "No, go home. Mark and I will stay here with Joyce and Karen until they decide where they are going to spend the night."

John announced that he and Karen would stay in his apartment after the prenuptial dinner. Karen's mother said she and Karen's father, who was joining her that night, would check into a hotel.

Al told me that I could stay with him. I envied Karen in that she was being rescued in just a few short hours. Still, it was comforting to know I wouldn't be alone.

I spent the rest of the day trying to feel better and preparing for the wedding. Karen's color was beginning to come back. "We'll meet you at the church at 6:30 for the rehearsal. Then we will all drive to the restaurant together after. Okay?" she asked me a trifle apologetically. "You'll be all right, won't you?"

I nodded. John drove Karen off. We had agreed that after the honeymoon she would empty out the remaining things she had in the apartment. Fortunately, she had already taken many of her possessions to John's. They would be living there after the wedding.

Al and Mark waited for me to pack. Both men were determined to stay close to me. Karen invited them to attend the rehearsal dinner and wedding service.

"Tonight we'd better wait outside," Mark replied. "Paul is supposed to be taking Joyce to the dinner and we'd be noticed. We'll attend church tomorrow. Even though he's supposed to be there too, it will be easy for us to be inconspicuous with all the people present."

I had forgotten all about Paul. He had said he would take me if he had the time off. I called his apartment and got his answering machine. Then I called the hospital and paged him.

Finally, he answered in that husky voice which made me remember him so well.

I flushed red. "Paul, this is Joyce. I hope I didn't disturb you."

"No. It's perfectly okay. What's up?" he asked.

"Well, Karen's wedding is tomorrow and the rehearsal dinner is tonight. Can you still go?"

"Oh, Joyce, I am so sorry. I really forgot. I agreed to work this weekend rotation. We're a little short around here."

Unexpectedly, I felt disappointed. "No problem, Paul. Thanks anyhow."

"Look, I really am sorry. I will try to make it up to you," he said softly.

"Paul, I understand," I replied. ."I'll see you the first of the week."

"Bye," he said, hanging up.

Trying to evaluate my mixed-up feelings, I realized I was disappointed, but I was also relieved. Now Al and Mark could stay with me until the wedding was over. I knew I was safer with them.

The officers talked among themselves. "I'll be with you all weekend, Joyce," Al offered. "We will have other agents close by, but I think we will give Mark the weekend off."

I nodded, trying to be brave. "I really don't need two of you."

"Look, if you want me to stay . . ." Mark said agreeably.

"No, really." I shook my head.

Mark thanked me. "Well, have fun and stay safe. I'll talk to you both later." He left.

Al helped me carry my clothes and bridesmaid's gown to his car. We agreed that I would take my car and leave it at his apartment.

Returning to Al's apartment and my old guest room, I almost felt at home. Then I realized life was becoming very complicated when I felt comfortable staying overnight at a police agent's apartment for the second time. I prayed that my ordeal would end soon. I wanted to get on with my own life.

The ivy-covered stone church was quaint and old. A white satin sheet would be rolled down the aisle for the wedding service the next day. The priest lined us all up and directed us when and how to walk down the aisle. He also made sure we would all go to confession in order to receive communion during the high mass ceremony.

I agreed to go to confession after the rehearsal. I wondered what I would say. Karen looked a little pale but happy as she walked down the aisle on her father's arm. I knew that tomorrow she would be the traditional glowing bride. Her mother was still disoriented. When she complained of a headache, we all understood.

Our appetites were small at the elegant dinner her parents had planned. The restaurant was a lovely, picturesque inn high on a hill overlooking the island. The food was four-star. Normally, I loved French food and vintage French wine, but that night the thought of piquant sauces and creamed desserts made my stomach queasy.

Karen and her mother felt the same. I merely wet my

lips as we toasted the bride and groom. My wine glass remained full all night. I picked at dinner and was glad when the evening finally ended at 11:00 p.m. Fortunately, the wedding was not until 2:00 p.m. the next day.

My heart had been pounding all day. I felt short of breath and kept having hot flashes along with a persistent nauseous feeling. Driving with Al back to his apartment I told him how unwell I felt.

"That's pretty normal," he replied. "Ether can cause some pretty strange reactions, you know."

"My entire body feels like it is still in overload. How long does this last?" I asked hoarsely.

"Until your liver and kidneys detox the stuff."

"I guess I knew that from training," I smiled faintly.

"Even professionals need reassurance once in a while," Al said gently.

Though I kept telling myself I was safe with Al around, when I did sleep it was fitfully. I had nightmares. The next morning I still felt tired and queasy.

When Al put scrambled egg in front of me, I pushed them away. "I just can't. My stomach is still upset."

"Just drink some clear liquids," Al advised.

"Now who's playing doctor?" I tried to joke. But I knew he was right, so I did. All too soon it was time for me to drive to John's apartment and help Karen dress for her wedding. For the last time, I buttoned the twenty-five pearl buttons up the back of her dress.

"You look gorgeous," I exclaimed, helping her adjust her headpiece and fix her shiny brown hair under it.

"I wish I felt a little better," she answered. "I can't tell whether I am nauseous because I'm nervous getting married or because of the kidnapping."

I concurred. "I don't feel so hot myself."

"Joyce," Karen cautioned, taking my hands away from her veil and holding them tightly, "I am worried about you. Do you have any idea how much danger you are in?"

"I know, Karen," I replied. "I can't tell you that I'm

not scared. I am. But I have to finish this job. If someone doesn't stop these people we all might be in danger. I have seen more than you can imagine."

"Like what?" she asked.

"I have seen one nurse actually injecting herself with drugs. I have been told that many more nurses, and doctors, here at the hospital do the same thing. I have seen nurses stealing drugs from their patients and giving them sterile water instead. I know how many drugs are exchanged in vials. Someone cuts the bottom off, empties the contents, and glues the bottom back on. The sterile ring on top isn't tampered with."

I paused to catch my breath. I wondered how much more I should share with Karen.

"Go on," she prompted.

"Well, I know how drugs are stolen in both our unit and in the OR. There is a crack built into the top of the medicine counter where nurses slide the drugs through. A metal box underneath catches them."

It was Karen's turn to be shocked. She sat down suddenly, looking pale and shaky.

"Are you all right?" I asked.

"I think so. But all this stuff you're telling me makes me feel very anxious."

"What I am telling you," I continued, 'is making me very angry. These drugs are removed from the hospital somehow. I don't know how yet. Then, they're sold. Apparently, many of our nurses are paid off for stealing them."

"By wasting them, you mean."

I nodded. "Yes. At the end of each shift, we co-sign the wasting of numerous drugs although we never really check to see that they are wasted."

"What else goes on?" Karen asked.

"That's about all I know about the drug ring. Except that I suspect that Paul uses drugs, too." I contemplated telling her about the butyl nitrite, but decided against it.

Karen stood up. Her long gown billowed out, white and filmy. She held her dainty lace sleeves out for me to button at the wrists. We were both silent for a few minutes until she finally said, "How would I know if a nurse or doctor was using anything?"

"Well, there are many signs and symptoms. Sloppy charting. Poor dress. Long sleeves even in the summer. Frequent trips to the bathroom. Giving more meds than others or asking to give meds more often than others. Wasting a great deal. Bloodshot eyes. Stuffy noses. Dilated pupils. Irritability. That's a pretty good list to start with."

"Some of those symptoms might be attributed to burn-out," Karen said.

"I know. But when a lot of them occur together it's probably not stress but drug-related," I said slowly.

"Why do they do it, Joyce? Why do they take drugs?"

"Al took me to an AA meeting to understand that one, Karen. Some people find living very painful. Drugs and alcohol make that pain go away, if only temporarily. Cravings and addictions are the by-product. Most of those who use crack or other stuff talk about how addicting it is and how they "Jones" when they don't have it. But they still mess up their heads and bodies with it."

"You feel pretty strongly about it all, don't you?" Karen asked.

I nodded vehemently.

"You are in the wrong part of nursing," Karen admonished. "I don't think you should stay in critical care. It sounds to me like you should go into psychiatry or chemical abuse."

"When all of this is over I am probably going to switch fields. I have been thinking about going back to school, too."

Karen nodded. "I think you should. I admire you, my friend. Just take care of yourself."

We embraced. One final hug of two women who had survived more than nurses' training. "I think we had better get you to the church."

"I am ready," Karen said mistily.

I handed her the basket of lavender roses she was to

carry. Grabbing my own bouquet, I stepped out of the bedroom close behind her. John had gone ahead to the church. Karen was determined that tradition remain undisturbed. He could not see her before the wedding.

Outside we paused by the limousines to have pictures taken. The other bridesmaids, who had dressed at Karen's mother's hotel room, joined us at curbside. There were three from high school and her flower girl, a twelve-year-old niece. Karen looked wonderful. I envied her the bliss and safety that lay ahead. A chill of fear tingled down my spine. Today I could relax and enjoy her wedding, but thoughts of Monday morning already frightened me.

Standing in the rear of the church I glanced around. Almost all of the pews were filled. Satin-ribboned candles on bedecked bronze stands lined the aisles.

Pink and lilac flowers were everywhere, on the altar and tied to the first three pews on both sides for the family members. The smell of sweet incense drifted down the aisle. It was to be a high mass.

John stood at the front of the altar looking nervous and excited. He stared down the aisle trying to catch a glimpse of Karen. She hid behind us. Her mother took pictures excitedly, outdoing the professional photographer hired for the day. I watched her closely for signs of illness, but she looked happy, healthy and joyous.

The bridesmaids began the slow, steady walk down the long aisle past faces straining to admire and see them. The flower girl scattering rose petals looked adorable. Whispers were heard everywhere. Weddings were always exciting.

I began my slow descent down the aisle looking directly ahead at John and his party. I avoided eye contact with the priest. My confession had been short and not quite truthful. I had left out most of the sordid details of my present life.

My knees were shaking. I could barely walk with a steady gait. Fears of walking down the aisle for my own wedding drifted through my mind. I thought about Karen. I knew she was nervous also.

I moved past the front pews. Both mothers smiled proudly. Corsages of pink roses and pink carnations with mauve ribbons matching our dresses were pinned on each. Each of the men had one small pink rose in his buttonhole. We smiled first to the left and then to the right. I felt as if my face would crack.

When I stopped in front of the altar, the traditional wedding march began. Karen began to move, hanging tightly onto her father's left arm. She walked slowly for all to see and admire her. Brides are always radiant and beautiful. Karen was no exception.

The service took nearly one hour. We stood, knelt, sang, prayed and took communion. Finally, the priest declared John and Karen "man and wife." Before he could tell them to kiss they were locked in a deep, passionate embrace.

The couple gleefully clung together walking back up the aisle towards the back of the church. I followed with my arm linked through John's best man, his older brother, Scott. Scott's wife, who was seven months pregnant, beamed at him from her place in the groom's front row pews. Scott smiled back.

We stood in the back of the church forming the traditional wedding line—greeting guests, being introduced, and shaking hands.

At the country club, the reception bubbled over with champagne and music. Al stayed with me the rest of the day, although I had to sit at the front table for dinner. Later, we danced together and mingled among the guests.

Wedding cake, champagne, toasts, gifts, dancing, and pictures finally brought the day to a close. Karen and John departed in their limousine. Mounds of pastel confetti flew on and about them as I watched the happy couple drive away.

"Shall we go?" Al asked, standing with me in the driveway as guests left to return inside.

"I'd love to," I replied wearily. "Do you think we can go home? To your home, I mean."

"Sure."

We said our "goodbyes" to the family. Karen's mother told me to "be careful." I knew what she meant.

Al and I left. I was glad that I had not caught Karen's bouquet. I knew I was not going to be the next single woman to get married. At the moment, I wondered if I would ever be married.

Entering the hospital on Monday morning I felt like I was being watched. I was still wired, but I felt the eyes watching me were not friendly.

The elevator doors closed and then re-opened on the first floor. I should have walked, I thought. A large, dark, heavyset man entered the elevator. He stared at me. Something about him seemed all too familiar.

I didn't want to stare at him. From my vantage point I could only see the large, hairy hands hanging next to his side. The ride to the third floor was making me more and more nervous. I felt myself to be in a time warp, afraid I would never arrive.

Finally, the elevator door opened. I raced out of the enclosed place and ran to the unit. Once inside I remembered why the man seemed so familiar. He was the man I saw with Dr. Jackson in the OR.

I wondered if he was the connection for taking drugs out of the hospital. I had overheard him telling Dr. Jackson something about quotas. I was scared. My heart pounded like a freight train in my chest. But it was only 6:45 a.m. I had fifteen minutes before I had to clock in.

I wondered where the man had gone. Could I find him? I left the unit headed back for the elevator hoping to see where it stopped. Unfortunately, it stopped at every floor. "What were the chances of my finding this man in the next few minutes?" I asked myself. Then I asked myself, "and if I did, then what?"

"Al," I whispered, touching my microphone and hoping he could hear me, "I just saw the man from the OR with Dr. Jackson. He was on the elevator with me. I might be crazy, but I think he was intentionally following me. I am going to retrace my steps to see if I can find him."

I pushed the down button on the same elevator. The door opened. I entered the filled car with other hospital employees and visitors. We all rode in silence to the first floor. The door opened. As I walked out into the lobby I noticed him.

He was in the hallway next to the radiology department. His back was to me, but I knew it was him by the hands. He stood talking to someone. I walked around the corner to hide from their view.

"I found him, Al," I whispered again. "On the first floor by the radiology department. He has a light blue suit on, is about 6'1" tall maybe 220 lbs, dark curly hair, and massive hairy hands."

I peered around the corner from my spot, glancing quickly across the room. Who was he talking to? I couldn't see the face clearly. A man, definitely, with a white lab coat on.

The clock on the wall said 6:55 a.m. I had to get upstairs. Turning from my place I pushed the elevator button again. Fortunately, the door immediately opened. I entered and pushed the number three for the third floor.

As the doors closed I continued to look at the man's back trying to see the full face view of who he was talking to. Suddenly, the man in the white lab coat turned his face towards me. So did the other man. Just as the elevator doors closed they both caught a glimpse of me. And I got a good look at them.

The dark-haired man was the same. The other man was Dr. Ralph Vorhees. Chief of Open Heart Surgery.

I raced into the unit. Marilyn and Lois were preparing for report. We had a full house again. I could tell that by the patient name board.

"Let's go, Strom," Marilyn called carrying the patient kardex into the nurses' lounge.

Report was always the same and always took close to an hour. Only the patients and their diagnoses were different. Today, however, one patient's name stood out.

Sara Kremantz had been admitted the previous day with a ruptured aneurysm. She was oriented and alert, although her pupils were sluggish. Her speech was slurred. Emergency surgery was done on Sunday night. A large bleeder was found deep inside her skull and clamped off. The neurosurgeon felt he had found the main bleeder, although her CAT scan and MRI showed another small ballooning deep inside the skull. The surgeon was unable to reach that one.

As the night nurse gave report on Sara she finally ended it by saying, "and you will all probably remember that she is Janice Dexter's older sister."

We all began to stir and whisper. I wondered what the chances were of having two sisters admitted in less than a month with the same diagnosis. One had died. According to report, there was now concern for Sara's life. And, if she survived, there was even more concern for her mental status.

Momentarily I forgot about Dr. Vorhees and the large, heavyset man. After report I returned to the unit. I was inside the cubicle of one of my two patients, giving a bedbath. Unlike most of the unit patients who seem to go from one crisis to another, this patient was going to be transferred to the floors for post-op surgical care.

He had ruptured two discs in his lower back. They had been surgically incised on a previous occasion. The man had continued to have problems and another herniation. His present surgery had been done to fuse his discs. He was stable, awake, and alert.

We were making small talk about his health and recovery when the cubicle curtains suddenly opened. Dr. Vorhees and Dr. Jackson entered. Both men looked directly at me.

"Good morning, doctors," I said trying to be polite and keep my nervous voice calm. "How can I help you?"

Dr. Jackson replied first. "Just checking on our patient." He looked at my patient lying in bed with his top partially exposed for his bedbath. "Good morning, Mr. Tiner. How are you feeling today?"

Mr. Tiner stated, "Fine, thank you. Are you going to get me out of this zoo today, doc?"

Dr. Jackson nodded. "Yes. You can be transferred any time."

"After your bath and morning care, Mr. Tiner," I interjected.

Dr. Vorhees continued to stare at me. He made me very nervous. He seemed to know it, too. There was no rationale for him to be there. He was not the surgeon on this case nor was he involved in any of the patient's medical problems.

I avoided meeting his eyes. Finally, the two men left. My hands were shaking. Mr. Tiner looked at me. "You shouldn't let those doctors get to you, Miss Strom. They are human, too."

I chuckled. I knew he meant well. He just had no idea why I felt so fearful.

The rest of the day passed fitfully. I could tell when Carol slipped drugs into the counter top slit and I could also tell when she had given herself an injection. One minute she would be nasty and irritable. The next, she was smiling, friendly, and passive. Her personality changes and mood swings were dramatic. I figured out that she must have injected herself twice on our shift.

Clocking out I whispered into my microphone that I was going off duty. I thought I was safe until I entered the elevator and found both Dr. Jackson and Dr. Vorhees inside. Thank goodness two visitors accompanied us on our elevator ride. On the second floor, I got out watching the doors close behind me.

Then, I raced to the stairwell trying to decide if I should go down or run up. They probably would be on the bottom waiting for me, I thought, so I chose to run up. At the fourth floor, I left the stairwell. I walked down the hall to the elevator trying to look as if nothing had happened.

I pushed the button and felt the elevator lurch to the first floor. The doors opened. I kept my finger on the button and looked out. The lobby was filled with guests and staff. I surveyed the area, but didn't see either physician.

Cautiously I got out. Suddenly I noticed them by the front door talking together and looking around the lobby. "I'm in trouble," I whispered frantically fingering the mike.

I raced down the hall in the opposite direction. Offices lined the hallway. I sensed that one or both doctors were on my heels. The only door I could safely enter was the small chapel.

I pushed the door to the chapel open and jumped inside. Panic set in. My heart raced. "Now, what do I do?" I asked myself. I was afraid to talk. Afraid of revealing my microphone and afraid of being overheard.

I suddenly slid under a pew laying my body lengthwise to hide it. From my hiding spot I could see their feet moving up and down the small aisle.

"I know she came in here," I heard Dr. Vorhees say.

"There is no other way out," Dr. Jackson added.

I was praying that the officers outside would overhear the conversation. I was also praying that the two doctors wouldn't find me. I dared not breathe.

"We know you are in here, young lady," Dr. Vorhees called out. "We are only going to give you a warning, so listen carefully."

Dr. Jackson spoke up. "Quit snooping around here. We don't like it. This time we're giving you a warning."

They stopped talking, still moving up and down different aisles. Both sets of feet were getting closer and closer to me. I was scared to death that they would find me.

"We don't want to hurt you," Dr. Vorhees added. "You can be a part of a good thing if you want."

"But we are watching you," Dr. Jackson added. "And, we will hurt you if we have to."

Both pairs of feet stopped. Right beside the pew I was lying under. Could they see me, I wondered. I held my breath and closed my eyes tightly.

Suddenly, I heard the chapel door open. I could hear voices entering the room. As the doctors prepared to leave one bent down towards my pew. "We are watching you," he whispered.

Chills raced up and down my back. The feet walked away. I heard them leave. A door shut.

"Are you all right, Joyce?" a familiar voice asked.

Moving out from under the pew I was relieved to see Al's face. I grabbed at him and began sobbing. "Thank God."

"Al, they have seen you now. They know something is up."

He nodded. "They don't know exactly what. They are not sure of you or what you know. But it's getting dangerous for you. Maybe we had better tell Sister Theresa this thing is over with."

I suddenly regained my composure. From somewhere, deep inside of me, I said "No. I will see this through."

THIRTEEN

Back at his apartment, Al and I talked the night away. I felt like everything was closing in on me. Both Dr. Vorhees and Dr. Jackson were threatening me. And Paul seemed to be avoiding me.

"Where do we go from here?" I finally asked Al while we washed the dinner dishes together.

"I'm not sure, Joyce. We still need to know how the drugs leave the hospital, and we need to catch Harry Cappuzzio with them. By the way, we did find one fingerprint on that last gift package you received."

"The box that arrived before the kidnapping?" I asked, shuddering as I remembered again the awful sight.

Al shook his head. "The same. The print did belong to Mr. Cappuzzio. Now we know we are on the right trail. Especially since your description of the man calling the shots during the kidnapping fits him too."

"If he's that involved," I interrupted, "he's probably going to make another attempt."

Sober-faced, Al met my eyes. "That's a pretty sure conclusion," he said. His calm, serious words had an edge of tension.

"Yes, I thought so." My voice sounded shaky. "I wonder what the real reasons are behind these men's connection to drugs.

Do you think more professionals steal drugs to sell them, or to take them?" I inquired out of curiosity.

Al pondered the question for a moment. "Frankly, I think the addiction rate is higher and most missing drugs are probably being taken by professionals for their own dependencies. This drug ring at your hospital has unusual aspects."

"Would hospital drug rings be going on elsewhere?"

"With a few innovations," Al said. "Just about the time we think we have all of the answers some criminal thinks of something new."

"So," I continued, "I go to work tomorrow as if nothing ever happened."

"You did agree to continue on with this," Al reminded. "Yes. Go to work. Keep yourself busy and surrounded by others at all times. And remember, we are not too far away."

As close a call as it had been in the chapel with the two doctors, Al was right. He had raced in to save me. I felt better and somewhat distant from the hospital's problems.

The unit, the next morning, brought reality back to me. It was business as usual: Marilyn receiving report, my assignment on the patient name board along with the other nurses, Carol still giving meds. I hadn't given meds to any great degree. Lois was careful to limit my exposure.

Melanie was on duty with me. It had been a while since we had talked about any of the unit gossip. I hoped we would have some time together during the day. If anyone knew what was going on, she did.

One of my patients, Mrs. Kendall, was a chronic emphysema patient who had a tracheostomy. She was connected to an MA-1 respirator. Mrs. Kendall was originally a patient on one of the medical floors. Her total lung capacity was only twenty percent due to the dead tissue in them. While on the floors she had a slight stroke and was transferred to our unit for observation.

Mrs. Kendall, who was seventy-two, was still alert

and oriented. She had petitioned the courts for the "right to die." She had requested her own "death with dignity." She had even gone as far as to ask to go home and die with the assistance of hospice care.

I respected and admired her willingness to fight for her belief. We took care of her physical needs, while her lawyers worked on meeting her spiritual and emotional needs. I spent time talking to her while caring for her. I tried to find words that would comfort and support her.

My other patient was a nineteen-year-old boy who had been thrown over one hundred feet from his motorcycle. Spring and summer had come—unfortunately, one of the signs of better weather was motorcycles. They caused traumatic injuries like the ones Brian had.

Brian had broken his first two cervical vertebrae in the fall. Crutchfield tongs pierced both sides of his shaven scalp. The tongs looked like they met somewhere in the middle of his head. Surrounding each tong were betadine-soaked gauze sponges. Heavy weights were suspended behind him. The sight looked painful; but we were assured that no pain was felt in the skull bones as no nerves go through the bones.

Brian was also on a respirator. If he survived the next two weeks he would also be trached. I noticed that his foley catheter still drained blood-tinged urine. The impact must have done some damage to his kidneys or bladder. We were infusing blood into him along with IV's. His mother was close by, tearful, anxious, and depressed. I could feel her pain as memories of other critically ill young people I had seen in the unit flashed before my eyes.

"Hi, Joyce," Melanie said, walking by me to find dressings for her patient. "How was the wedding?"

I spun around. "Oh, it was beautiful, Melanie. Maybe I will get to tell you about it at lunch."

"I hope so," she called back.

We met in the nurses' lounge for a coffee break at

10:15 a.m. "It's pretty busy around here again," I commented.

Melanie said, "It sure is. We had one hell of a weekend, as you can see."

"Worse than what is out there today?" I asked.

"I am afraid so," she replied. "We had two codes on Saturday. One patient died. Your patient tried to disconnect her respirator all weekend and nearly succeeded during the codes. The patient in number ten, a fresh post-op gastrectomoy (removal of part of his stomach) bled out on Sunday. Plus, we admitted your young motorcycle accident just before clocking out on Sunday. What a weekend."

"It sounds awful," I grimaced. "I'm glad I was at a wedding."

"So, tell me about it," Melanie said excitedly. "I love weddings."

I described the bridesmaids' gowns and Karen's. I told her about the rehearsal dinner and reception at the country club. But I didn't tell her I was attacked or that Karen was drugged just before the event. I also didn't tell her I was not staying at home.

"What else is happening around here, Mel?" I asked, hoping she had some gossip and would share it.

Melanie paused for a minute. "Well, let's see. Did you know about the resident in anesthesia who was busted for possession?"

My ears perked up. "No. Who?"

"A doctor by the name of Hamilton. I don't know him personally. Apparently he was a transfer from General. All I know is that he had a lot of pills on him. Valium. Librium. Tuinal. Seconal. And," she added, "he also had a syringe and an ampule of morphine."

"What's going on around here!" I exclaimed. "Tell me more."

Melanie continued. "There has been nothing in the newspapers, though. Strange, huh?"

"I don't think so, Mel. No one wants to talk about our internal problems. We do protect our own."

She agreed and then she changed the subject. "Paul has been looking for you."

"Paul? Why? He knows I was at Karen's wedding. He had to take the weekend rotation."

Melanie's smile twisted into a mischievous one. "But he says he hasn't been able to reach you all weekend. He wants to know if you are dating someone else?"

I had forgotten to check in with my answering machine. I wondered who might be worried about me, like my mother. "I'm not dating anyone else," I replied.

"You really like Paul, don't you?" she asked.

"Yes." It was true. I did. I was torn between what was right and ethical versus my passion and desire. My mind wandered to Paul and to our intense moments.

Melanie sensed my straying thoughts. "It's time to go back to work, Strom," she announced, standing up and gently punching me on the leg. "Save the memories for off duty," she laughed.

I was taking care of Brian, doing his morning care and changing his dressing, when Dr. Peters, making rounds with the interns, entered the unit. The routine was always the same. Dr. Peters would stop at each bedside and review the chart, especially the nurses' notes. Doctors are dependent upon us to document and record everything. We are their eyes and ears. Dr. Peters would then ask the interns rapid-fire questions about the patient, the diagnosis, the prognosis, and the treatment.

Dr. Peters was strict. He always embarrassed and reprimanded the students in front of everyone. His rationale was to make them each a "top quality doctor," but as he stood yelling at one young female intern I couldn't help thinking about "Code Pink." I was almost tempted to call one. However, I was not on sure footing myself, so I kept my mouth shut.

I was lost in thought and grateful when they finally moved from Brian to their next patient. My IV was off and

I was checking the needle site to make sure it was still in the vein.

"Good morning, Joyce," a soft, famliar voice cooed in my ear.

I could feel chills of excitement running up and down my spinal column. "Good morning, doctor," I replied, trying to sound indifferent.

"I have been looking all over for you," he whispered as he moved closer to my back and touched my hair lightly with his fingertips.

I tried to continue my work. The IV site looked like it had come out of the vein. I was going to have to pull it and begin a new IV. "I was busy," I answered.

"I know. Karen's wedding. How was it?"

"Very nice. Sorry you couldn't make it," I added, tearing down the IV in Brian's hand. "I have to stick him again," I announced, turning away and hoping he would leave me alone. My hands were trembling. I was thankful that Brian was still unconscious. That made my work a little easier.

"Need help?" he asked again, adding, "and I am sorry too."

"No thank you. I can manage." I began to take the IV tray off the bedside stand. Opening a new sterile IV tubing I connected it to the IV bottle and let the fluid drain to clear air out of the line. Then I opened my needle and prepared to look for a good vein site.

Paul stood watching me. The hair on the back of my neck was standing up on end. He watched me wrap the tourniquet around Brian's arm and palpate the area for a bulging vein. I soon found one and prayed I could stick it on the first try. Swabbing the area, I gently, but firmly, put the needle into the vein. Blood immediately came back. I breathed a sigh of relief as I connected the IV tubing to the needle. Sticking a patient on the first try was the mark of a pro. I could perform the task under the worst of circumstances. And to me, at that moment, the worst of circumstances was standing behind me.

"Good job," Paul remarked watching me dress the IV site and write on the bandage the date and time I had changed it. Then I documented the infiltration and re-start in my nurses' notes.

"I am sorry, Paul, but I really don't have the time to talk to you right now."

"So, when will you have?" he asked, again moving his body closer to mine.

I could smell the Calvin Klein. "Damn," I thought.

"Where will you be when I get off duty?"

"Page me," he whispered. As suddenly as he was there, he left.

I caught a glimpse of his tight buttocks walking out of the unit. Dr. Peters and the interns also left. The unit was noticeably quieter. I was glad that the noise level had been so high when Paul was there.

I looked around and caught Marilyn's eye. Then I turned back to my work.

The rest of the day went smoothly. Melanie and I had lunch together, but she didn't offer any new information on any subject. If she had heard about Dr. Jackson and Dr. Vorhees, she didn't let on. I ate in silence, listening to her babble about her life.

I paged Paul when I got off duty, but he answered to tell me that he was in the ER and all hell had just broken loose. I told him I would call him later.

"Quiet day," Al inquired matter-of-factly.

"Yes, except for Paul."

"I could hear your heart pounding," he laughed. "You really like that guy, don't you?"

"I wish I didn't. It would make all of this so much easier. Unfortunately, my heart can't tell the difference like my mind can."

"Love is blind," Al quipped.

"Al," I said, changing the subject, "tell me about a

resident by the name of Hamilton. Melanie said he was arrested for possession over the weekend."

"True. But he is not part of this conspiracy. He is just your typical doctor looking to make life's pain go away."

"You know, I keep hearing about life's pain," I retorted. "My life has had a lot more pleasure than pain."

Al made sympathetic noises. "It is a matter of perspective. Believe me, Viet Nam was painful—overrun with death and violence. We never knew who the enemy was over there. Coming home, we didn't know who the enemy was here," Al said fervently.

"I can understand how you would feel that way then," I said, immediately empathizing with him. "But basically life is wonderful, or should be."

"Well," he continued quietly, "not everyone thinks so. Drugs and alcohol make the pain go away."

I worked on Tuesday and Wednesday. Thursday was my scheduled day off. Since Lois had given me the previous three-day weekend off for Karen's wedding I was working the evening shift Friday, Saturday, and Sunday.

I had also made the decision to go back to my apartment. Al was fighting me on it.

"The lines to your alarm can be cut again," he stated.

"What about the microphones you planted?" I asked. "They didn't help either apparently."

"They found the microphones," he finally admitted with embarrassment. "We hid them in the usual and obvious places."

"So, hide them some place not so usual and obvious. I am going home." I was headstrong when I wanted to be. And I wanted to be home.

Paul and I kept missing each other. My weekend on was his weekend off. He wanted me to come over Saturday night. It would be midnight before I could arrive. I thought about it all day Saturday and then phoned him from the unit at 7:30 p.m. telling him I was too tired.

I really didn't want to have to deal with facing butyl nitrite again, or anything he may have decided to offer me. Avoiding him for now was my way of coping with him. I couldn't confront him yet.

Melanie worked with me on the weekend, too. "Did you hear about Sally?" she asked during our coffee break on Sunday.

"No," I answered. I grinned. She was a walking newspaper.

"She was discharged from the psych unit last week. She resigned. Word has it she may never go back to nursing again. She really flipped out, didn't she?"

"Yes. Would you call that a nervous breakdown?" I asked.

Melanie nodded. "Yes. She keeps talking about killing patients. She's crazy if you ask me."

I didn't answer. Apparently Sally's secret had been well kept. Melanie didn't know that Sally's "hallucination" was real. I pondered Dr. Jones' position, wondering why he kept on protecting her. Perhaps he was part of the in-house conspiracy, too.

Mrs. Kendall was my patient again. I liked her, so it didn't bother me that she was assigned to me as often as she was. Her attorneys spend more time in the unit than her family.

I overheard one of them tell her, "The judge is going to make a decision and ruling on your case by Friday, Mrs. Kendall. Personally, I think it looks real good."

Mrs. Kendall nodded. She could write notes to the men, her family and the nurses on a board we had given her. She wrote furiously and they answered her questions.

After the attorneys left, along with her son, I prepared her for her evening care. I drew the cubicles, rubbed her back, tightened her sheets, and changed her gown. When she was relaxed and comfortable I sat down next to her and talked with her.

She enjoyed our time together. Usually, I told her about the world news or the weather outside. Tonight, however, she wanted to tell me the subject of conversation.

She took her pencil and board and wrote, "Something very strange happened to me. I want to tell you, but you must promise to keep it to yourself."

I just looked at her and finally said, "Yes. I promise."

Mrs. Kendall then wrote, "I was lying here in bed last night when suddenly, I felt myself floating out of my body and up to the ceiling. I looked down and saw my body in this bed."

She showed me the board. I thought she was having a bad dream, but I decided to humor her.

She continued. "The next thing I knew, I was in a tunnel. I saw a light, like a pin point, straight ahead of me. I was being pulled to the light. And, the light kept getting bigger and bigger."

I read this paragraph slowly. "Did you see anyone?"

"Then, I was in the light and my husband, Jerry, was standing there waiting for me."

She began to cry, at this point, and put the pencil down. I held her hand.

After a few moments she picked up the pencil and began writing again. "He looked so handsome. He was wearing the brown suit I gave him for our wedding. And he looked just like our wedding day picture."

I was familiar with Elizabeth Kubler-Ross's works on death and dying. For my nursing class, this was a mandatory course. Kubler-Ross had often said that we could visualize our departed loved ones in a dream. I was sure that Mrs. Kendall had such an experience.

Mrs. Kendall continued. "I could see through the light past Jerry's head into the most beautiful field I have ever seen. I saw green mountains, and colors that I can't even describe. I felt the most wonderful peace."

Her tears came again. This time heavier. Suddenly, she began to choke. I immediately suctioned her trach, helping her to bring up the thick mucus.

Mrs. Kenndall looked searchingly at me. I sat quietly. "Then, Jerry told me I had to go back. He said it wasn't my time. Suddenly, I was back here. I don't want to be here," she wrote in large letters. "I have seen death and it is nothing to fear. I want to die."

I comforted her and talked to her about how wonderful it must have been to see her husband. I couldn't answer her questions, or explain her experience, but I tried to reassure her that she wasn't crazy.

She told me she knew she wasn't crazy. Only angry. She was angry to be in a pain-ridden feeble body when she had felt peace and "unconditional" love, as she worded it.

Her experience stayed with me all night. While I never told any of the unit nurses about it, because I didn't want them to think she was crazy, or I was, I did decide to do some research.

Later that night, back in my own apartment, I found Gary Feinberg's business card. I decided to call him in the morning. Maybe he could give me a psychological explanation of what had happened to Mrs. Kendall.

D̲r. Feinberg returned my call Monday morning. Our conversation was brief and friendly. I discovered that he was married and had a newborn baby daughter. I also learned of a phenomenon with which I was unfamiliar.

"Have you ever heard of the Near Death Experience?" he asked.

"No," I answered honestly.

"Well, research on it is pretty new. I suggest that you read two books by Dr. Raymond Moody," "Life After Life," and "Reflections of Life After Life." I purchased both on my way to the hospital that day.

During the afternoon break, I grabbed a few minutes to read one or two case histories that Dr. Moody presented. In the unit I raced over to Mrs. Kendall excitedly.

"You are not crazy," I told her. I showed her the books and explained what a near death experience was. She nodded and wrote she was happy that I had told her.

The shift progressed quietly until Mrs. Kendall respiratory arrested at 9:15 p.m. Feeling heartsick but determined I intentionally did not call the Code. I left the drapes around her bed until she was asystole. When the Code was called it was too late.

I said a silent prayer for Mrs. Kendall. I felt her presence looking down on me, thanking me. She was at peace now and with her husband.

We learned later that evening that the judge had ruled in her favor. She was to be removed from life support. I felt no guilt or remorse.

The next two weeks flew by rapidly. Undercover officers continued to watch my apartment. Neither Dr. Vorhees nor Dr. Jackson spoke to me, but I knew they were keeping an eye on me. I was unable to learn anything new about the drug pilfering. So, I just did my job and stayed out of everyone's way.

On the unit, our patient, Sara Kremantz, responded better than any of us ever expected. She was partially alert and oriented, even though she was progressing slowly. The cranial surgery had left some motor weakness in her left side. Her memory was impaired, especially her short-term memory, but she knew her family and friends.

We transferred her from the unit to a rehabilitation hospital. Her stay there would be long-term, but we were all optimistic about her prognosis. Most of all we were very happy to see a healthy patient leave the unit. It was a cause for celebration. So celebrate we did!

We purchased a large white-iced pink-rosed sheet cake with the words "Goodbye and good luck" scrawled on top of it. Her family joined us in the party. Every medical professional who came into the unit shared our joy. It was an exhilarating feeling, and I was glad to be there to be a part of it.

I was scheduled to work the Memorial day weekend, so I had the second weekend off in May for a long weekend to make up for missing the holiday. It was nearly one year since I had begun working as a nurse in the unit.

I telephoned my mother and told her I was coming home.

"It is about time," she said over the telephone. "I thought you had forgotten us."

I couldn't tell her on the phone about my life during the past year. Hopefully, in person I would be able to talk to her about it.

Just before my weekend off, Sister Theresa approached me in the hall and asked how things were going.

"Fine," I said, trying to make my tone upbeat. She must have known I needed reassurance.

"Please stop by my office when you have a chance. I want to give you some copies of board actions to read."

"I'm taking this weekend as a long weekend," I said. "Can I take the reports home with me?"

"Surely," she answered. "Just keep them to yourself. I want you to know just how things are progressing, and how important your work is. I think you will find the reports interesting. I know you will find them shocking."

Later that week I stopped in her office. Her secretary handed me a sealed envelope. I took it with me, in my purse, as I left the hospital. I was glad to have the chance to leave town for three days. I was tired and feeling burned-out. I was also eager to read the documents that Sister Theresa felt were so important.

I drove home for the long weekend. The drive out of the smoggy, industrial cluttered city towards lush green hills made me feel secure again. Owasco Lake, cloistered and blue, nestled in the middle of the Finger Lakes region, looked warm and inviting. Our summer cottage looked out on the serene waterfront. It was there, on Friday morning, as the sun rose radiantly over the east side of the lake, that I began to read the documents Sister Theresa gave me.

I spread them out and picked up the first. They were copies of administrative complaints and actions recently taken on nurses by the State Board of Nursing.

"Date of birth: May 20, 1935. License issued by endorsement from Kentucky. Complaint: On three occasions, February 24, 1976, March 3, 1976, and March 18, 1976, while employed as the Director of Nursing at East Shore Hospital, New York, the Respondent diverted controlled substances from her hospital employer, and sold those controlled substances to undercover police agents. Respondent was arrested on March 18, 1976, and charged with four (4) counts of possession of controlled substance, three (3) counts of sale of controlled substance, two (2) counts of delivering a controlled substance. When Respondent was arrested, she had in her possession a small quantity of cocaine in a cigarette case."

On April 7, 1976, the "order of emergency suspension of license" was given. The formal hearing took place before Officer P. L. Brock on July 15, 1976. There was a note attached to see the transcript. I flipped through several pages of documentation with testimony presented by the officers, witnesses, and the D.O.N. (Director of Nursing).

The final recommendation handed down on December 18, 1976, was: "that the Respondent's license be revoked." The Respondent also faced criminal charges that were not covered in this memorandum.

I reflected on the contents of the transcript and summary while sipping my coffee. The sun rose higher in the sky, casting a bright yellow hue across the lake. Birds flew from trees to our outdoor feeder. As I watched nature begin her daily dance I wondered how a nurse, especially a Director of Nursing, could take such a risk by stealing and selling drugs. The full reality of the impact of the problem in our profession was sinking in. For the first time, I contemplated leaving nursing.

I pulled out the next transcript and summary. "Date of birth: July 21, 1953. License by examination. Administrative complaint: On or about August 30, 1976, while employed as a nurse at General Hospital New York, Respondent told police informant Mark Yacolla that she would provide him with controlled substances diverted from her place of employment. During July, 1976, Respondent delivered fiorinol, a controlled substance, to police informant Mark Yacolla. Neither Respondent nor Mark Yacolla possessed a valid prescription for fiorinol."

Administrative action: On March 29, 1976, Respondent's license was suspended with a provision that she could apply for a reinstatement after the elapse of one year and that reinstatement would be granted upon a demonstration of rehabilitation.

I wondered how a nurse could demonstrate rehabilitation. Nothing in our state gave any guidelines or examples to follow. Appalled and shocked, I continued to read.

The next five transcripts and summaries were similar. Nurses caught using drugs on duty and/or stealing drugs to either use and/or sell. One male nurse diverted morphine and would inject himself subcutaneously in the abdomen, rotating the sites in the same way diabetics do. He was using 130 mg. to 140 mg. a day, plus which he was taking fiorinal, percodan, and p.o. (oral) demerol, as many as ten a day with the injections. Initially, he stated in the transcript, he would be euphoric. By the time he was arrested, drugs only gave him an "artificial energy."

The packet also included two summaries on physicians. One was a cardiologist who used alcohol and barbiturates to "deal with the long hours and stress." The doctor named in this action stated, "We're supposed to act like God and not let our patients hurt or die. We have to keep our feelings inside." Later, he stated, "The availability of drugs is easy. Pharmaceutical companies send samples," which he would take. Writing fake prescriptions for himself was another way he obtained the drugs.

The second physician was found guilty with another RN. The nurse worked in psychiatry. The physician was a psychiatrist. The doctor's drug of choice was the benzodiazapenes (sedatives and tranquilizers). He would ask the medication nurses, usually this one RN, for p.o. (oral) or IM (intramuscular) valium several times a day. He would take this medication while the nurse charted a prn (whenever is necessary) order to a patient. The patient's record would reflect the medication given, the time, and the effect (a standard nursing process), but the entire documentation was both fraudulent and in violation of the Nurse Practice Act.

As I continued to read the transcripts I discovered that this same nurse was now under psychiatric care and had been diagnosed a manic depressive. She had a history of wasting medications without witnesses, including over 100 dalmane capsules, 25 mg. to 100 mg. of demerol on several occasions, and had even diagnosed two nurses' aides as having high blood pressure. She then prescribed and gave each nurse lasix, a potent diuretic. Both nurses' aides became violently ill.

Other case transcripts discussed the mode of ingestion of drugs. Besides taking pills by mouth or injecting medications subcutaneously or intramuscularly or intravenously, I learned that nurses gave themselves injections in ways that couldn't be easily detected. IM and IV shots leave bruises, but injections between the toes, in the balls of the feet, under the fingernails, and even in the vein under the tongue were all too common.

My mother, now retired from nursing, joined me at 11:00 for her second cup of coffee. "Joyce, I haven't asked you anything, but I know something is the matter. You haven't come home in a long time. You know I'm glad to see you. But do you want to tell me what is going on?"

I sat back and told her the story for the first time. She listened quietly. I felt better sharing everything with her.

"These," I pointed to the packet spread before me, "are cases acted upon by the Board and I have to make a decision."

Mom looked through the papers. She looked shocked.

"What decision?" she asked, looking more carefully at the case histories. "In my hospital we always 'knew' which doctors and nurses had a drinking problem, but nothing was ever done about any of them. No one knew how to help or intervene."

"Actually, I have to make two decisions. The first is whether to approach Lois or Marilyn, who are head nurses in our unit, and tell them what I know."

Mom was apprehensive. "Why would you do that?" she asked.

"Because the only way I am going to find out anything more is to get on the inside. I can't go on much longer. I am emotionally stressed and exhausted. I am also frightened." I looked at Mom with tears in my eyes. "I have to stop this nightmare."

She nodded and seemed to understand. "And your second decision?"

"I am thinking about leaving nursing." Now that I had said it I felt a relief.

"I've suspected that," she said quietly. "You know, not everyone in our profession has a problem. Just a few. Perhaps you could find a way to help professionals deal with these issues."

I shook my head. "Maybe, but not right now. I am going to apply to graduate schools and look at other options. I just can't deal with nursing and its problems much longer."

During the remaining part of the weekend Mom gave me time and space to think. She left me alone for hours at a time as I lay floating on the lake in my large truck tire inner tube. I loved the calm, clear beauty of the water. It felt cool next to my body. I loved the feeling of the sand beneath my toes. It is a shallow lake—I could walk a hundred feet out and still be in water only up to my knees.

I remembered childhood days when I would swim to the raft a third of the way out and lie on the boards, feeling like Tom Sawyer on my private barge. I loved water skiing on the lake and memories of our high school parties. Our beer parties had been part of normal adolescence but, for the first time, I wondered how many of my friends had drug or alcohol problems.

In the winter the lake would freeze and I could ice skate. In the winter our front lawn and the water seem to merge. We would skate for hours and then retreat inside to the fireplace and hot rum toddies. Amazed, I realized for the first time that all of our functions included alcohol. I never craved the stuff. I never consumed much of it either, but I was becoming more and more frightened of it.

Late Sunday afternoon I reluctantly packed my car to leave. For a brief few minutes I was tempted not to go back, to just make a phone call and say "I quit." Responsibility to my patients, my co-workers, and myself took over. I kissed Mom and drove away from my quiet retreat of home back into a city now filled with terror for me.

Monday morning, I was on the day shift. I hadn't worked days in a long time, the day shift's being the most requested by nurses. I didn't like it; I would be around everyone I was most afraid of. However, it was the perfect time to approach Lois. I told her after report that I wanted to see her sometime during the day. She probably thought I was going to resign. At 2:00 p.m. she came for me. This time she took me to her private office. It was the first time I had ever been there.

Lois sat in silence waiting for me to bring up my subject. I took a deep breath and began. "I asked to talk to you because I know what is going on up here and I want to be a part of it."

Lois was cool. She never batted an eyelash when she asked, "What do you mean?"

"I know about the drug pilfering. I found the box and the hole in the medicine counter top. I even found that same thing in the OR. I know Carol uses, but she also steals drugs and gives patients either sterile water or diluted drugs." I paused to take a breath and gather my courage. Lois stared at me, her pupils becoming more and more noticeably constricted. As she reacted, my heart pounded harder. Somehow, I continued.

"I went to Miami with Paul and I carried figurines filled with crack back. If we had been caught I would have been arrested for possession. I have seen many of the nurses using cocaine at parties, like Marilyn's Christmas party. I have also seen Dr. Jackson and Dr. Vorhees make contact with a man I believe takes the drugs out of here and pays for them."

Lois sat mute. She looked agitated. I knew I had put the pieces together. She knew it too.

"I think you are all getting paid for what you steal. I'm tired of being an underpaid and overworked nurse and I want in." My voice was becoming stronger, more assertive. For my final manipulation I added, "And I know you have a drinking problem."

My last comment shocked her. "I do not," she retorted. Lois regained her composure and control. "Well, you certainly have surprised us, Joyce." At least she didn't call me by my last name this time. I knew I had her. "We never thought you could be trusted. Initially, we were afraid you were a narc. Then we decided you were just plain nosey."

"I was," I interjected. I repeated my request. "I want in."

Lois lit a cigarette and nodded. "Okay. I agree. I'll have to discuss this with the others. And if they approve, you are in."

"Thank you," I replied, standing up. I wanted to leave before my fear showed. I needed to be in control. I had not discussed this plan with Al. I was afraid his officers would be angry with me for forging ahead without their agreement. But at least I had Lois on record agreeing with me. "I'd like an answer by tomorrow."

As I turned the door handle she smiled and said, "You will have it." She then added, "Welcome."

How ironic it was that after a year I was finally being welcomed into the unit. Not as a fully qualified nurse, but as a co-conspirator in a large internal drug ring. I cursed my naiveté under my breath as I walked back into the unit. I also pledged to be out of nursing and into graduate school by the fall. I didn't know what I would do, but I was determined to end this nightmare and leave the state.

For the first time in months I felt better, stronger, more in control. Perhaps now my future plans would fall into place, instead of crumbling as had those I'd formulated in the past.

FOURTEEN

The following morning, I arrived on duty at 6:45 in the morning. Lois signaled me to come into her office. "You're in," she announced.

I smiled. "Thanks. What do I do now?"

"You are on meds today. Give them out like you always do. Tina has been on all night, so when you count with her and she asks you to co-sign her wastes, just do it."

I nodded. Now I knew that Tina was in on it. "Do I waste any meds during my shift?"

"Yes," she replied. "Use common sense. Take drugs only from those with more than one order or from the unconscious ones. You know where the opening is: just slip the vials or ampules through."

"When do I take the box out?" I asked, hoping she would give me the information I wanted.

"Don't let that bother you now. The box will be removed later."

"Lois, who can I trust besides you and Tina?" I was intentionally pushing. I hoped she wouldn't feel threatened.

She paused, looking at me strangely. "Well, you did help Paul on the Miami trip, although we all honestly thought you had no idea about that."

"I knew something was going on," I lied. "I agreed to go with Paul because I was hoping he would tell me just what." I lied again, adding "Paul and I had something once, but we're just friends now."

Lois succumbed. "Paul is one of ours. Dr. Vorhees and Dr. Jackson have the outside contact."

"The heavyset man I saw with Dr. Jackson in the OR."

"Yes. You certainly have done your homework," she exclaimed. "There are several of us. In the unit you can depend on Marilyn and Carol. Terry, the Respiratory Therapist, is also available."

"We are not the only department, are we?" I asked, hoping to sound innocent enough for her to continue. Apparently I succeeded.

"Of course not. You already know about the OR. The ER, the Recovery Room and CCU (Critical Care Unit) all work together. So does psychiatry and two of the medical-surgical wards."

"I didn't know we were so big," I proclaimed in genuine shock.

"This is a big business, Joyce. Every hospital in the area contributes."

I chose my words carefully. "There must be someone who helps us in nursing, isn't there, or do we just report to Dr. Vorhees?" I prayed she wouldn't think I was too inquisitive.

There was a disconcerting silence. "You're asking an awful lot of questions," Lois said with a sulky hostility.

I hesitated, trying to sound less demanding. "Sorry, but my license is on the line too. Besides, I am already guilty."

Lois nodded her head. "Well, that's true," she said low-voiced, with expression. "Look, I'll tell you this much. If you ever have any problems in this facility and none of us are around to help you, you can go to Nursing Service."

"Nursing Service!" I repeated and could not keep my

voice from quivering. Who could possibly be part of this scam in nursing service, I wondered.

She read my thoughts. "The Assistant Director of Nurses."

I stared at her incredulously. "I'm shocked. Mrs. White works with us?" I thought about the board transcripts and summaries I had read over the weekend and felt an undercurrent of concern. A mental picture of the Director of Nurses crossed my mind.

"Yes. She coordinates everything for us with the physicians. We take what we steal to her and she passes it along somehow. I don't know everything, Joyce. There is not much more I can tell you."

I hardly knew the Director of Nurses, Mrs. White. She was young, slender and attractive. Her husband had terminal cancer and was a patient in a local hospice center. I tried to rationalize her behavior. His medical expenses must be exorbitant. "What about Miss Holcomb or Sister Theresa?" I asked.

"No. Neither one of them. Sister Theresa is in her own little world of outdated values. Miss Holcomb does administration. Frankly, neither one of them needs the money."

"Speaking of money," I said casually since she opened the door, "what is my share?"

Lois answered coldly. "We divide the proceeds among ourselves according to how much we take out of each unit."

I listened attentively as she went on. "You can also have any drugs you want, but not until we turn them in to Nursing Service. As you know, we are having a problem with Carol. She is using more lately than she is confiscating. If you want drugs, let us know. We can provide you with cocaine and pot too. That's always a bonus."

As calmly as I could, I said, "That is a bonus. When I need some I'll ask.

"Marilyn and I keep the count and record books," she continued.

So, there were record books. My ears perked up. If our unit had some then everyone else probably did also. I leaned forward, hoping she would continue.

And she did. "When the transfers are made and Dr. Vorhees pays us, we divide it. Therefore, you owe a responsibility to everyone in the unit to carry your weight. We do not compete against each other. We work together. There really is plenty to go around, Joyce."

I felt absurdly dazed but forced a smile. "I know. You can count on me."

She nodded and looked at me cautiously. "You had better go to work now."

"Thanks," I said as I opened the door to her office. Back on the unit, Tina and I counted, and I co-signed the drugs she claimed to have wasted. The numbers astounded me. On the night shift alone she wasted ten vials of demerol, five of vistaril, eight vials of valium, and five vials of morphine. She also "discarded" four sleepers: nembutal, placidyl, seconal, and dalmane. Tina nodded approvingly at me as I signed my name. I hoped that Al's promise of legal protection for me included my license.

The day shift went smoothly. Marilyn was almost friendly to me. Not at all like my first day in the unit. She invited me to have lunch with her. In spite of the illegal things she was doing, I found that she could be very nice when she wanted to. It was pretty scary to me.

At lunch, Marilyn whispered in low tones. "How much have you diverted so far?"

"I have been able to discard three demerols, three morphines, and two valiums. It has been pretty busy in the unit today. Is it always difficult on the day shift?"

"Yes," she answered. "Evenings and nights do better, because there is less traffic, fewer interruptions, and fewer people around. But you have done well so far."

"Thanks." I picked at my lunch. I really had no appetite. Fear was inhibiting it.

"I was pretty rough on you when you began, Joyce," she added. "I want to apologize."

"I understand, Marilyn. You had to be careful. I really don't blame you."

Well, we thought you were a narc from Nursing Service. Mrs. White always knows firsthand who is placed there, but she was confused about you. She couldn't get any information on you for a long time. So, we didn't trust you."

"You set me up, didn't you, to test me?" I asked, probing for more details. I had learned more in the past two days than in the preceding months.

She played with her salad. "You mean the trip to Miami with Paul?" A flush suffused Marilyn's face. "Yes, we set you up. How did you catch on?"

I hesitated only briefly. "Just my own intuition. I'm tired of being underpaid for my work too. Nursing is not as rewarding as I thought it would be. It's too stressful. The public doesn't even know what we do. In fact, they don't really know what doctors do. I overheard a patient ask an ER physician if he did surgery?"

She laughed. "You're right. Everyone thinks that all nurses are pretty and sexy while all doctors perform surgery and deliver babies. They think all doctors drive limos and nurses work for the love of it instead of money. Well, you won't be poor anymore."

"How much money can I expect to make?" I hoped I sounded greedy. I also hoped that Al was taping my every word.

"At least three bills a week."

"Good grief!" I was shocked. I only made $450.00 every two weeks. After taxes that left me with $328.00. Overtime might give me another $50.00 of spending money in every pay period. Here was Marilyn telling me that I could bring home $300.00 extra a week. I could see where the money would be tempting.

"I have made as much as $600.00 a week," she announced proudly. "Also, Terry and I live together, as I'm sure you know, and he brings home the same."

My curiosity rose. "What do you do with all of that money?"

Momentarily Marilyn's temper flared. "What makes you ask that?"

"Curiosity," I answered ruefully. "You don't have to answer."

Marilyn laughed uproariously. "I don't mind. We are saving it. We plan on retiring in another year and leaving the state. We want to live in Hawaii. It is expensive out there. I don't want to work and Terry really doesn't want to either."

"That sounds tempting, but aren't you ever afraid you will get caught?" I asked.

"No. Lois and I keep the books, but we don't steal anything and we never sign anything. In fact, if any of us got caught the Board would probably slap our hands. Our lawyers tell us we probably would get probation. You see, we can all plead that we were all in it together."

I regarded her with what I hoped was a sympathetic expression. She looked pretty composed. She was right about her signature. It wasn't on anything. And I was surprised that she had already consulted with an attorney.

"Well, I'll help in any way I can," I offered. I looked down and noticed my hands were trembling. I hid them under the table.

"Good," she purred.

The rest of the afternoon went smoothly. I stole more drugs, feeling guiltier with each one. As long as I could waste narcotics I felt I could handle it. But I wanted to find out more about swapping sterile water for them. I knew I couldn't give a patient nothing and chart that I gave medication, or give normal saline as I knew others did.

To my surprise, Marilyn came over to me at the end of the shift. She had Annette give report for her so only the skeleton staff was in the unit. "I'll tell you how to empty the box now and take it to the nurses' lounge."

I felt excited. I was beginning to make real progress. "Just tell me what to do."

She responded sharply. "Take one of the syringe boxes marked for disposable needles. Empty the contents and bring the box into the locker room. I'll meet you there."

She turned and left. I surveyed the room. Everyone was busy charting or doing vital signs. I leaned down and opened the cabinet door. Filling the syringe box was quick and easy. When I stood up I placed another syringe box marked for disposal on the counter top and took the one I had into the locker room.

It really was easy. Something not routine, since Central Supply usually picked up the disposables, but not uncommon either since we emptied our bedside wastebaskets frequently, not waiting for housecleaning. Soaked chuxs, dressings, and tubings were all tossed into pastic liners. One of the nursing chores we did to help decrease contamination was to discard those plastic filled liners by lining them up near the unit door. Housekeeping picked the tied bags up at least twice on every shift.

So taking a disposable syringe box was not unusual. I walked into the locker room. Marilyn called to me, "I've checked to make sure we're alone." I shivered. If she only knew about the times I was hidden in the back of the room, waiting.

She walked me over to the second row and pointed to a locker. Turning the combination she opened the door. I gasped.

The locker, number thirteen, was filled with stolen syringes, kelly clamps, bandages, IV tubings, assorted instruments, and boxes of medication.

"You take instruments and tubing too?" I asked, mesmerized.

She said, more serious than before, "If you can. Just shove extras in your pockets and bring them in here. We sell these too."

My voice broke the ensuing silence. "I guess you had better give me the combination."

She did. "Five to the right. Seven to the left. And nine to the right. Locker number thirteen is believed to be an unlucky number, so no one requests it," Marilyn said wryly. "You can bring items in here anytime," she stated.

"How do you get all of this stuff out of here?" I asked. "These are pretty large amounts."

Marilyn laughed. "That's easy. We have help in both Central Supply and housekeeping."

The pieces began to fit together. Of course, both areas would go in and out of the locker room with no questions asked. And both groups could facilitate the removal from the hospital.

"This is really remarkable, Marilyn," I said as I placed the syringe box in the locker. Closing the door I tried the combination finding it worked on the first try. I glanced at Marilyn over my shoulder.

She smiled again. "You did well, Strom. Go home and rest. By next Friday you will have your first paycheck."

Keeping my voice low, I asked, "Is that when these things will be removed from here?"

She shook her head. "No. Lois and I will count and record them on Tuesday. The transfers are made on Wednesday or sometime after that. But as a rule, we all get paid on the third Friday of every month."

"Good," I interjected, "I really need the money."

Her face visibly relaxed. "We all do, Strom, for one reason or another."

I patted her shoulder. "Thanks, Marilyn. For everything." I left to count meds with the afternoon nurse, Mary, who was not part of the scam. She didn't have to co-sign my wastes, however. Annette had done that automatically while I was at lunch. I now knew she also was one of the group.

Leaving the hospital I decided to avoid Sister Theresa's office. I would contact Al later. All that was left was to find the record books and have Al tell me when they would make their arrests.

"We're getting closer," I remarked to Al later that afternoon. "In fact, I am learning more all of the time."

"Our adrenaline is flowing now, Joyce. We want to wind this up before too much longer, for your sake and ours."

I started telling Al about some of the Board procedures I had read. "Some were damn serious," I remarked, "but others were ridiculous."

"Like what?" he inquired, half listening to me.

"One of the cases involved two medical/surgical nurses who were working a floor of twenty-five patients by themselves. One of the nurses became violently ill and was vomiting. She called the supervisor to cover for her and let her go home from the hospital, but the supervisor was already covering in another area. So the other nurse filled a syringe with phenergan and injected it into the first nurse to help her get through the shift."

"Where is the problem? I don't understand your drugs or what they do to you."

I continued. "The board ruled that nurses cannot prescribe for each other because it is a violation of the Nurse Practice Act, and that I agree with. However, they also stated that taking the phenergan from the hospital supply was stealing. Al, I can't tell you how many nurses take drugs from the hospital supply or from patients' drawers. I know it is wrong, but we're talking about aspirin or tylenol. Not narcotics."

"It is a gray area," he remarked.

"No," I said. "It is very black and white. And I myself am guilty of taking aspirin from the unit drawer. There is another problem I am discovering," I mused.

Al was still listening with only half an ear, but I needed to talk whether he listened closely or not. "What's that?" he said.

"Doctors are always screaming or shouting orders for patients at nurses. Or we call them on the telephone and they order something verbally. We write the order and they sign it the next time they come into the unit. On many floors there are standard orders. The nurses decide which orders to give, write them, and then call the doctor to cover them afterwards. Of course, if there is a problem, the nurse is responsible."

Suddenly my words caught Al's attention. "Can you give me an example?" he asked.

"Sure. My friend, Roberta, works the pre- and post-op surgery floor. There are standing post-op orders for demerol 50 mg. to 75 mg. and vistaril 25 mg. to 50 mg. every four hours as needed for pain. There is also a standing order for one or two percocets by mouth every four hours as needed for pain. Roberta tells me that the nurses decide how much pain medication to give and how long to keep the injections up before starting the oral meds. She complained that most of the nurses start too high with the meds. She starts low, feeling you can always go up, but you cannot come down."

Al's face tightened. "In other words, patients are being overmedicated and some may become addicted because of these decisions."

"Yes." I shook my head impatiently. "Or nurses steal and take drugs; some of these medications may be charted as having been given, but in reality, the patient may have received the lower dose while his nurse took the remainder."

Al had eased forward in his seat. "What other pieces of information have you learned?"

I smiled faintly. "The floors now have a relatively new pump called the PCA—patient control analgesic pump. Actually, it is a wonderful concept and works well. A 50 cc vial of demerol or demerol mixed with vistaril is placed in the pump. The doctor writes the order for the maximum injection, such as 10 mg. an hour. The patient can push the button as many times as he wants, but he will still only get his 10 mg. in an hour."

"That is a super way to control the drugs. The patient

gets his drug without someone taking it," Al said excitedly.

"I agree, but there is still another problem."

"Okay," he said dejectedly. "Go ahead and tell me."

"The pharmacists don't want to be bothered preparing these 50 cc syringes every time a PCA is ordered. They have decided to let every floor have three filled syringes and have the nurses keep them locked in their own narcotics boxes."

"I am confused," he said, scratching his head.

"Demerol is a clear liquid." I grimaced. "How does the floor nurse who takes one of the syringes know that it contains demerol? There is only a needle on top that is meant to be removed by the nurse. She can remove all or part of the contents. Vistaril can be added or even sterile water. Who knows?" At length I raised my eyes and met his.

Slowly, Al nodded. He finally understood. "So, by leaving 50cc syringes supposedly filled with demerol on the floors it is an open invitation for anyone with access to the keys to have a field day."

"Right. Including the pharmacist. Let's not exclude this group from addictions. They have problems, too."

"Brilliant." He paused, obviously thinking about the enormous intensity of the problem.

I interjected, "There is one other recurrent problem we have among nurses."

"Another one?" he asked, exasperated. "Is there ever an end to any of this?"

I continued. "It is difficult for nurses, who are trained to alleviate suffering, to care for dying patients in so much constant pain, so sometimes they aid death along by giving overdoses."

"Overdoses show up on autopsies," Al said skeptically.

I nodded. "Correct, only not all patients have a post. In our hospital we need the family consent, or documentation that the patient died at the incompetent hands of another."

Now Al was listening closely and intently. "Then most "mercy" killings go undetected."

I nodded again.

"I almost hate to ask, but is there anything else you want to tell me?" he quipped.

"Just one more thing," I said, a touch whimsically. I had been reading articles in the nursing journals and newspapers predicting nursing shortages. Everyone had a solution or suggestion. Al was the prime target on whom I vented my frustrations.

"Nurses have many internal problems. At one time every hospital had a school of nursing. Student nurses were paid to work for that hospital on a twenty-four hour rotation. The shortage of nurses was the same, but the students were there running the facilities. Of course, malpractice and other legal aspects soon made hospitals realize that this was a dangerous practice."

I paused for a moment and then continued. "Large teaching hospitals, like Trinity, still have interns and residents. Again, these are doctors working the twenty-four hour rotations, while the attendings get to go home after work. Some hospitals are beginning to look at this as a problem law suit area."

Al smiled. "I think you're on a roll. Go on."

I smiled back. "Nursing schools moved to the community college level and university level. The trend now is to have our LPN's—Licensed Practical Nurses—earn the associate degree from the community college and the RN's—Registered Nurses—earn a Bachelors in Nursing from the University."

The sharp note in Al's voice brought me back to the present. "So what is wrong with that? It would seem like you would have more knowledge and respect."

"True. But, I feel we should have a minimum of a Master's degree in a specialty area and function as independent practicioners under the direct supervision of an M.D."

"Won't doctors think that you are moving into their territory?"

I experienced a surge of anger. It showed in my voice. "They already do feel that way. Al, there's something I've been meaning to discuss with you."

"I thought so," Al said, his eyes meeting mine.

I took a deep breath. "I want to leave the unit by August 15. I have been researching graduate school programs. I think I am going to get a degree in psychology and become certified in psychiatric nursing. I would then be able to work independently and help more clients, especially nurses."

Al nodded. "I knew you were preparing for a major life change. Of course, I had hoped it would be law enforcement. Even the FBI is recruiting women."

"Al, I just couldn't do it. Doing this job has been exciting and rewarding, but I don't want to hide in closets the rest of my life. And I've realized I don't want to be just another set of hands at someone's bedside either. I want to do something about the problems I've seen here, something that will count."

"Maybe you should go into politics," Al joked.

I laughed. "I'll do my political action with my pen," I stated. "We need to develop confidential monitored programs for impaired professionals to help them detox and then continue to work, while not losing their licenses."

"Like a probation status?"

"Yes. I have begun to find out what other states are doing. Apparently, a few states like California and Georgia are creating an impaired professionals program."

"And you've applied for graduate school?" he asked.

I nodded. "In Florida."

"Would you go to California or Georgia afterwards?"

"I don't know. Graduate school is two years and a lot can happen in that time. Maybe I can even come back here."

"Maybe." Al was quiet for a moment. And, so was I. Then he said, "I am impressed with you and with what you have done. I will really miss you when this case is over."

Tears began to fill my eyes. "Al, I will miss you, too. But I feel it's important for me to begin to implement some of the things I've learned. Or at least to try—I hope I can accomplish something worthwhile."

"Everything new requires a risk," he offered. "You have certainly taken some heavy risks up until now. I pray you never stop."

Al had become my moral supporter. "I only have one major stumbling block right now," I remarked.

"What's that?"

"I don't know what to do about Paul."

Al looked at me soberly. "That may be out of your hands, Joyce. If Paul is one of the conspirators, he will be arrested and treated like all of the others."

"I know," I said gloomily. "But, I wish it could be different."

Al patted my hand. We sat together silently for quite a while. I knew he felt helpless. I also knew he couldn't give me the answers I so desperately wanted. And I wasn't ready to hear those he could give.

FIFTEEN

I searched everywhere for the record books Al needed to tie the case together. At home I constantly formulated ideas and plans for finding them. I kept focusing on both Marilyn's and Lois's offices, wondering if they would possibly leave them there. They were always locked. But even under lock and key that seemed very dangerous. Where would I leave record books if I were stealing drugs? I racked my mind and kept looking, but without success.

I began working the evening shift. Annette gave meds while Carrol co-signed her wastes. Carol was the charge nurse. Annette went to dinner first with Melanie and I went with Carol. The unit was quiet.

Carol was in an upbeat mood. I suspected she had recently medicated herself. "Well, Strom," she began suddenly, "it sure is comforting to know that you are one of us. God, were we surprised."

"Thanks, Carol," I replied, not looking her in the eyes. She made me nervous. She was being too nice. I didn't trust her, even though she now seemed to feel she could trust me.

Dinner was filled with small talk. We walked back to the unit together as if we were good friends and buddies.

Later that evening, I found the time to work my way

towards Lois's office. Opposite it, the nurses' lounge was empty. The smell of stale, strong coffee filled the cove. Putting my hand on her doorknob I tried to turn it, but it was locked. Marilyn's office was next to the unit, on the other side. Her door was also locked.

I was becoming discouraged and convinced that I would never find the record books. I thought about Mrs. White and how she would come into the unit once or twice on the day shift. I had never thought of her appearance as being unusual. She was Lois's direct supervisor.

At 10:00 p.m. the ER called to say they were sending a patient. I had an empty bed so Carol told me the patient was mine. I prepared the cubicle area and set up supplies.

"What are they sending?" I inquired as Carol sat at the desk taking orders off.

"A four-year-old girl with slashed wrists."

My stomach turned. Pediatrics was my most difficult work assignment. There was something about small, sick, helpless children that I couldn't seem to deal with. I became too emotionally involved. In training, while working my OR rotation, I had witnessed a tonsillectomy on a tiny three-year-old boy. The surgery was routine and normal. It was also very bloody. I had passed out cold, on the floor, from the sight of both the small, helpless child and the blood.

"Who slashed her wrists?" I asked.

"We don't know," Carol answered, keeping her head down and writing furiously. "The ER suspects child abuse."

I cringed. Child abuse made me even sicker. I had seen too much of that in training also. The unit doors flung open. An attendant pushed the stretcher. I saw the tiny head of a tousled-haired blonde girl sticking out from under the cover. She was sobbing quietly. Running beside her were her parents. Walking up to them I saw tears in their eyes. I looked first at one, then the other, wondering which had hurt this sweet little child.

"Hi, there," I said to her as the attendant lifted her into my waiting bed. "My name is Joyce. What's yours?"

She sniffled and looked up at me. I tried to communicate my compassion. "Chelsea," she whimpered.

"What a pretty name," I exclaimed and then, noticing the torn doll she was holding I asked, "and what is her name?"

Chelsea beamed as she looked at her doll and then me. "Chrissie," she replied.

Her parents began pleading with me to help her. Guilt seemed to exude from both of them. "Why don't you wait in the waiting room outside until I have her cleaned up," I said trying not to let my distaste show. "Then I will let you visit for just a few minutes and say goodnight."

The couple reluctantly left hanging on to each other. Her mother was crying. I kept looking at Chelsea to see if she would make any unusual response to their leaving, but she didn't.

We medicated Chelsea for pain, which also put her to sleep. I allowed the parents to kiss her goodnight. When they left I felt both helpless and relieved. The sight of the frail, wounded child upset me all night. I had forgotten about the record book.

The unit was still quiet the next afternoon. I walked in just as the nursing supervisor, Mrs. White, was leaving. She smiled and said hello to me. I nodded in return.

I immediately looked for Chelsea. She was sitting up in bed with both wrists bandaged and playing with her doll. I wondered if she would be my assignment again, but then I noticed that I was on meds. Carol was in charge. Apparently Annette had called in sick. Melanie was on duty along with a new nurse, Jenny.

"Watch the new one," Carol cautioned as we prepared for report.

Tina had worked days. I co-signed her wastes when we counted the narcotics together. Al was on duty outside.

Report was fast because we only had five patients. When Marilyn came to Chelsea she reported that the social worker had make some picture drawings with the little girl. She showed us the pictures done on white paper with crayons. Chelsea had drawn a picture of her family. Her mother was on one side, crying. Her father was on the other side, screaming. Chelsea was in the middle. Large tear drops fell from her eyes to the floor. Her hands were raised. Large red drops of blood mixed with the teardrops and fell to the floor. A broken dish lay alongside them.

In telling the story about her picture to the social worker she had stated, "The mommy and daddy are fighting and the mommy is crying and the daddy takes a dish and breaks it and cuts the little girl's hands."

My heart wrenched thinking of Chelsea and all she had seen and endured. I felt dismayed, thinking of my own close family, that her father had abused her, and amazed to find out what the social worker had been able to elicit from her art play. I made a mental note to learn more about this technique when I returned to graduate school.

"Chelsea is being transferred to peds," Marilyn continued. "Social services has already reported the abuse. Her father will not be allowed to see her."

I was relieved. Relieved that her father couldn't see her, and relieved that she was being transferred. The stress of seeing her in the unit was more than I could bear.

Carol went to dinner with Jenny while Melanie and I stayed in the unit. Again I tried the locked office doors, with no success. I also went into locker thirteen, but found it empty. The pick-ups had gone as scheduled. Only the day shift drugs and two kelly clamps were in the locker. I closed the door and returned to the unit.

I decided to check the OR out when I got off duty. After Mary and I counted—Carol had already co-signed my wastes—I clocked out. Whispering into my chest I said, "Al, I am going back to the OR and see if their box is empty. I don't know what I will find, but I want to try."

I knew he was probably swearing at me for further imperiling my own safety, but I wanted to find out just what was going on.

The OR was quiet. Black. Only the hall night lights were lit. I left the elevator and listened for any sounds. Hearing nothing, I deftly made my way down the corridor towards the medicine counter.

My fingers slid across the counter top. I found the opening, just as before. Reaching under the cupboard I removed the box gently expecting it to be light. Instead, the box nearly fell from my hands because it was so heavy.

Laying the box on the floor I could see it was nearly filled with drugs—vials, ampules, and pills in individual packages. "Al, I'm in the OR in the medication room. The box is full, but I can't find any signs of record books. I am going to put the box back. I will be out shortly."

I replaced the box and stood to carefully close the cupboard door. Deciding that I had done everything, I turned to leave the area as I found it.

I looked up and down the hall carefully. No one was there: feeling relieved, but eager to get outside of the hospital, I shut the door.

Suddenly, a strong hand grabbed me from behind. Another hand slapped something over my mouth. I tried to let out a muffled scream. Then, I felt dizzy. The room began to swim. Nausea was my next sensation as I fought hard against the weight of the hands.

The men laid my body on the floor and began to remove my uniform. They quickly found the hidden microphone in the center of my bra. Taking the microphone, one man walked over to the unit autoclave and placed it inside. Neither man spoke as the first set the dials and turned on the switch. The steam and high temperatures quickly melted the device.

They returned to my partially clad body on the floor. "Is she out?" the first asked.

The man checked me. "Yes. She is unconscious. Ether still works wonders."

Actually, I was semi-conscious, but I pretended to be out cold, afraid that they would give me more ether. I felt nauseated and had all I could do to lie there quietly.

"Okay, doc, now that we've got her, what are we going to do with her?" The voice was that of Harry Cappuzzio.

Dr. Vorhees replied. "Kill her, but not here. She was in contact with someone outside. We have to find out who and find out how much they know."

Harry agreed. "Leave that to me, doc. The guy must be around here someplace. I'll find him."

"Fine," Dr. Vorhees replied. "I can always count on you, Harry. She would have to walk in just as you were doing the weekly pick-up. Damn fool. I was always suspicious of her. Even though Marilyn and Lois had assured me of her desire to work in the group, my own gut feeling said otherwise all along. Just help me get her out of here," he commanded. "She has caused us a great deal of trouble."

"What are you going to do with her, exactly?" Harry asked. From the way he asked I could tell he would love the chance to waste me, having messed it up the first time.

Dr. Vorhees grinned. "You screwed it up the first time, Harry. We need to find out what she knows before you get a second chance."

Harry looked pleased. "Just so I take charge of disposing of her."

Vorhees nodded. "We wil transfer her to our privately-owned sanitarium and keep giving her enough drugs until she talks and is fully addicted. You can have her when we're done."

Harry leaned over my body, touching my forehead. I tried not to shake or let them know I was hearing everything as he whispered "You and I will have some fun first, honey, before you die."

My heart pounded, but I had to keep calm to protect myself. My mind raced trying to think of a way out of this predicament. I could only pray that Al had overheard enough to help me.

"I'm damned angry," Vorhees said. Picking up his telephone he dialed a number. "Get the ambulance here immediately," he ordered. "One shipment for the sanitarium."

The attendants arrived within minutes. "Take the stretcher to the OR by the OR's 'Surgical patients only' elevator," Vorhees instructed.

"What have you got?" one of them inquired.

"Bad news," Dr. Vorhees answered, nodding towards me. I could tell as I squinted through my eyes.

When I was a small child I became quite good at pretending to be asleep while peeking through my eyelids to watch the Tooth Fairy or Santa Claus come to my bedside. I did the same thing now, forcing my mind to pretend that I was small and safe in my own bed.

The attendants lifted my inert body onto the stretcher. They covered me with a blanket. Taking the private elevator down, the attendants moved out through the emergency room doors. The ER was busy. I thought of screaming but knew I would never find out the truth if I did so, despite my fears, I kept still. I knew the removal of a "patient" would go unnoticed, especially when two attendants and Dr. Vorhees were escorting it.

The men asked for instructions. "Take her to Green Hills Clinic," Dr. Vorhees said. "I'll follow you in my car."

"With sirens or without?" the driver asked.

Dr. Vorhees smiled. "Turn the siren on, George. Enjoy yourself. Just keep the radio on so I can stay in touch. Harry also has a radio. He has gone to look for the guy she was talking to."

I prayed Al was smarter than they were and close on our trail. Suddenly I overheard a scuffle. Paralyzed with fright, I saw Harry open the ambulance door and push a heavy body in. Through my slitted eyelids I saw Al thrust into the stretcher beside me. Harry stood over him. Flipping the body over, he used Al's handcuffs to lock his wrists behind his back. Then Harry removed Al's service revolver, still inside the holster under his arm.

Blood oozed from a cut over Al's eye. I could see his

chest heaving up and down. I said a silent prayer. He was still breathing.

I kept my eyes glued shut, fighting back the tears. I had never felt so hopeless or lost in my life.

Our ambulance sped through the night, with both the sirens and lights flashing. The attendant called Dick was in the back watching me and making sure I didn't regain consciousness. Sometimes he would pinch me, but I bit my tongue so as not to respond.

Dick kept watching me. He didn't think that I could hear him as he talked about how he almost felt sorry for me. I had crossed Dr. Vorhees and from the conversation between he and George, I wasn't the first one. He and George had taken care of a couple of nurses a year earlier. Dick remembered and spoke of Maria. A tiny, pretty little Italian girl. Looking at me he said, "It is a shame that so many pretty nurses betray them and have to be killed. Eventually."

Harry Cappuzzio drove the ambulance. He called back to his two conspirators, "We're lucky to have caught the two of them. I wonder who else is in on this conspiracy to break up our drug ring. I'm getting tired of these damned games. Vorhees better watch himself. I'm not as young as I used to be and I'm more impatient."

"Dick, you know I've seen the little nurse before."

"Where was that, Harry?"

A pause. "Shit, I know. The night of the Christmas party at Marilyn's apartment. I knew I didn't like her then. She was nosing around too much. But I fixed her later."

"You mean she was the one we gave the crack to?"

"Yes, you jerk, even though you got the wrong girl first. We still got across our message."

"The dead rat, you mean," George interrupted.

Harry laughed. "She's a dead rat all right. Both of

you keep your eyes on her and the cop. I'll watch Vorhees. He's in the car right behind us. I'll give him quite a race. Let him find out what it's like to tail someone."

The roads were black. Occasional street lamps illuminated the highway. But there were no cars around anywhere.

Harry called back. "All right. I see Green Hill Clinic ahead, just over the next hill. I'll let Vorhees pull in first. After all, he's the owner of our little facility."

Al began to stir. He moaned loudly. "Hey, that guy is beginning to wake up." Harry looked back over his shoulder. "I am tempted to kill the cop right on the spot," he announced, adding, "how I hate cops."

I could tell by the tone of his voice that he meant it. He kept talking about how he loved to kill and about every time he watched the breath of life leave someone how he felt a streak of pleasure. Like a good orgasm, his body would react. He was eagerly looking forward to killing us.

The more he rambled on, as if talking to himself, the more frightened I became. I hoped Al, with all of his training, would wake up and know of some way out of this dilemma. I prayed that someone else knew of our fate, too, and that we were not really as alone as I was feeling.

Harry swung the ambulance through the gates which had been unlocked for his admission and that of the car following. I could hear the security guard, recognizing Dr. Vorhees, letting him through also.

Harry rolled the window down. "Hi, Stan. Just me, with a new patient in the back."

"Go ahead," Stan replied, opening the gates for the ambulance and car.

Stan knew something was up. "What's going on?" he asked, "usually it is very quiet around here at this hour of the night."

I heard the gates close again. I felt trapped.

George and Dick took Al and me out of the ambulance on the stretchers. Dr. Vorhees pulled his car up and parked it right behind us. All three men watched in silence.

A night nurse called out to all of them. "Hey! Where are you taking them? The man has an injury over his eye," she declared, noticing the blood still oozing down Al's forehead.

Dick knew the nurse. "He'll be all right, Tracey. We have orders to take them directly to special rooms."

Dr. Vorhees came through the door at the head of my stretcher, with George at my feet. Tracey smiled. "Good evening, doctor. Can I help you?"

"Thanks Tracey, but we have it. We'll take them to number six."

Dick laughed. "The padded room," he said. "And a soundproof one, too."

"What about him, doctor?" Tracey asked. She had seen the handcuffs. "I'm not sure how the rest of my staff will feel about having a criminal here."

"I'm responsible," Dr. Vorhees admonished. "We'll take care of both of them. In fact, I will be calling in the private duties for these two cases."

"Fine, doctor," Tracey answered. She sounded glad that she didn't have to do the admissions or patient care for two more people.

Harry and Dick brought us back to a small windowless office. They put Al on the couch.

"Everything okay here, boys?" Dr. Vorhees asked, entering and removing his suit coat. "I'm dead tired," he continued. "It's been a long day and I still have surgery at 8:00 a.m. That's less than seven hours away. So let's get a move on here."

"I'll think we'll be able to get rid of these two soon," Harry replied.

"You're damned right," Dr. Vorhees retorted angrily, "but not until they have told us everything we want to know." He bent over Al's body and checked the left eye. It wasn't serious. I watched them apply some salve and gauze to the wound.

Al let out a groan of pain. "Don't worry, cop," Dr. Vorhees announced. "You'll be all right for the time being.

You and your nurse friend have certainly caused us a lot of problems. We intend to put a stop to that. Forever."

I knew that Al was groggy and I saw him squinting as he tried to focus his eyes on the man administering first aid to his forehead. I wondered if he also had a throbbing headache. "Where am I?" he asked hoarsely.

Just hearing his voice, so close to me, made me feel that I was less alone. I was still counting on him to save our lives. I lay on the stretcher near the doorway. No one seemed to be paying any attention to me at this point in time.

"In the hospital, of course," said Dr. Vorhees in a professional tone. "But, I am afraid you are going to be quite sick for some time."

George and Dick looked at each other and smiled. Al began to look around the room. "Where is Joyce?" he asked, suddenly concerned for my safety. Then he noticed me.

Dr. Vorhees said soberly, "She is safe and with us. But she is also going to be sick for a while."

I could feel everyone's eyes on me. I still pretended to be unconscious.

"What have you done to her?" Al shrieked, trying to struggle to his feet. They pushed him back. His hands were locked behind him. I guessed he had figured out he was wearing his own handcuffs and wondered if the key was still in his breast pocket. I knew that was where he kept it.

"Now, don't panic," the doctor said in a cheerful, detached voice. "We will keep you advised as to her health." The doctor turned to the attendants. "Take them both to number six, boys. I want them to be together so they can watch everything." Chills raced through my body.

The two men nodded as they lifted the groggy Al from the couch. "My head throbs," Al said. The men had to hold him up. "Look guys, the room is swimming and my knees are buckling under."

Then Al began to wrestle against the handcuffs and the two attendants. Dr. Vorhees called out. "Hold it. We're trying to help you." Reaching into his black bag he produced a vial and syringe. Deftly and quickly, he withdrew the contents of the vial into the syringe. Both men held Al firmly as the doctor swabbed Al's arm with alcohol and then injected the needle.

Al yelled, "My arm feels like it's on fire."

"What did you give him?" Dick asked, obviously taking pleasure in the painful sight of Al squirming from the injection.

Dr. Vorhees said, "One hundred mg. of thorazine. It will knock him out."

"What's wrong with him now?" Dick said disgustedly.

"Thorazine burns tissue. We usually give 25 mg. dosage injections into the buttocks. I injected all the solution into his arm," he added.

"Give him thorazine every thirty minutes until he is out," he ordered, "and get them to their room."

"Sure, doc," George answered. "It will be our pleasure."

The men unloaded both of us into hospital beds and pulled the siderails up. Minutes ticked by. Geroge eagerly looked at his watch. When thirty minutes were up he drew up more thorazine and injected it into Al.

Al squirmed and screamed. I could tell that the damn shots hurt like hell. I realized, as I lay there helplessly, and still "asleep," that we both were in deep trouble. Knowing as I did the results of thorazine injections, I watched Al terrified. I knew that his tongue felt thick and that he was unable to swallow. The lights overhead must have been blinding his eyes. He continually blinked. If it were me, my last conscious thought would be fear of choking to death. I wondered if Al felt the same way.

George removed the handcuffs. Dick undressed Al and put a patient's gown on him. I didn't like the way Dick liked looking at Al's naked body as he left it exposed for a few moments.

"For God's sake," George ordered. "Cover him up."

I watched George clasp Al's wrists to the bedside rails using leather restraints. Dick started an IV in Al's left wrist and then attached a bottle of normal saline. "Let's put a posey vest on him," Dick said. "We'll be sure he's securely locked in place."

George left the room. "They are all yours," he said to Dick. "I'm going to crash for a little while."

Dick nodded. He took Al's blood pressure and recorded it. Then he administered another injection of thorazine.

He checked on me and stroked my hair. "Well now, pretty thing. We really did a good job on knocking you out, didn't we?" I held my breath, not letting him know I was fully awake now. I was afraid of having him give me any kind of an injection. With Al out of commission I had to stay alert and keep my mind going.

Dick seemed to feel the need to talk. He spoke of how Dr. Vorhees had hired him for the clinic giving him the opportunity to ride the ambulance and work these "special" cases. "I love this job and all of the fringe benefits," he said. "Especially since I used to be a nurse just like you." He nodded in my direction. "Then bad luck set in. First I tried to help a patient, gave him a little more blood thinner than the doctor ordered. The damned guy seemed to be getting better when he started to hemorrhage and died." Internally I gasped. He had killed the man!

"After that everything went downhill. One night when I was a little high like almost everyone else, I forgot to connect a suction tube, and when I went off duty the patient choked to death. They all blamed me for it. Well, I got out of there and let them take the blame. Unfortunately, they pushed it on me and I lost my license. Now the only time I get to practice is here."

"I hope neither one of you is killed too soon," he said

softly. Remembering how he had looked at Al's naked body, I winced. Finally, Dick fell asleep at our bedsides.

Streaks of light passed through the drawn window shades. Daylight was fast approaching. I could hear the nursing staff beginning to finish their early morning procedures. No one paid any attention to Al or me. We had both been classified as "privates" under the direct care and supervision of Dr. Vorhees.

Dr. Vorhees checked on us once more. "I'm going home," he said to Dick. "You'd better find out who all of their contacts are. After my surgery this morning I'll call Paul in."

I cringed. So Paul really was one of them. I wondered if he would hurt me. But, to my surprise I heard Dr. Vorhees say that he didn't trust Paul. He said that Paul had always been there and even done the run to Miami without asking any questions. "But there's something about Paul I can't put my finger on. Maybe it's just his relationship with her," he announced.

Dr. Vorhees went on, "I'll bring Paul back with me to the clinic and let him administer the sodium pentathol." As an afterthought he added, "And I have also decided to let Paul watch you waste both of them."

I wondered if Paul could or would really do that. I lay barely breathing and stiff from not being able to move. My bladder was full, but I couldn't let them know I was awake. My life, and now Al's, depended on me.

SIXTEEN

Dr. Vorhees returned to the clinic early. I was surprised to see him show up in our room because he had spoken about an 8:00 a.m. surgery he was scheduled to perform. There was a large clock on the wall close to Al's head.

Dr. Vorhees looked first at me and then at Al. I could no longer pretend to be asleep. My bladder was so distended that it hurt and I finally said so.

"So, you are back from the world of the unconscious," he said smiling.

"Where am I?" I asked, acting as if I were confused and dazed. Then, before he could answer, I said, "and I really need to go to the bathroom."

"Give her the bedpan, Tillie," he commanded looking over at the heavyset nurse who had walked in almost behind him. "Then put a foley catheter in," he ordered.

"Please," I begged, "I'll behave myself. Please don't catheterize me."

"Where am I?" I asked again.

"In my private clinic," he said. "And," he nodded toward the still-sleeping Al, "your cop friend is right beside you."

I tried to play stupid. "What cop friend? Who is he?"

"Don't give me that," Dr. Vorhees snarled, but the

surprised look on his face gave him away. I could tell that I had caught him off guard and that he was momentarily wondering if perhaps he did have the wrong man.

Suddenly he looked up at the clock. "Damn. It's late. I'd better phone the hospital."

He walked over to a telephone near me and picked it up. "I overslept," he offered apologetically to a voice on the other end of the line. "I'll be there shortly. By the way, is Dr. Parker around by any chance?" Looking over at me, and holding his hand over the mouthpiece, he said that he could always have Paul do the hernia repair waiting for him in the OR if he couldn't find his associate. For some reason, he seemed to take a delight in telling me everything he was doing.

"Just a moment, sir. I'll ring him." I could hear that the operator had put him on hold and dialed Dr. Parker's extension.

"Dr. Parker here," came his punctual reply on the first ring.

"Just a moment please, Dr. Parker. Dr. Vorhees would like to talk to you. I'm connecting you now." I was so close to the telephone that I could even hear the operator plug the lines in allowing the men to talk. I wondered if I should call out help or try to grab it. But the realization that Dr. Vorhees would stop me, or perhaps controlled the person on the other end, stopped me. I decided my best idea at the moment was to play dumb, listen, and do nothing.

Dr. Vorhees explained the situation to his associate. Dr. Parker sounded excited at the news. "It's about time we got her. You stay there . . . with her . . . and I'll supervise everything from this end. By the way, what is your patient's name?"

"Gerald McGee," Dr. Vorhees answered. "I'm at the clinic if you need me. And," he paused, "thanks Phil. I owe you one."

"Don't mention it. I'll be around later to see you. Meanwhile, I'll observe our patients," Dr. Parker added.

"Good. See you then." Dr. Vorhees pressed the button. I heard the dial tone, then he dialed again. "This is Dr. Vorhees," he stated. "Could you please page Dr. Paul Thompson."

From the silence I knew she was looking at the resident on-call board. "I'm sorry, sir. Dr. Thompson is not in the house today."

"Thank you." Dr. Vorhees hung up the phone. "I'll have to find Paul later," he commented watching me. I said nothing.

"How's our other patient this morning?" he asked Dick.

Dick, who had been asleep in a nearby chair, awakened with a start and an apology. "Sorry, sir. I guess I was just dozing."

"That's okay, Dick. You deserve it. Besides, our man is sleeping like a baby. Just watch his vitals, though. I don't want him to respiratory arrest. Not yet, anyhow. He knows too much and we need to find out everything he does know."

Dick gave him a report on how well Al had slept all night. Actually, both Al and Dick slept well. I had lain awake.

Tillie, the private nurse Dr. Vorhees requested, flashed a wide grin revealing a missing front incisor. She looked rather goofy to me.

"When was his last sedation?" Dr. Vorhees questioned, skimming the chart with his eyes.

"I believe it was at 5:20 a.m. I haven't given him anything since then," Dick announced. Tillie stood mute apparently waiting for her orders.

"Good," he commented. "Let him wake up. I need to talk to him. Just watch both of them though and you had better keep them both restrained." He looked at me, adding, "she might be violent."

Tillie immediately placed a posey restraint and leather straps on both of my ankles and wrists. She then started an IV and moved the tubing out of my reach and behind my head.

Dr. Vorhees began to check on Al. "He's asleep, but he has very shallow respirations and a weak and thready pulse," he said thoughtfully.

"How's the girl?" Dick asked, changing the subject. He didn't seem to want to antagonize Dr. Vorhees as he looked over at me and asked the question, although he should have known how I was.

"Fine. I'm going to give her some pentathol before I do anything more. I'll probably give him some, too," he said nodding towards the unconscious Al. "See you later," Dr. Vorhees rang out cheerfully as he left the room.

Dick adjusted the IV, checked the remaining fluid and then took Al's pressure. He said to Tillie, "It's dropped considerably, probably from the massive doses of thorazine. He'll probably sleep for quite some time. I'm going to take a break and go for breakfast." She nodded as Dick left the room. Hunger filled me as he talked about how hungry he was.

My tongue stuck to the roof of my mouth. I realized I was very dry and thirsty. I tried to move my hands and legs, but they were tied. I began to panic. "Look, could I have a drink and something to eat?" I asked Tillie.

"In a few minutes," Tillie answered. "You can have your breakfast, if you just lie still and cooperate."

"I promise," I lied, hoping she would untie me and allow me to eat on my own. But something deep inside me knew she would probably feed me.

I had been correct. Tillie brought a tray in and set it on the overhead table. She then began to spoon-feed cold cereal into me. I hated cereal, and told her so. "It's what the doctor ordered," she said matter of factly. "So just be a good girl and eat it all." I knew she was right. I was their prisoner and I was going to need all of my strength to get out of my dilemma.

Just as she finished feeding me, Dr. Vorhees returned. He pulled a chair close to the bedside and sat down, leaning close to my face. "Now, why don't you and I have a little talk?"

"NO!" I screamed. "I will not talk to you." I was trying to be loud and scare him away. I had managed to loose the restraints on my left hand. I reached out and tried to scratch his face. I missed the face but caught his chin.

"Damn you," he muttered moving his chair back. Then he starerd at me again and tightened the restraints. "Go ahead, Joyce. Scream. No one can hear you. This is a private clinic. You are in a soundproof room. And you have a private nurse. The staff here thinks you are criminally insane, so they will only ignore all of your pleas and screams." He smiled with satisfaction. "Now, why don't you settle down and just save your energy."

"Never!" I spit at him.

Dr. Vorhees was losing his patience with me. "There are ways, my dear. First, I can use sodium pentathol. Then, I will have you repeatedly injected with addictive drugs. I might even have to perform exploratory surgery on you."

I tried to act brave. But I knew my situation was dangerous. Obviously, he suspected my narc role in the drug trafficking, and I was no longer considered part of the in-group. I thought about Bob Morgan and wondered if I was going to die in the same fashion. For the first time, the reality of my death seemed eminent and terrifying. "Why surgery?" I weakly asked.

"Oh, an abdominal exploratory, I think, so that we can intubate you, keep you on a respirator and keep you sedated. Your death will be slow and uncomfortable." Dr. Vorhees shrugged. "Quite frankly, you have caused too many of us to suffer."

Fear was flowing through my body. I wrestled against the restraints, uselessly.

"Fight all you want while you have the strength to do so." Dr. Vorhees turned to Tillie. "We'll give it to her IV," he ordered.

Tillie nodded and prepared the syringe to inject the fluid. I could see the IV over my head and out of my reach. How was I going to get out of this dilemma? I wondered who would or could save me. I lay sobbing hysterically.

Suddenly, Tillie spun around calling out to Dr. Vorhees. "Excuse me sir, but your other patient is having tremors. He's spastic. He's having difficulty breathing." There was a panic in her voice as she said, "I see that he has been receiving thorazine. It looks like the beginning of tardive dyskinesia."

I was all too familiar with the common side effect of thorazine. A toxic dosage causes a patient to lose muscle coordination that can ultimately lead to muscle rigidity. There may also be tremors and grotesque motions. Usually the patient complains of a swollen tongue first, but Al was in no position to complain about anything.

"Where the hell is Dick?" Dr. Vorhees bellowed angrily.

Tillie sighed nervously. "He went to breakfast. Can we give this man some artane or cogentin?" she asked. Either of these two drugs would immediately counteract the side effects of thorazine.

I knew that what she was saying was true. Thorazine did cause tardive dyskinesia and without an antagonist, Al could respiratory arrest. I cried hysterically as I watched Dr. Vorhees and Tillie race to his side.

Dick entered just as Tillie gave Al an injection of cogentin in his right hip. Dick noticed the airway protruding from Al's mouth.

An irate Dr. Vorhees spun around looking at the male nurse. "And, where in the hell have you been?"

Dick was stunned. "Ah . . . breakfast," he replied meekly.

Dr. Vorhees began to calm down. "Okay. But we just had a near emergency. Our patient was going into tardive dyskinesia and you know how dangerous that can be."

Dick looked pensive. I wondered if he did remember the side effect and its symptomology. I could also tell by

the wounded look on his face that he was intimidated by
Dr. Vorhees. Dick's whole demeanor changed when he was
challenged by his boss.

"Sorry I yelled at you," Dr. Vorhees suddenly, and
almost politely, offered. He added the rest of instructions.
"I ordered cogentin. Keep it up." Dr. Vorhees and Tillie
then spun around to look back at me.

Dick was obviously shaken, but began taking Al's
vital signs. He left the airway in place. Al continued to
sleep. He looked in a deeply comatose state.

Dr. Vorhees returned to my bedside. Tillie handed
him the syringe. "That was a close call," he reported to
me. "Your friend had a reaction to the thorazine. He'll be
okay. For now."

Dr. Vorhees punctured the tubing with the syringe
needle. As he pushed the plunger in I knew my life was no
longer mine. I would be forced to tell him everything he
wanted to know.

The medication seemed to take effect quickly. One of
my last thoughts before losing consciousness was that I
hoped I could die and visit the same wonderful place Mrs.
Kendall had told me about.

"Scalpel! Retractors! Sutures!" Dr. Vorhees's voice
called out the perfunctory orders loudly. I felt frightened
remembering his earlier threat of performing surgery on
me. Was he pretending or really going to do it. Panic
stricken I waited "Number 8 oral endotracheal tube," the
nurse anesthetist bellowed, adding, almost as a last minute thought, "and for God's sake, turn on the respirator!"

The breathing machine filled the room with loud, life-
giving swishing sounds. The doctor's panicking voice
could barely be heard above it. "Thrust the jaw forward.
Now, insert the tube." Commands kept coming.

Finally, a gag reflex occurred. "Good," the doctor
said. A sigh of relief passed through his lips. It was still
too soon to totally relax. Too much could still go wrong.
"Slide it in very carefully," he instructed. "I think we have

it. Attach the life support to the machine and set the dials for control. Pentathol stat."

The needle penetrated the IV tubing already in my vein. I thought it was my right arm and wondered if I was correct. *What did it feel like?* I questioned myself in a sleepy daze. *Perhaps like a slippery, smooth snake winding its way through a dark tunnel.* My hand wanted to move, but I was paralyzed. Something heavy lay on my wrist, like a brick.

"That's fine," the familiar voice praised quietly. "Go slow and make this as real as you can," he cautioned.

The voices were clear but distant. Far, far away. I could hear my lungs filling and emptying with the life-sustaining air. Air sounds like wind in a tunnel. *No control,* I thought. *I have no control. Perhaps I am dying. Maybe this is the near death experience I have heard about. It is so peaceful here.* I wanted to stay.

"Nasogastric to low suction." A nurse's voice penetrated my thoughts. I recognized the voice. Soft. Commanding, yet deferential, knowing her place on the team. The voice was reassuring. I felt the slippery snake passing through my right nostril into my stomach lining. A frightening noise permeated my quiet space. Suctioning turned on and off at regular intervals. My stomach rumbled; I began to retch violently, trying to cough up the tubes that filled my breathing and eating passages. I felt another tube emptying urine from my bladder; others filled my veins with painkilling medications.

"Where the hell is more pentathol?" the doctor's voice bellowed angrily again.

Yes, bring me drugs, I thought as I began gasping for air. It wasn't peaceful anymore. I was frightened.

"I'm coming," the nurse answered. She didn't sound so reassuring. "I'm injecting it now, doctor, into the main fluid IV."

"Thank God. We nearly lost this mean-aarterial line, and we still have to put the swanz gans pulmonary wedge line in." The doctor seemed to be talking to himself. "The next time I call you, young lady, you had better come running." *You always have to tell the nurses what to do, doctor,* I thought. *Put them in their place.*

Peace suddenly fell over me. My mind went blank. *Where am I?* I asked in the last momentary split second of consciousness. In that split second in time I remembered who I was.

I know. I know. My mind raced back to the injection Dr. Vorhees gave me. Then my body went flacid, succumbing to a deep, drug-induced state; my mind was no longer on earth or in heaven. My spirit lingered someplace in between.

I have no idea how long I lay unconscious. At some point I began to awaken. I was in a fog, at first, and momentarily thought I was home in my own bed. I attempted to sit up. When I couldn't, I quickly realized I was in Dr. Vorhees's clinic.

I could see a smile on the doctor's face as he sat next to my bed. "You were superb," he cooed. "And we thank you for all of your help."

Apparently, from the way he went on talking, Dr. Vorhees had learned everything he wanted to know. He knew of my involvement with Al and the DEA. I had told him about Mark Gibson, and the State Attorney, Leonard Elliott. He even ascertained Sister Theresa's role in the process. Dr. Vorhees was nervous. He told Tillie and Dick that far too many people had become involved and seemed to know what was going on.

He knew that I never caught on until after the trip to Miami with Paul. Apparently, he was satisfied with what I told him about Paul, although he was relieved to know that Paul had kept a lot of information from me.

He was surprised to learn that Paul and I had never discussed the real reason for the trip to Miami or my feelings about Paul's usage of drugs. He also discovered that we had both done butyl nitrite together. He and Tillie laughed uproariously at that one. My face flushed with embarrassment. I felt vulnerable and fully exposed, wondering just how much of my intimate moments with Paul I had revealed.

Dr. Vorhees sat by my bedside. He looked lost in thought. My thoughts flashed back to Bob Morgan's death. Bob Morgan was killed before anyone knew whom he was in contact with. Now I had apparently told him what he needed to know. My future seemed precarious.

Dr. Vorhees apparently began to feel optimistic. "With both the cop and the nurse out of the way," he said quietly, as though he were speaking only to himself and no one else in the room, "we could still work for a while longer." He talked about some changes he needed to make and some new precautions. "It should work out," he announced proudly.

Although I was groggy, I was also becoming more and more aware. The pentathol was wearing off, although again I played the part of someone who was confused, dazed, and disoriented.

Dr. Vorhees's thoughts were interrupted by the sound of footsteps. He smiled as he recognized Dr. Phil Parker entering our room. "It's nice to see you," he beamed.

"Your hernia went just fine, Ralph," Dr. Parker stated, seating himself in front of the doctor between our beds. "I let Blowers do it. The kid does nice work."

"Great. Thanks for your assistance."

"So," Dr. Parker began, stuffing his pipe and lighting it, "what has been going on around here, Ralph?" He glared over at me and then at Al.

"We just played surgery," Dr. Vorhees said jestingly.

Dr. Vorhees described the entire series of events. His associate sat and listened quietly, puffing on his pipe and nodding in approval. I, too, lay quietly listening with my eyes closed as if I were sleeping soundly.

"Have you given the policeman any pentathol yet?" he inquired.

"No. I am still waiting for him to come around. We really loaded him up with thorazine." Dr. Vorhees paused.

"Do you want to check on both of them and grab a bite?" he asked.

Dr. Parker put the pipe down in the glass ashtray. "Sure. We can talk some more over lunch." He reviewed both charts and took both of our pulses. Then the two men left the room.

I fell asleep and slept peacefully for a brief period of time. I was so tired that I was dead to the world. My last memory was of Tillie sitting, reading a mystery novel.

"Don't give her any more sedation," Dr. Vorhees ordered as he and Dr. Parker returned from lunch. "We want her alert.

I overheard him, but dozed off again as I heard Tillie reply.

"Yes, doctor," Tillie answered.

Somewhere, deep inside a dark tunnel, I could hear the voices and laughter. I just couldn't find my way or see anything clearly. I was suddenly too tired, but my last thoughts were of obtaining some rest in order to find a way out of this dilemma and help Al.

When I next woke up I saw Dick sitting silently twiddling a ball of paper. He was throwing wads of towels into the wastebasket across the room.

Dick nodded to the two doctors and stood up as they walked over to the bedside nurses' notes. "His pressure is coming back up," Dick reported, adding, "and I removed his airway twenty minutes ago."

"Let him wake up," Dr. Vorhees reported. "We'll talk to him later. The nurse gave us a lot of information. We hope he will be as informative as she was."

Dick nodded.

When I overheard the doctors talking I forced myself to consciousness, although I still pretended to be asleep. I used my old trick of peering out from under my eyelids.

"I talked to Marilyn and Lois this morning," Phil Parker stated, "before I left Trinity."

"How did they react?" Dr. Vorhees asked.

"Shocked. Just like us, but glad that we caught her."

"Damn, we've had a very successful operation here," Vorhees snapped.

"Do we stop now, Ralph?" Dr. Parker inquired. He paused, taking a long, deep breath before continuing. "My own personal expenses are more than I can support on just the surgeries." His statement shocked me. He went on to reveal his problems.

Apparently, he and his family lived way beyond their means. Also, he liked to gamble: the horses, football, Las Vegas. He had large debts and was always working on paying them off while still accrueing more.

"I don't see why not," Dr. Vorhees answered. He, too, enjoyed a quality life style. He talked about how his wife no longer met his emotional needs, but she wore the finest of clothing and jewelry. She was active in social circles, and the couple travelled lavishly and frequently.

The doctors were becoming impatient and tired as they waited for Al to wake up to fill in the remaining missing pieces of information.

Al was not responding. "Damn," Dr. Parker muttered. "It will be a few days before he detoxes all of that thorazine." The men looked at each other. "Well, we will just have to wait."

"Do we let the nurse live for a while, too?" Dr. Vorhees asked of his friend as they looked over at me.

"Why not? She is worthless to us dead. Alive, we can bargain with her."

I felt better just hearing those words. The two doctors informed Dick and Tillie that they were going back to Dr. Vorhees's office.

Sometime later another nurse entered my room looking at Tillie. Tillie was dozing. Momentarily startled, she looked up, "What can I do for you?"

"I am your relief," the nurse answered with a smile.

"Oh," Tillie smiled, "you must be Sharon."

"Yes. Just fill me in and I'll let you go."

Tillie looked at her watch. I looked at the clock on the wall. It was already 6:45 p.m. Both nurses were taking twelve-hour shifts. Tillie was surprised that she had fallen asleep and missed dinner. But, she was grateful to the relief nurse. "I'll leave a little early and pick up a large, double pizza on my way home," she said.

Tillie gave report. "Thanks, Sharon. See you in the morning." I watched her pick up a heavy sweater and novel, stuffing them into her large, black purse. "See you in the morning," she chirped again, leaving the room and letting the door close behind her.

After Tillie left, Sharon approached me. She leaned over the bed, silently watching me breathe for a while. I was frightened. I was also groggy but awake.

"Dont say a word and don't scream," Sharon warned me, whispering. "I am an undercover officer. You are going to be all right. Do you understand me?"

I nodded, feeling a sense of relief. "Yes," I whispered. "What about Al?" I asked.

Sharon began untying my restraints. I stretched my arms and began to rub circulation back into them. I had been in the same position for nearly fifteen hours. My entire body ached.

Sharon looked over at Al and asked what I knew about him as she was cutting the extension from my foley and letting the saline drain from it to deflate the balloon inside my bladder. Before I could answer she said, "Take a breath."

I did instinctively, and felt the rubber snake being gently pulled from my body. "He is still unconscious. Dr. Vorhees and Dr. Parker have him medicated with thorazine."

"Look," she said, "I want you to stay here until I tell you that everything is all clear. We have this place surrounded, but we want to apprehend everyone." She then wrapped the restraints around me without tying them. She taped my foley to the bed sheet.

I forced myself not to cry. "How did you know where we were?" I said, pleading for explanations and answers.

"You can thank me for that," a male voice said, walking through the door. I looked up in time to see Paul.

"It's okay," he said offering reassurance. "I have never been too far behind you." He began to soothe my head. "Everything is fine now, Joyce."

Shock filled my entire body. I looked up at Paul. Paul standing there to rescue me. Paul with those same beautiful sky blue eyes and thick, dark, shiny black hair. One curl fell off his forehead clinging to his right eyebrow. I wanted to reach out and brush it away.

Paul, the man who had made passionate love to me unlike any man I had ever known. As he stood before me my mind flashed and reminisced. Our first meeting at the disco. Dancing and holding one another close. Our Italian meals, vintage red wines, nights of romance and days of teasing. Our trip to Miami. Even the silk scarves raced through my memory. Then I remembered our trip to Miami and how close I had come to being arrested.

Anger was beginning to replace the shock. Anger at Paul for using me and not including me in whatever it was he was doing. I soon realized that the angry emotion was really fear. I was frightened and confused.

As Paul removed the IV from my left hand, he gently caressed it and then asked, "Can you stay in this position for a little longer?" His eyes met mine. Somehow, I sensed the unspoken message. In that fleeting moment I knew that Paul loved me. Later I would pray that he realized just how much I loved him. I always have and I always will.

I nodded as he taped the IV tubing to my arm. At least, the needle was no longer in my arm. Now I was just play-acting a part. There was no time for me to ask questions. Paul looked at Sharon. "Stay with her," he cautioned.

The officer nodded and showed both of us a service revolver in her purse.

Paul waited until Dick returned from his dinner a few minutes later. Dick jumped, but recognized the young resident whom he had seen on many previous occasions. "Hi," he called out. "What's happening?"

Paul replied, "Oh, I just heard about our newest kidnaps. I wanted to be in on everything."

"Sure," Dick nodded.

"How is he?" Paul asked the nurse.

"Better now," Dick stated. "He was pretty heavily overdosed on thorazine. The docs want him to wake up so they can question him."

Paul nodded. "I want to be a part of that," he retorted, adding, "and I am sorry I wasn't a part of the interrogation with the nurse."

Dick chuckled. "It went well." He looked over at me. The restraints were loose around my wrists and the foley lay inside the sheet covers. He didn't seem to notice that even the IV was no longer really in my wrist. It had been replaced to look as natural as possible.

"Did you know she had the hots for you?" He laughed again, nodding towards me.

Paul blushed as he looked over at me. "Yeah, but you know how it is. I had to check her out. Can't be too safe these days."

His icy tone along with the words stung. Was I imagining everything, I wondered. Perhaps Paul didn't really love me. Perhaps he had only used me, then pretended to frame me, and was part of the conspiracy. I wanted to scream out, to ask a thousand questions. At the same time, I wanted to yell obscenities at Paul and then hold him in my arms for one more time.

Dick nodded in agreement.

"Hey," Paul announced, no longer looking at me or noticing the moods on my face, "Do you want me to stay here with you until the doctors come back?"

"Gee, that's nice of you, doc. Sure. Thanks." Dick picked up the papers strewn around the wastebasket, the ones he had missed.

Paul and the nurse talked and laughed among themselves for a few moments. Then Paul suddenly stood and opened the door of our room. Dick was caught off guard as two policemen entered.

"Hey," he bellowed, "what's going on here?"

Paul drew a gun, as did Carrie. They held the gun on Dick and watched as he was immediately arrested by two uniformed officers.

Dick tried to resist, but handcuffs were placed on his wrists and tape across his mouth. I heard his rights being read to him as they took him out of the room.

"One down," Paul said, looking at both Carrie and me. "Now, we need to find Dr. Vorhees and Dr. Parker."

"They went to their offices," I offered.

"Okay," he replied.

"Paul, let me go with you?" I asked.

"No way," he declared. "It is too dangerous."

I begged. "Please. After what they did to all of us, I want to be there to see them get arrested."

Paul didn't answer as he checked on Al. His vital signs were doing better than he expected. "Sorry, sir," he whispered, "but you will be all right now. Joyce is fine, too." He nodded towards me.

Paul removed the foley catheter and IV from AL. He took off the restraints and kept poking the man to wake up. Finally, Al responded. I was glad to see proof that he was alive and well. "Good work, son," he said groggily to Paul. "What's happening?"

"We're about to move in for the kill, sir," Paul replied with a politeness I had never heard. "We're going after Vorhees and Parker."

Al nodded. "You know the plan. Make sure you are arrested too."

Once again I was overwhelmed with the dishonesty of this conspiracy. I had been used and lied to by both of them. My face flushed with pain and rage. I wanted to throw something at both Al and Paul.

"You bastards," I spit out vehemently. "You both used me. How could you do this?"

"We couldn't let you in on everything," Paul stated,

looking over at me. "It was too dangerous for you and for us. I am really sorry, Joyce. I never wanted to see you get hurt."

Although I had many questions, I realized that now was not the time to ask them. My thoughts turned to Al's well-being and health. "Al, are you okay?" I asked, changing the subject.

He turned and looked at me, nodding his head. "And you?" he inquired with genuine concern.

"I'm fine," I exclaimed, adding with a determined tone to my voice, "and I'm going with these two."

"No, you are not, young lady," Al tried to bellow, but I knew he really had no strength to fight me. Our eyes met. There was no stopping me.

"Who has a better right?" I said in a low tone. "You owe me a lot of explanations. Right now you can begin by letting me participate in the windup of this nightmare. I have come this far," I cautioned, "and I intend to see it through to the end. At least let me have that satisfaction."

Al nodded at Paul and Carrie. Al understood my determination. It was also apparent to me that he was still the man in charge.

Carrie and Paul helped me to my feet. I was wobbly, but determined to walk. In the hallway we found our policemen. Two helped Al. I followed the others until we were right outside Dr. Vorhees's office.

I felt euphoric and eager to see the tables turn on both of them. Waiting outside the office, we could hear the two doctors engrossed in conversation.

"I'll be glad when this is over," Phil Parker said to Ralph Vorhees, sitting in the dictor's spatial office. He sighed. "I love this room with its warm, massive oak furniture, heavy velvet drapes and, in the winter, the fireplace crackling. It's peaceful and luxurious—my style."

Dr. Vorhees nodded. "Me too. We will interrogate the cop, and when we know who else is on to us, we will have Harry do the dirty work."

"Harry's getting a little old for all of this, don't you think?" Dr. Parker questioned.

"Probably. Who isn't?" Dr. Vorhees retorted. "I don't want to keep this up much longer myself, Phil. It is getting too complicated. Sometimes I have visions of losing my license and going to prison. It's a recurring nightmare. I wake up at 3:00 a.m. sweating and restless. Then I toss and turn the rest of the night."

Paul knocked at their door. "Who is it?" Dr. Vorhees called out.

"Paul Thompson," he replied.

"Good. Come on in, Paul. The door is open."

I stayed in the hall with Carrie as Paul entered, leaving the door ajar. I couldn't see the men clearly, but I could overhear everything.

"I understand you were looking for me at Trinity this morning," Paul said.

"Yes," Vorhees answered cheerfully. "We caught your nurse friend in the act last night. Apparently, she is our narc."

"Where is she?" Paul questioned as if he knew nothing.

"Room six. And, we have a cop in there too."

"Great," Paul exclaimed, trying to sound delighted. "Has she told you anything?"

Dr. Parker and Dr. Vorhees both chuckled. "I am afraid so," Vorhees said mysteriously.

I knew Paul was nervous. I suspected that he wondered just how much I knew and what I might have told them. "Tell me," he said.

"Shall we start with the butyl nitrite or end with it?" Dr. Parker laughed.

Dr. Vorhees told Paul everything I had repeated. I sensed Paul breathing a sigh of relief as he apparently realized that his cover had not been blown. Just as Dr. Vorhees finished we gave another knock on the door. Knowing that it was time for us to move in for the arrest my heart quickened again. Only this time, I felt a pulsating sense of excitement.

Paul walked over and opened the door before either Dr. Parker or Dr. Vorhees could respond. I watched him being greeted by three officers, with guns drawn, and two undercover agents.

The three doctors froze. Both Dr. Vorhees and Dr. Parker exchanged glances.

One officer walked over to each man and instructed them to raise their hands. "You have the right to remain silent" another began. "If you give up that right . . ."

Dr. Vorhees heard nothing more. He quickly looked over at Paul and noticed his hands were up and that he, too, was being arrested. He then saw me enter the room. Our eyes met, but we never spoke. I remember feeling a tremendous relief that the nightmare was over.

The three men were led away in three separate squad cars. I was escorted to a waiting vehicle. Al was waiting for me, looking pale, but I was grateful that he was okay.

Al seemed still weak but alert. "You guys sure took your time," he reprimanded his men.

"We had to make sure, Al," Mark Gibson answered.

"Did you get them all?" Al asked Mark, who was sitting next to him in the unmarked police car.

"We sure did. And the record books too. You did a nice job," Mark stated.

"I damn near died," Al retorted angrily. Then he looked at me. I had been sitting in silence listening to both of the men. "How are you?" he asked me in a softer tone with genuine concern.

Tears filled my eyes. I was fully aware of our close call with death. Trying to be brave I answered, "I'm just fine," but it would be a long time before I would really feel that way.

Al and I sat in a quiet corner of a busy coffee shop deep in the heart of the city. It had been one week since the arrests took place at the clinic. Al looked better, although he said he had taken several days off to recover from the effects of the thorazine.

"What are your plans now?" I questioned him while he played with his spoon in a cold cup of coffee.

Pausing to look at me, he said, "We have already completed a lot that you don't know about. I was angry with you for making that decision to go back into the OR without discussing it with me first. But I have to admit that we couldn't have made the arrests without your help."

"So, is this what a narc does?" I inquired. "It's tough going. It has taken me a few days to get my own feet back on the ground."

"Yes. And, you have done it well. I'll ask you again," he said, "would you like to reconsider and make a career out of law enforcement, Joyce. A lot of medical professionals do work for both the legal system and at their jobs. Some nurses and doctors are expert witnesses, testifying at cases for lawyers and fighting crime."

"Al, I'm sorry, it's not for me. Thank you anyway. I never wanted to play the role of an undercover agent. All I want now is to end this and get on with my life."

"Okay. Let me tell you what we have done so far." Al pushed the coffee cup away and bent his head closer to me. "We planted undercover officers in maintenance, laundry, housekeeping, and central supply. All of the nurses' lounges and lockers have bugs planted in them."

"When did you do all of this?"

"In the past week. Sister Theresa has also ordered an in-house camera system to be installed. There will be cameras focused on every area within the hospital and they will be monitored by security. The system is not one hundred percent foolproof, but it will decrease a lot of drug problems in the future."

"The Big Brother concept," I interjected. "It plays havoc with my old ideals about medicine and our roles as heroes. Well, I guess everyone else uses them. Why not hospitals?"

Al nodded. "Ideals and reality sometimes conflict." He looked searchingly at me. "Sometimes but not always, Joyce." He patted my hand with his own. "Don't you lose touch with either one." He smiled, a gentle smile.

"I'm going to try like hell not to," I said, returning his smile. I swallowed hard, blinking back tears. "Now tell me what's going to happen to Marilyn and Lois and Carol and the others. Will they be arrested?"

Al grimaced. "You don't give up easily. No, not now. Charges will be filed later, but on an individual basis. Some charges may not be filed at all. Sister Theresa can't hire and train nurses fast enough to replace them all."

Actually, I was relieved. One of my nightmares was the picture of a large arrest with all of the nurses knowing I had caused it. Al seemed to have read my mind.

"Narcs are not exposed, Joyce. We go to great lengths to protect them."

I was still concerned about the nurses I had seen, the many who were users. Stealing and selling was one thing, but nurses under the influence were damned dangerous. I told Al that.

"You nurses are going to have to find ways to help each other. Drug and alcohol addictions are a disease and need to be treated. I can't help you there and I can't authorize arrests of abusers unless they are caught in the act of stealing and using. Of course, the camera security system should help somewhat."

"Who are you going to arrest? What are your plans?" I pressed. I still wanted a resolution.

"We are going to arrest Karen White, the Assistant D.O.N. We found her records, so we have plenty of evidence on which to prosecute her. And Dr. Vorhees left his records in his office. Harry Cappuzzio works for the local mobster, Joseph Bertollini. Mr. Bertollini and his family are the laundering source. They are the ones who arranged for pick-ups in Miami. You brought cocaine back to them."

"And Paul's role in all of this?" I still had feelings for Paul that bordered between love and anger.

Al understood my confusion. "Paul is one of ours. An undercover narc who always wanted to be a doctor. The department paid his medical school expenses. He is a brilliant detective and a good doctor.

A chill shuddered through my body. I was excited and relieved to know that Paul had not really misused me. "Is his name really Paul Thompson?" I asked. Before Al could reply I also asked, "And will I ever see him again?"

"No to both questions," Al replied soberly. "He changed his name for reasons I am sure you can understand. I can't tell you his real name. And I doubt that you will ever see him again. We have to keep him undercover. His arrest was staged, and he is being charged along with Dr. Vorhees, Dr. Parker, Dr. Jackson, and Mrs. White. He will never go to trial, however. He will be transferred to another part of the country and begin the same job again."

Al noticed me beginning to cry. "I am really sorry, Joyce. I know you cared for him."

I could only sniffle and nod. My affair with Paul was obviously over. Somehow I had been grasping at straws, praying that a resolution to this experience would allow Paul and me to begin a life together. That dream had been my fantasy all along. I wanted to be with Paul. To live with him. To love him singularly and passionately for the rest of my life.

Now that Al had told me the hard, cold facts my bubble was burst. There would be no romance or life with Paul, or whatever his real name was, for me. In reality, I would never even know who he really was. For the rest of my life he would remain in a corner of my mind and heart hiding there until resurrected by a thought or a dream or a glimpse of someone who looked like him on the street. I would never forget Paul. I also knew that I could never stop loving him.

Finally composing myself, I asked, "What do I do now, Al? Will I have to testify or anything?"

"No. Now you can get on with your life, just as you requested. We're very grateful to you for your help. Sister Theresa will give you a recommendation wherever you go, although she is hoping you won't resign."

I shook my head sadly. "I have to. Critical care nursing is not for me. I miss the patient contact. I don't like the necessary detachment from feelings. I am going to leave nursing and go into psychology. Maybe there I can learn more about people's motives and personality traits. Besides, I can't go back to Trinity now."

Al's eyes met mine. "Sister Theresa expected you to say that. I can't say I blame you, either. And you're right—you really can't stay at Trinity, anyhow." Al paused. "Well, it is your choice," he finally connceded. Al signalled to the waitress for the check. "I think we can wrap this up."

In the parking lot he paused by my car. "Thank you for everything," he said, taking my hand and shaking it. "We couldn't have done this without you." Then, suddenly and impulsively, he pulled me close and hugged me.

Neither one of us spoke. I knew the hug meant "goodbye." I would never see him again.

One week later, sitting on my porch at my parents' lake home, I opened the local morning newspaper and found a small article about a drug arrest at Trinity Hospital.

A Mrs. Karen White, the Assistant Director of Nurses, was arrested for the stealing and selling of drugs. She was found with a notebook of all transactions on her. Dr. Ralph Vorhees, Dr. Phillip Parker, Dr. Leslie Jackson, and Dr. Paul Thompson were also arrested. There was no mention of evidence found on any of the men. There was also no mention of anyone else having been arrested. I never heard another word about the drug ring. And, to this day, I have never seen or heard anything more about Paul Thompson.

Two weeks later my acceptance to graduate school arrived. I moved to Florida on August 20, 1977.

FINAL EPILOGUE

I graduated from Nova University in Ft. Lauderdale, Florida, in May, 1980, receiving a Master's degree in Counseling Psychology and Psychomotry (Psychological testing). In 1981, I took the American Nurses Association's national exam and became certified as a Psychiatric Nurse Clinician. While completing graduate school, I worked as a critical care nurse in many local Florida hospitals. I never left nursing. Nursing was too deep in my blood.

In December, 1980, I began a private practice offering nurse support groups. Nurses were slow and reluctant to come. Fearing self-disclosure, they felt unable to trust other nurses. Gradually, however, word began to spread. By 1982, nurse support groups were ongoing and meeting several times a week. At the present, groups continue to meet weekly or bi-monthly. They meet in our offices, or on-site at hospitals, nursing homes, home health agencies, and public health nursing divisions. It is my fervent hope that schools of nursing will soon provide support groups to students during their training.

In October, 1983, the Florida State Board of Nursing created the Impaired Nurses Program. The program, later titled the Intervention Project for Nurses, helps nurses who have a chemical addiction or judgmental/emotional impairment to comply with the IPN requirements. Besides detox, AA or NA meetings, as well as random urines for chemical addictions, the program requires participation in ongoing nurse support groups. The minimum probationary period is two years. Licenses are not acted upon and nurses continue to work with the knowledge and written support of their employers. Nurses are given the choice of entering the program on a voluntary basis or going before the State Board of Nursing and possibly having their licenses acted upon.

Since the inception of the program, Florida has treated close to five hundred nurses. Hundreds of others have voluntarily entered treatment before getting caught, and have voluntarily entered nurse support groups. The majority of nurses treated have done remarkably well. Relapses among addictive nurses have been minimal. Nurses with emotional/judgmental problems have been given intense individual and group psychotherapy. Recovery has been widespread. Results have been positive.

Hundreds of other nurses still join support groups to cope with stress, burn-out, internal nursing problems, and frustrations. Nurses in the programs learn to trust each other, like each other, and work together.

Since beginning my private practice and support groups, I have personally worked with or supervised over five hundred and fifty nurses on either an individual or group therapy basis. I have gathered data on the value of nurse support groups and presented it at numerous national and international nursing and psychological workshops. The only other available studies done on the value of nurse support groups, to date, have been limited to critical care areas of specific hospitals.

Our nurses come from all phases of the profession and all settings. Our groups are comprised of nurses from hospitals, home health clinics, doctors' offices, and private duty. They also include Directors of Nursing, nurse managers (head nurses), staff nurses, RN's and LPN's, nurses' aides, ward clerks, X-ray technicians, and Advanced Registered Nurse Practitioners. All barriers are dropped in these groups. Cohesiveness has been the goal and by-product, and it has worked.

However, our national nursing organizations still have only small numbers that belong or participate in these groups. Hopefully, as nurses find they can understand themselves and others more, they will unite for common goals. In the meantime Florida, like a few other states, is to be commended for the way in which it helps nurses.

There is also an Impaired Physicians Program in the State of Florida for doctors who abuse and misuse chemicals. Other professional subgroups, including psychologists, have also created similar programs. I genuinely hope that this book will enlighten and encourage other states and professions to look at those of us who are "helping the helpers."

Finally, this story is true. The entire book is a composite of my experiences as well as those of my clients and associates. All names, dates and places have been changed to protect their privacy.

Today, I am proud to be a nurse. I am the Nursing Administrator for Psycho-Awareness, Inc. in Ft. Lauderdale, Florida, where I supervise both the Intervention Project for Nurses program in our facility and our continuing education programs for nurses. I continue to personally run five nurse support groups and I was instrumental in the creation and publication of "How to Start Nursing Support Groups."

I am proud to teach nurses and other health and psychological professionals, continuing education programs at the community college level. The classes I teach include: New Age Psychology: An Overview of the Near Death Experience, Past Life Therapy Theory, and the Theory of Spiritual Possession; Dream Analysis; Suicide and Depression; and Neuroses, Psychoses, and Crisis Intervention.

I did become actively involved with Near Death Experiences following an intense workshop in 1984. I have published numerous articles on this subject and spoken at International workshops. Many of my Near Death Experiences are Viet Nam Vets.

I am proud to be functioning as a primary therapist to nurses both individually and in group therapy. I am listed as a nurse entrepreneur (with both the American Nurses Association and the National League for Nursing). As an entrepreneur I was instrumental in helping to create Psycho-Awareness, Inc., a full service, out-patient, psychiatric and psychological facility.

I am proud to have staff privileges at two Ft. Lauderdale area hospitals where I admit patients and administer my psychological and psychiatric therapeutic skills. I sign third party insurance forms under my Psychiatric Nursing license. I make judgment calls, nursing diagnoses, and work closely with the medical community in my treatment plans.

As a lecturer and consultant I educate lay people and nurses alike on what nurses do and how much we know. I advocate the increased educational requirements I feel nurses need to gain respect in addition to the knowledge base they already have. I also feel that we nurses should seriously consider a name change to help recruit men into our profession.

Nursing is a wonderful profession. We are in the midst of many positive changes. Nurses are becoming as independent as physicians have always been. And, most importantly, nursing is looking at all phases of illnesses and treating our own.

Over the past eight years I have witnessed abuses in the psychiatric and psychological professions. I have become familiar with and treated sexual abuse, physical abuse, and emotional abuse. Some of the damage has been inflicted, unfortunately, by my own professional associates.

In addition to our support groups for chemical impairments, I now work with nurses who have been found judgmentally impaired. I work with personality disorders, and dual diagnoses among many of my clients, including nurses. I have seen the psychological after-effects of sexual abuse, incest, and inappropriate professional care by psychiatrists and psychologists who have not worked through their own emotional histories.

I am now completing my Ph.D. in Clinical Psychology, and am more cognizant of the internal processes and problems in my profession. Now and in the future, I hope to take an active part in finding solutions for these critical problems so that tragedies like those depicted in *Medical Treason* won't be repeated.

GLOSSARY

AA: Alcoholics Anonymous

AMA: American Medical Association

ANA: American Nurses Association

Amyl nitrite: a blood dilator, usually used for angina attacks. Sold in sex shops as butyl nitrite, it is popular for the flushing and dilation of the major blood vessels, especially during sexual intercourse.

Arterial shunt: a tube placed in the artery often at the wrist, for kidney dialysis. The exchange of blood through the dialysis machine is done through this shunt.

BP: blood pressure. A side effect of too much demerol is a decrease in respirations (breaths) and a decrease in blood pressure.

Bilirubin: the bilirubin, a pigment from the liver, is analyzed in the blood with the concentration level telling the medical team about the liver and presence of disease.

CVP: the purpose of the Central Venous pressure is to see how the right side of the heart manages the body fluid load and becomes a guide for fluid replacement in the critically ill patient.

Chloral hydrate: a commonly ordered sleeping pill used by drug users to quickly bring them down from their high state.

DOA: dead on arrival.

DRG's: Diagnostic Related Grouping was enacted by the Federal government to control and decrease the amount of time a patient stays in the hospital. Medicare, in particular, was seeking a way to cut costs and unnecessary added hospital expenses.

Dalmane: a commonly prescribed hypnotic sleeping pill used for people with severe or chronic insomnia who have difficulty falling asleep or staying asleep. Drug abusers use it to help counteract the effects of their drugs and/or alcohol and allow them to sleep.

Demerol: an analgesic that produces a sedating, or calming effect, in some people, and elation in others. Side effects are nausea and vomiting.

Detox: to cleanse the body from wastes and poisons, also called toxins.

Dilaudid: a pain killer that causes drowsiness and changes in mood while easing severe pain. It is taken illicitly to ease emotional pain and cope with psychological stress and demand. It can cause severe depression and burn skin tissue if it is repeatedly injected into the skin.

Dopamine: a medication used to increase the heart rate by increasing the muscle contractions of the heart. It is frequently used after a patient has had an MI (myocardial infarction known as a heart attack), CHF (congestive heart failure where the bottom of the heart is filled with too much fluid) or Open Heart surgery.

Downs syndrome: Mongoloids born with an extra chromosome.

Electrolytes: the body's chemical system.

Endocardium: covers the heart valves and the surface of the heart.

Hemodialysis: the removal of the body's wastes through the arterial shunt when the kidneys do not adequately cleanse the body's wastes and toxins.

ICU psychoses: the mental confusion exhibited by a patient who has not had enough sleep or whose electrolytes are too high or too low in the blood system.

IV: intravenous—tubing or needle placed within a vein.

Laparotomy: an exploratory surgery of the abdominal region where the incision is closed after the surgery.

Lasix: a diuretic used to help the kidneys give off fluid buildup and avoid heart and lung fluid overload problems.

Lidocaine: used for the acute management of cardiac (heart) arrythmias (irregular heart beats). Lidocaine will return the heart beat to a normal sinus rhythm.

Luminal: hypnotic barbituate used by drug abusers, especially alcoholics to help them avoid tremors and agitation.

MAP: mean arterial pressure tells the medical team how the blood vessels are working, especially in the top part of the heart.

MF IV: main fluid IV.

Mannitol: a drug used to reduce fluid in the brain.

Morphine: narcotic (opium) which slows pain and causes drowsiness. Morphine puts some people to sleep, while others state they feel calm and able to cope.

NA: Narcotics Anonymous.

Narcan: a drug antagonist used to counteract opiate intoxiation, i.e., narcotic (opiate) drug overdoses.

Nembutal: a hypnotic sedative with an onset in fifteen to twenty minutes. It has a calming effect and allows some people to function without feeling emotional pain.

Nubaine: a strong painkiller that works both for and against other narcotic painkillers. It will cause common narcotic side effects of nausea, vomiting, and stomach disturbances.

OB: obstetrics.

OD: overdose.

Output: the hourly rate of urine flow.

PRN: as needed.

PVC's: premature ventricular contractions. The bottom two chambers of the heart are known as the ventricles. Normally, the top part of the heart, the atriums, contract, pushing blood through and then the bottom part contracts. When the bottom contracts first it means the top part is no longer contracting properly, if at all.

Percocet and percodan: narcotic analgesics that kill pain and sedate, causing a calming effect.

Pericardium: the membraneous sac lining the outside of the heart.

Phenergan: used to alleviate the nausea and vomiting associated with many illnesses. It also may contain codeine, a narcotic used for decreasing pain. The combination for a drug user allows the emotional "high" from the codeine while alleviating the physical side effects of nausea and vomiting.

Placydil: an hypnotic drug that causes sleep in fifteen minutes to one hour and lasts about five hours. Placydil is a commonly prescribed sleeping pill that is used to bring a drug user down quickly from the "high" they are feeling and give the body a chance to sleep.

Potassium Chloride: replenishes potassium lost by the patient, especially through the kidneys. The heart muscle needs potassium chloride to pump and contract properly.

Pseuydomonas: a bacterial infection.

Ringer's lactate: a fluid replacement used after the kidneys have been assessed as it is more isotonic than D5W (water with sugar).

STAT: immediately.

Seconal: hypnotic sleeping pill used to induce drowsiness. It also helps alleviate nausea and vomiting associated with habitual use of narcotics.

Skull series: a set of X rays done on the head from all angles to view any abnormalities.

TPR: temperature, pulse, and respirations.

Talwin: a strong painkiller with a sedating (quieting) effect which works within fifteen to twenty minutes after the injection or ingestion (swallowing) of the medication. Talwin burns skin tissue when repeatedly given in the same injection site. It is normally used to reverse heart, breathing, and behavioral depression caused by morphine or demerol.

Tardive dyskinesia: a side effect of thorazine in which the patient loses muscle coordination causing muscle rigidity. There may also be tremors and grotesque motions. The tongue's swelling is one of the first signs of this side effect from thorazine.

Thorazine: a major tranquillizer used to stop vomiting and psychotic thought disorders. A central nervous system depressant, it can mimic psychotic and confusing thoughts.

Toxemia: the severe state of pre-eclampsia. Both are diseases unique to pregnancy where the patient's blood pressure can suddenly rise and cause the death of the baby, convulsions, and/or coma in the mother.

Tuinal: barbituate called a "downer" for its sedating and calming effects.

V-tach: when the bottom chambers of the heart no longer contract in a normal rhythm. The increased rate, called tachycardia, or tach for short, means the heart muscle will give out soon if action is not reversed.

Valium: an anti-anxiety drug used for the short-term relief of tension, anxiety, and the agitation of alcoholics in withdrawal. It relieves muscle spasms along the skeletal (bone) system. It is highly addictive and causes depression, although many abusers love the calming feeling they obtain following the initial orgasmic rush.

Vistaril: tranquillizer which works to decrease anxiety, tension, agitation, apprehension, and confusion for people with acute emotional problems, especially before surgery, childbirth, or in the critical care arena. As a street drug it is used to help alleviate the side effects of the other narcotics, these includes nausea, vomiting, and stomach disturbances. It also decreases agitation, apprehension, and confusion brought on by other drugs.

ABOUT THE AUTHOR

Joyce E. Strom-Paikin, MS, RN, C is a Certified Psychiatric Nurse Clinician with a License in Marriage and Family Therapy. She is also Board Certified as a Fellow Diplomat for the American Board of Medical Psychotherapists. Mrs. Strom-Paikin is in private practice in Ft. Lauderdale, Florida, and is an adjunct professor for Broward Community College. She is a free lance writer, consultant, and international lecturer. Ms. Strom-Paikin earned her nursing degree from the State University of New York, her Bachelors and Masters Degrees from Nova University, Ft. Lauderdale, Florida, and is currently a Ph.D. candidate at Saybrook Institute, San Francisco, California. She is listed in numerous "Who's Who" including the inaugural edition of "Who's Who in American Nursing."

HICKSVILLE PUBLIC LIBRARY

3 1911 00044 6139

362.293 S
Strom-Paikin, Joyce E.
Medical treason

Hicksville Public Library
169 Jerusalem Avenue
Hicksville, New York
Telephone Wells 1-1417

Please Do Not Remove
Card From Pocket

HI